Beyond Innocence
and Redemption

Beyond Innocence and Redemption

CONFRONTING THE HOLOCAUST AND ISRAELI POWER

Creating a Moral Future for
the Jewish People

MARC H. ELLIS

1817

HARPER & ROW, PUBLISHERS, SAN FRANCISCO

New York, Grand Rapids, Philadelphia, St. Louis
London, Singapore, Sydney, Tokyo, Toronto

Library of Congress Cataloging-in-Publication Data

Ellis, Marc H.
    Beyond innocence and redemption: confronting the Holocaust and
Israeli power: creating a moral future for the Jewish people/Marc
H. Ellis.—1st ed.
        p.   cm.
    Includes bibliographical references.
    1. Holocaust (Jewish theology) 2. Israel—Moral conditions.
3. Jewish-Arab relations—Religious aspects—Judaism.   4. Judaism
and social problems.   I. Title.   II. Title: Holocaust and Israeli
power.
MB645.H6E43   1990
296.3—dc20   89-45954
                                                                          CIP

ISBN 0-06-062215-6

 90 91 92 93 94 RRD(H) 10 9 8 7 6 5 4 3 2 1

This edition is printed on acid-free paper that meets
the American National Standards Institute Z39.48 Standard.

To my son Aaron
sign of innocence and redemption

All I wanted to say is this: The misery here is quite terrible; and yet, late at night when the day has slunk away into the depths behind me, I often walk with a spring in my step along the barbed wire. And then time and again, it soars straight from my heart—I can't help it, that's just the way it is, like some elementary force—the feeling that life is glorious and magnificent, and that one day we shall be building a whole new world.

Etty Hillesum
Westerbork Transit Camp
3 July 1943

I see these images of burning children
This time they are not our own
Or are they
Burning everywhere.

A young Jewish poet
Jerusalem
December 1988

Contents

Acknowledgments

This book could not have been written without assistance from many quarters. First and foremost, I owe a special debt of gratitude to those who have encouraged my work over the recent years, Richard Rubenstein, Rabbi Michael Robinson, Nyaela Ayed, Rabbi Marshall Meyer, Agnes Ballesteros, Jean Zaru, Rosemary Radford Ruether, Leopoldo Niilus, Herman Ruether, Dale Bishop, Susannah Heschel, Rev. Charles Kimball, Gabriel Habib, Dan Leon, Jonathan Kuttab, John Wilkins, Robert Gormley, Kathy Bergen, Jan Abu Shakarah, Samir Abu Shakarah, Rabbi Jeremy Milgrom, Rev. Naim Ateek, Muhammad Hallaj, Leon Howell, Vivian Lindermayer and Gail Hovey. I also wish to thank the Maryknoll School of Theology and the Middle East Council of Churches for their encouragement and support, which helped facilitate the research and writing of this book. A special word of thanks is due James O'Halloran, librarian at the Maryknoll School of Theology. Research assistance and advice have come to me through a variety of people, especially Mark Chmiel. The manuscript was typed by Kathleen Jones, and extensive editorial assistance was provided by Ann McDonald and by William Newell, consulting editor at Harper & Row. For all, I am grateful. Finally, encouraging responses to my ideas in written and oral form in the United States and around the world, from Jews and non-Jews, allow me to persevere through difficult times and speak what I perceive to be the difficult truths of contemporary Jewish history. To all those known to me by name, and those who have remained anonymous, I am grateful.

Introduction

Every author contemplates the blank page with a sense of terror, as if it will prove impossible to convey the ideas that seem so logical in the mind or that, once set down on paper, they will turn out to be superficial. A subject like the one addressed in this book, the need for Jews to come to grips with the history we are creating in Israel and through Jewish responses worldwide to the Israeli-Palestinian conflict, engenders a second and more profound anxiety: the possibility that one may be wrong and the certainty that one will be accused, by at least some Jews, of betraying one's people. My own anxiety, however, is tempered by my hope that in clarifying my position within the context of Jewish history and tradition, I might somehow, along with other writers, activists, and religious leaders, contribute to a renewal of the Jewish moral and ethical tradition.

Thus this book, first and foremost, attempts to clarify the essential dynamics of contemporary Jewish life in relation to Jewish suffering in the Holocaust and the empowerment of the Jewish people, particularly in the state of Israel. The urgency of this clarification hardly needs discussion in the face of the Palestinian uprising, the brutality of Israel's response, and the divisive, bitter debate within the Jewish community. Several commentators have described the Israeli-Palestinian struggle as in reality a civil war, and the internal Jewish debate in Israel and North America assumes similar attributes. The stakes are extremely high, and the participants seem to understand this at a very deep level. It is not too much to say that the future of the state of Israel, of Judaism, and the Jewish people are being determined in the most decisive way since the destruction of the Temple in 70 c.e. Jews can hardly afford to be mere spectators in this drama, and few are.

Yet the emotional level of discussion, the almost irrational quality of charges and countercharges among and against dissenting Jews lends little to the search for a clarification so crucial to deciding the paths before us as Jews. Are we after our difficult history in Europe becoming a warrior people? Is it possible that the yearnings for a haven from persecution, paid for so dearly in the past, will justify the expulsion and dispersion of another people? Can we continue to protest our innocence—no matter how loudly we insist upon it—while daily betraying it in dislocation and murder? Though Jews rarely speak in overt theological terms, the nuances of our discussions, our hopes and aspirations intimate an intense yearning for a moral and religious framework within which to address these issues. Here I speak of theology in terms of its task rather than its speculative or systematic dimensions, that is, theology as nurturing the questions a people needs to ask about the history they are creating. Do the parameters of our present theological discussion, what I call Holocaust theology, nurture those questions? Does the dialectical tension of Holocaust and empowerment—Holocaust mandating empowerment but also constraining it by ethical demands—so ably articulated by Holocaust theologians in the 1960s and early 1970s still exist? Or has that tension been shattered; has Holocaust increasingly becoming a servant of empowerment, justifying almost any form of empowerment including occupation and the beating, deportation, and humiliation of the Palestinian people? In speaking of our innocence and redemption does Holocaust theology remain naive about the history we have created in Israel even well before the Palestinian *intifada*? Are the categories essentially developed in the ecstatic days after the 1967 Six-Day War useful in dealing today with what now must be counted as the third decade of that war? And finally, in looking at these questions, can we properly see them in their full complexity without including those, Jewish and non-Jewish, who have in the past and continue today to dispute Holocaust theology's interpretations of events? Don't we need, for example, to speak of historical figures who were Zionist in their search for a Jewish homeland but were opposed to the creation of a Jewish state, people like Judah Magnes and Hannah Arendt, without dismissing them as idealists made irrelevant by Arab intransigence? Shouldn't we speak of the Jews in contemporary Jewish life, political analysts like Arthur Hertzberg and Noam Chomsky, who present truth to us if we will only listen? And don't we need to listen to Palestinians like Muhammad Hallaj and Edward Said who see their experience of dislocation and death as similar to ours, without insisting that no one should ever equate their experience to the Holocaust of the Jews? Finally, shouldn't we listen to

Jews in Israel like Israel Shahak and Yossi Sarid who have made and who today make intuitive connections between Nazi and Israeli policy that make Jews shudder but that also might take us beyond innocence and redemption to a more sober view of the choices before us as a people?

The argument made in the following pages presents these issues and figures as crucial to the future of the Jewish people. It is a call to Jewish moral and religious thinkers who functioned brilliantly when confronting the oppression of Jews in Christian Europe, but who are now quiescent in the service of Jewish state power, to speak before it is too late. Though the occupation and its policies are now in their third decade, not one major Jewish theologian has said what is obvious to many Jews and non-Jews alike:

> What Jews have done to the Palestinians since the establishment of the state of Israel in 1948 is wrong.

> In the process of conquering and displacing the Palestinian people, Jews have done what has been done to us over two millennia.

> In this process Jews have become almost everything we loathe about our oppressors.

> It is only in the confrontation with state power in Israel that Jews can move beyond being victim or oppressor.

> The movement beyond victimization and oppression can only come through a solidarity with those whom we as Jews have displaced— the Palestinian people.

The task of Jewish theology is to establish a new relationship to the state of Israel rather than to challenge its legitimacy. Like any other state, Israel exists because of its ability to govern a specific territory and population. This ability to govern is in turn based on Israel's having sufficient power and consensus to exist and govern. No state in the world, including Israel, can, despite its rhetoric, claim a moral legitimacy beyond its power and consensus. The situation is no different for Palestinians. A Palestinian state will come into being when a sufficient power and consensus is available to govern a specific territory and people.

The function of Jewish theology is to evaluate critically the history the people are participating in, and the structures that promote or hinder the Jewish struggle to be faithful. Palestinians, Muslim and Christian, will face a similar theological task when they achieve statehood. Because the Jewish struggle occurs in diverse communities where Jews find themselves historically and in the present, communal structures are to be judged within this same diversity of experience. Communal structures, then, rather than being delegitimized, are relativized and demystified. At the same time, structures that serve the people in one era may hinder the people in another era. That which mobilized energies for building new structures at one point in history may, at another point, need to channel the same energies to transform those structures into something else. Jewish theology, then, needs to be wary of absolutizing any structure through uncritical support or silence.

Ultimately, a question of purpose is being posed here. What is the essential mission of the Jewish people? Is it to build Israel as an exclusive Jewish state? To serve that state in the United States by lobbying for Israeli economic and military aid? Is this a choice faithful to a history filled with suffering and struggle? Can such a choice be maintained over time without changing the essence of what it means to be Jewish? Can Jews continue to pretend to an innocence (as oppressed victims through millennia) and redemption (by recovering a land of their own) when actions of the state of Israel closely replicate the history of suffering that Jews sought to escape? These are the questions that confront Jews as a people and Jewish theology. Can we say that any theology that does not address these questions as central is a theology that leads to torture and murder? One that threatens the very tradition of suffering and struggle that Jews inherit?

In the coming months, as in the previous years, many of these questions will remain unasked, at least in public. Those who raise them in public will be vilified. Jewish theologians will continue to legitimate Israeli policies or, when this is no longer possible, at least equivocate. But the consequences of Israel's attempt to disperse and to destroy the Palestinian people are too serious to be ignored. The day of reckoning will come. By then, however, we as Jews might survey with Walter Benjamin the treasures of victory, which have an origin that "we cannot contemplate without horror." That is the day their children will relate with tears the history the Jews of today have bequeatherd to them. To minimize that horror we must act now. We are very nearly too late.

Beyond Innocence
and Redemption

CHAPTER 1

The Birth of Holocaust Theology

One of the first radio broadcasts from the newly discovered death camps in Eastern Europe in 1945 began with the following sentence: "I have something to report to you beyond the human imagination." The reporter was surrounded by corpselike figures who smiled weakly and by rows and rows of actual corpses stacked one on top of another waiting for cremation. The next few weeks featured discoveries like these in camp after camp, as well as the hundreds of thousands of Jewish refugees wandering within and between the devastated remains of European civilization.[1]

The discovery of the death camps startled people the world over and called for a reevaluation of the prospects of Western civilization. Of course, mingled with the introspection was the need to rebuild Europe, to get the world back on its feet, to go on with life. In the rebuilding and in the ensuing cold war, new challenges and enemies arrived, and many of the questions posed by the death camps were, like much of the great European architecture, buried under the weight of war and redevelopment.[2]

For the Jewish community, with almost one-third of its population lost, with entire historic areas of Jewish life vanished forever, the European catastrophe posited both a continuation of Jewish history and a radical break with it. The suffering of the Jews in Europe was hardly novel, but its scope and intensity brought the history of Jewish suffering to a new, more horrific level. At the same time, for all practical purposes, the history of Jews in Europe, especially eastern Europe, had within a decade come to an end. In short, it was impossible to go home because home had become a nightmare without escape.[3]

The end of eastern European Jewry also signaled the end of Jewish theologies and secular philosophies that had emerged in the nineteenth century and competed for Jewish allegiance even in the European ghettos and concentration camps. If these ideas continued at all, it was in name only, and their framework shifted considerably. For years after the war what we now know as the Holocaust was for the most part unnamed by Jewish thinkers and theologians, as if the pain was too great and the historical events too close. There was also a fear, understandable, as it turns out, that the surviving Jewish world might become so overwhelmed by grief and disoriented by the destruction so as to never recover. The questions of Jewish survival were practical, seen in the swelling refugee population, and theoretical, expressed in questions about the continuation of Jewish life and God's efficacy and care for the Jewish people. The future of Jewish life was to combine politics and theology, but the articulation of this synthesis awaited a generation able to speak to these issues. It is hardly surprising that the generation formed in the early part of the twentieth century, that is, those who were formed before the onslaught, ultimately contributed little to this necessary and almost unprecedented synthesis. Rather, the task fell to those formed in the crucible of the European catastrophe.[4]

In the end it was the trial of Adolph Eichmann in 1961 and the lightning victory of Israel in the 1967 war that provided the opportunity for articulating the Jewish response to the European catastrophe. Holocaust theology was that response.

Holocaust Theology

To begin to analyze Jewish life in the present and the themes that are important to Jews and Jewish communities around the world, it is important to articulate theological underpinnings. The work of Holocaust theologians such as Elie Wiesel, Emil Fackenheim, and Rabbi Irving Greenberg is crucial here, for they have articulated a theology that speaks in a profound way to the Jewish people, one that has become normative in Jewish conversation and activity.

When looked at closely, Holocaust theology yields three themes that exist in dialectical tension: suffering and empowerment, innocence and redemption, specialness and normalization. Though they exist side by side, they also are sequential, the first two themes emerging at the time of the Arab-Israeli war in 1967, the third in the 1980s with the Israeli invasion of Lebanon and the Palestinian uprising against Israeli occupation of the West Bank and Gaza.

The themes of suffering and empowerment came to the fore at the time of the 1967 war. In those heady times, there was a collective awakening in the Jewish community, exemplified by Elie Wiesel and Emil Fackenheim, that is hard to describe. But the literature is clear: the experience of Israel in 1967 elicited an articulation of specific themes of contemporary Jewish history for the first time since the European catastrophe. It is in light of the 1967 war that Jews articulated for the first time both the extent of Jewish suffering during the Holocaust and the significance of Jewish empowerment in Israel. Before 1967, neither was central to Jewish consciousness; the Jewish community carried on with a haunting memory of the European experience and a charitable attitude toward the fledgling state. After the war, both Holocaust and Israel are seen as central points around which the boundaries of Jewish commitment are defined.

Yet if the emerging Holocaust consciousness saw Jewish suffering as mandating empowerment in Israel, it also recognized some of the dangers inherent in empowerment. The lesson of Jewish suffering is indeed empowerment, but suffering also constrains the forms of empowerment. Jewish suffering is unacceptable after the Holocaust, but also no people should have to suffer as Jews have. Thus for Holocaust theologians, at least in the early stage, the Holocaust had both particular and universal meaning; the lesson of the Holocaust is that Jews and all people should be empowered to the point at which it is impossible to inflict massive suffering upon them.

Within the theme of suffering and empowerment lies the corollary of innocence and redemption, and this too developed in the wake of the 1967 war. For Holocaust theologians the victory in the Six-Day War was a miracle, a sign that an innocent people so recently victimized might be on the verge of redemption. That is, a subtheme of Jewish suffering in the Holocaust is the total innocence of the Jewish people and thus the innocence of those who defend the lives of Jews in Israel. For Holocaust theologians, the victory of Israel in 1967 is a victory of the innocent trying to forestall another catastrophe, another holocaust, and the redemptive sign is that this time Jews will prevail. The celebration of victory is therefore seen within the context of an earlier devastation: a helpless people abandoned by the world now ensures its own continuity and survival against a new enemy. Of course, in this formulation the transference of European history to the Middle East is complete; insofar as Palestinian Arabs and the Arab world in general attempt to thwart Jewish empowerment in Israel, they symbolize to Holocaust theologians the continuity of the Nazi drama. The 1967 war symbolizes a shift in the

physical geography of the drama; the internal landscape remains
the same. In the literature written immediately after the 1967 war, the
feeling is clear: this time Hitler lost.

Still, there is a tension. As with suffering and empowerment, the
dialectic of innocence and redemption remains problematic. Though
there is no doubt about the innocence of suffering Jews in Europe and the
innocence of Jews in Israel, the fully redemptive quality of victory remains elusive. Holocaust theologians stress at this point that Israel does
not atone for the Holocaust, is not a fulfillment of the devastation, nor
does Israel replace suffering with joy. If Israel is a response to the Holocaust, it is not an answer. The European catastrophe remains central in its
horror and in the questions it raises.

Within suffering and empowerment, innocence and redemption, is
the difficult question of God. Holocaust theologians are bold in asking
how Jews can relate to God after the Holocaust. Can Jews believe in a
God of history who allows such devastation? Can Jews relate to a God
when over one million innocent Jewish children were killed? In essence
Holocaust theologians conclude that there are no definitive answers to
these questions and that thus the religious duty of the Jewish community
cannot simply revolve around belief in God. Rather, the survival of the
people takes precedence, and because empowerment is crucial to that
survival, empowerment takes on religious connotations. Holocaust theologians therefore articulate a religion beyond prayer, ritual, and certainty about God and place that religion in the historical progression of
the Jewish people, symbolized in post-1967 Israel. In this way, Holocaust
theologians challenge and ultimately replace the normative religious
ideals of rabbinic Judaism, or at least provide a new focal point for
rabbinic Judaism.

The third tension, specialness and normalization, exists already
within the first two, but becomes more explicit as the ramifications of the
1967 war become clear. Already in 1967 the tension is felt as Jews re-
emerge on the world scene in a position of power. Holocaust theologians
celebrate what this power ensures: continuity and independence. Even
in victory, though, they argue that the 1967 war represents a "unique"
type of victory. This uniqueness is seen in a number of factors, beginning
with the particularity of Jewish existence and history, a return to the land
of Jewish ancestry, and, especially, renewed access to the old city of
Jerusalem and the Temple Wall. To be reunited with those symbols of
ancient Jewish heritage after a two-thousand-year exile, an exile that
culminated in the catastrophe in Europe, is to recover the special character of the Jewish people. Thus for Holocaust theologians the 1967 war is a

sign of specialness, and the description of Israeli soldiers as reluctant warriors, as restrained conquerors, is part and parcel of this special quality.

Yet it is at this point that there arises the question of normalization—what form power is to take and how it is to be exercised now that Israel is an established nation-state. For the miracle of 1967, as Holocaust theologians view it, did not carry with it the occupation of the West Bank and Gaza—or at least there is little mention of such an occupation in the early post-1967 writings. It is only in the 1980s, when it becomes obvious that the occupation is a semipermanent part of the Israeli policy, and when the war in Lebanon explodes on the front pages of the international press, that the reality of normalization takes on importance. In fact, the arrival of the third part of this dialectic of specialness and normalization divides Holocaust theologians themselves. Elie Wiesel and Emil Fackenheim, for example, argue the themes of suffering and empowerment, innocence and redemption, but have little to say about the dialectic of specialness and normalization. That is, they argue from the European catastrophe about the need for empowerment, but their main focus is on the former. It is Irving Greenberg who realizes that the miracle of Israel has now arrived at center stage and that the reality of Israel beyond the miracle now has to be addressed. We might say that in the 1970s and 1980s Greenberg both synthesizes the themes articulated by earlier Holocaust theologians and ventures beyond them: Jews are no longer innocent (because of the power Jews wield and the way they wield it), and the cost of empowerment is for Jews to become more like other nations and peoples. For Greenberg, this normalization of the Jewish community is probably the most important and most difficult reality for Jews to accept. Jews who expect too much of the state, who apply the prophetic norms that grew up in situations of powerlessness, thus threaten the survival of Israel, because no state, Jewish or otherwise, can survive on prophetic ideals.

As we enter the last decade of the twentieth century, Holocaust theology has reached its final articulation, having moved from a deep, almost poetic paean to Jewish suffering to an expression of international normalcy; Israel is to be measured by the same standards as any other nation. And yet the glaring weakness of this constraint that Holocaust theology has developed comes into focus with this dramatic shift. In all of Holocaust theology there is never an attempt at a critical history of Zionism or of Israeli state policy. Jewish dissenters are rarely mentioned by name, nor are the positions they held discussed. Thus the Jewish tradition of dissent, Zionist and non-Zionist, vis-à-vis Israel is lost, and the variety of lessons to be drawn from the Holocaust remain in the background or disappear altogether. The strength of Holocaust theology is also its weakness: a univocal view of history that, as often as not, is ahistorical.

It is important to understand that Holocaust theologians face constraints that all theologians, regardless of faith tradition, face when asked to legitimate state power. That is, Holocaust theologians helped to make normative—as a religious commandment—empowerment in Israel. Because Zionism existed long before the Holocaust, and the state long before Holocaust theology, Holocaust theology was, even in its own incipience, legitimating something already in existence. A further complication is that the theology that articulates a general sense of Jewish identity and affirmation in no way controls or even directly influences— nor could it retroactively change—Israeli state policy. Thus Holocaust theologians are called upon and feel responsible to articulate and defend, or to explain as essential and normal, state policies that are presented to them. There is little question that the 1967 war was easier for Holocaust theologians to explain than the Lebanese war, and the Lebanese war a bit easier than the brutal suppression of the Palestinian uprising. Explanations attempted by people such as Irving Greenberg are strained, and the quest for an understanding of a normalcy that most Jews feel to be intensely disturbing finds an increasingly narrow Jewish audience. We might say that the Palestinian uprising signals the end of Holocaust theology because Holocaust theology in its inception articulated a much different sense of Jewish purpose, that of an innocent, suffering people in search of their destiny.

Eichmann and Jerusalem

In February 1961, a young and relatively unknown Elie Wiesel traveled to Jerusalem as a reporter for the *Jewish Daily Forward*. His task—to cover the trial of Adolph Eichmann, the mastermind of the Nazis' "final solution"—was a difficult if not impossible assignment for one who just fifteen years earlier had barely survived Auschwitz. But in Wiesel's articles one finds a young man searching for a language to speak of the horrible crimes he had witnessed. And within these terse, somber, and often angry dispatches can also be found a people trying to articulate the massive experience of suffering we now know as the Holocaust. In the courtroom where Wiesel imagines an audience of the entire Jewish people, a theology is being born.[5]

In his first report of 27 February 1961, Wiesel discusses the appointment of a Jewish Israeli lawyer, Mendel Short, to serve as an adviser to Eichmann's German attorney. From a logical point of view, the appointment makes sense: an expert on Israeli law ensures a fair trial by advising a foreign attorney on the intricacies of Israeli law. There is also a certain logic in the public arena: Eichmann's lawyer cannot argue that he was deprived of competent counsel, and thus a full and fair trial. Yet for Wiesel "everything pertaining to the Holocaust is devoid of logic." Eichmann's trial is different; his crimes require new terminology and new laws. Wiesel wonders about the ability of a Jewish lawyer to advise Eichmann's attorney. "Where does he find the strength to approach this trial logically? Where does he get the courage to stand, even from a strictly legal point of view, in the same camp as the exterminator of the Jews? How does he justify to himself the fact that he, a Jew and a lawyer, is not among the prosecutors?" Wiesel had never thought it difficult to understand a Jew. But he could not understand Short. "Can it be that our understanding also was consumed in the fires of Auschwitz?"[6]

Six weeks later, in April, Wiesel anticipates the beginning of the trial in the courtroom of the House of the People. Eichmann, in his glass cage, is surrounded by seven hundred and fifty people, mostly the press, the prosecution, the defense, diplomats, and official visitors. But, in Wiesel's view, these are the least of those present. To begin with, the victims are present. For Wiesel, the trial is less for the living than for the dead and, among the living, for the survivors. The collective judgment of the Jewish people is taking place: "From every corner of the world, Jews, dead and living, will leave their cold graves and their warm homes and stream toward Jerusalem," Wiesel writes. "Millions of people will face Eichmann as witnesses, as accusers, as judges." And those who were complicit in the destruction of the Jews, all who assisted, actively or passively, are present as well in the person of Eichmann. The trial is therefore a monumental event that brings an ancient and suffering people face to face with its own history and a complicit world. When the chief justice with his gavel signals the arrival of the hour of justice, Wiesel calls for silence to envelop the world. For Wiesel it is a holy hour. "Soon will begin the eternal dialogue between the Jew and his murderer, between good and evil, between man and the devil. Soon the dead will arise and shout their accusations into the face of the German, into the face of the world."[7]

Though Wiesel anticipated a collective judgment by the Jewish people, he realized that old wounds would be reopened and illusions shattered, and that pain, becoming articulate, would intensify. There was, of course, the difficulty in reliving the past through the simple presence of

Eichmann. The prosecutors' questions to the survivors, logical questions in any other courtroom, were equally painful. A month after the trial began a witness was asked why the Jews had not revolted against their Nazi enemy. Wiesel reports the scene in vivid imagery:

> The witness choked with tears, as though yesterday had him by the throat. The scene he described shocked observers in the courtroom. Because a little Jewish boy sang a Russian melody in a concentration camp, he was sentenced to death by hanging, and all the prisoners were forced to witness the execution. Armed SS men walked up and down the rows and beat anyone who turned his eyes away from the black gallows.
>
> The little boy did not arouse God's pity: if he had, he would not have died more than one death. The first time, the hangman did not throw the noose properly around the boy's neck. The rope tightened but the boy lived. So the hangman tried a second time.
>
> At that point in the testimony the prosecutor interrupted the witness and asked why the prisoners had not revolted. At first the witness stammered in confusion: How can anyone ask such a question? Finally he said that anyone who had not been there could not understand.
>
> Why, indeed, had fifteen thousand prisoners not attacked the murders and torn them to bits? True, the Germans were carrying machine guns. True, hundreds, perhaps even thousands, of Jews would have been killed as a result. But they must have known, in any case, that death was lying in wait for them. Would it not have been better to die as heroes, to sacrifice themselves and spare a little Jewish boy such agony?[8]

These were not just the prosecutors' questions, for Israeli youths often asked the same questions. For these youths, the testimony aroused feelings of shame and resentment. Israeli sabras believed in heroes rather than victims and martyrs; for them, six million Jews should have become an army of insurrection. For Wiesel, however, the answer to the questions of Jewish passivity had little to do with psychology or even military strategy, but rather with a sense of abandonment by humanity and God, who "looked away while the bonfires blazed." When asked why the Jews did not revolt, Wiesel replied, "If the intellectuals, the lovers of mankind, and the proclaimers of ideals had not slept peacefully while the sky over Auschwitz was aflame, we would not have had to ask the question: Why didn't the Jews revolt?"[9]

On 4 June 1962 Eichmann died on the gallows. Wiesel reports that some American Jews expressed shock that Jewish hands had carried out the "commands of justice." Clearly Jews were not accustomed to this. For thousands of years crimes against the Jewish people had gone unpunished; this was the first instance in which the Jewish people had brought their tormentor to justice. There were other critics as well, anti-Semites who saw Eichmann as the "victim of Israeli avengers." To both groups Wiesel answers: "When millions of Jews were listening for one voice of conscience, those now protesting were dumb and blind. Today, when it is a question not of saving the lives of millions of innocent victims but of preserving the tainted life of a mass murderer, they have suddenly found their tongues and their sensitivity. Let those who were silent then remain silent now." To be sure, there was no punishment befitting Eichmann's crime, a crime that included the murder of one million children. For Wiesel, it was enough to execute him for the murder of one child and let history be his judge for the rest.[10]

1967: The Miracle

If Wiesel's coverage of Eichmann in Jerusalem provided the first aspect of an emerging theology—the public articulation of Jewish suffering and the complicity of the world in that suffering—his trip to Jerusalem in the midst of the June 1967 Six-Day War addressed the second aspect of that theology, the miracle of empowerment.

Like his writing on Eichmann, Wiesel's prose again has the immediacy of one who has entered into an experience and is almost overwhelmed by it. Wiesel begins with a confession: as war became imminent, he did not believe Israel would win. On the contrary, he thought Israel would lose the war, and that this would be the last war of the Jewish people, "the end of our march to eternity." For Wiesel, the Israeli experience was much too beautiful to last, but could he live— could the Jewish people continue—if Israel disappeared? Wiesel quotes Raymond Aron, the French sociologist, as illustrating his own thought: "If Israel disappears, I do not wish to survive." Thinking this to be the end, Wiesel flew to Israel on the second day of the war as an act of defiance and solidarity. As it turns out, he was not alone. On the plane to Israel, he met an old friend who was motivated by the same conviction, that the Jews were heading toward a reenactment of what happened in the Warsaw Ghetto, and he, like Wiesel, wanted to be on the inside. "But the tragedy did not occur. We have all been saved. Had Israel lost the war, we would all have been doomed. We simply could not have gone through another catastrophe—two catastrophes would have been too much for one generation. The Jewish people would have survived for centuries to come, even if Israel had not been established in 1948. But now that Israel does exist, our people is so linked to it that we could not survive its disappearance."[11]

Holocaust imagery is ever present. Wiesel records in his diary that in the moment of anguish Israel was alone, as before in Europe, "during its night." The indifference of friendly or neutral governments was the same; as before the Vatican remained silent; the invocation of total war, this time by the Arab governments, was familiar. Israel was a ghetto again, and the war recalled the uprising of the Jewish survivors in Warsaw. "The inhabitants would resist until the end, and the so-called Christian nations, civilized and progressive, faithful to their tradition, would watch—and do nothing." And for the Jewish people everything would have to begin again, "except that no longer would we have the strength or desire to begin again."[12]

And thus the victory is seen as a miracle. "The people plunged suddenly into the unreal, outside the realm of time and thought. They no longer knew the day of the week, the month, the century. At times, they seemed to be reliving the trials and triumphs of the Bible; the names and battles had a familiar ring. At other times, they felt themselves thrust into a far away messianic future." Wiesel first recognized this mystical dimension of victory as he entered the old city of Jerusalem and watched thousands of Jews approach the Western Wall, the sole vestige of the Temple. He was struck by the silence that pervaded the scene. "This is my first time here, yet I feel that I have been here before. I have already seen these Jews, heard their prayers. Every shape seems familiar, every sound as though it has arisen from the depths of my own past. But there is a difference. Before, there were no young men and women milling about in uniforms. What are they doing here? And why are they crying? I do not know. They themselves neither know nor say. They see nothing except the Wall before them. But it is theirs, for it is they who bore it on their shoulders year after year and generation after generation. And their tears—their tears are the Wall's."[13]

As in the trial of Eichmann, the entire Jewish community, past and present, is united in Jerusalem, this time to forestall destruction and to experience the miraculous. The enemy is defeated by the sum total of Jewish history. Two thousand years of suffering, longing, and hope are mobilized for the battle, "just as the million of martyrs of the Holocaust were enlisted in the ranks." Like the biblical pillars of fire, the martyrs of the Holocaust came and shielded their spiritual heirs. And the possibility of Israel's defeat is reversed, for what enemy could ever conquer them?[14]

The passion of Wiesel's writing makes it clear that for him, as for Jews around the world, everything changed with the war. Wiesel describes this period as a watershed for himself. "I became a child again, astonished and vulnerable, threatened by nightmare." It is also a watershed for the Jewish people. "Suddenly all Jews had again become children of the Holocaust." The watershed involves a military victory and a religious manifestation to be interpreted, in Wiesel's words, by poets and kabbalists. Indeed, the details of the war, if they are known in their totality, can hardly describe "the great mystery in which we are encloaked, as if by the command of the Almighty." Religious and secular Jews alike interpret the experience of victory as a religious one, compelling each Jew to "confront his people, his past, and his God." The war was a matter of the survival of the Jewish people, and a unity emerged that Wiesel describes movingly: "University students flooded embassies to enlist for the fight; the Hasidim of Williamsburg declared days of fast and prayer; youngsters from assimilated homes organized fund raising drives and joined in protests; millionaires cast aside their businesses and took off for Jerusalem; community leaders went sleepless night after night because of their great efforts and profound anxiety. Never was the Jewish people so united, never so moved and anxious, never so ready and prepared to offer and sacrifice everything it had, its 'might, heart and soul.'"[15]

For Wiesel, there is another miracle involved in the Israeli victory, and that is the humanity of the Jewish soldiers, who fought without hate. Despite the "poisonous incitement" over Arab radio, the Israeli soldiers, except for rare instances, exhibited no cruelty toward Arab prisoners of war or toward civilians. "I have seen many armies; none more humble, more humane in its victories. I have seen Israeli paratroopers crying before the Wall. They were sad rather than proud." For Wiesel those soldiers sum up his sense of Israel as a moral victory. In a lecture three years after the war, he enunciated this theme.

> To me Israel itself represents a moral victory. In the Jewish tradition a victory is never linked to defeat. That means one can be victorious without defeating the enemy. Judaism recognizes only victory over oneself. If I feel pride that Israel exists today, it is not only because it can take in Jews who need one place where they are wanted, not just tolerated. And it is not only because it creates a renewal of history. And certainly it is not because of the military victories. I have no admiration for military men, either in Israel or in America, if they are only military. My pride is that Israel has remained human because it has remained so deeply Jewish. During the Six-Day War the Jewish fighters did not become cruel. They became sad. They acquired a certain maturity, a very moving maturity, which I simply cannot forget. And if I feel something towards them, the child-soldier in Israel, it is profound respect.[16]

ThoughWiesel is less a systematic thinker than a storyteller, by 1967 he had brought to the surface several of the major themes foundational to

Holocaust theology that exist in dialectical tension—the suffering of the Jewish people in Europe and the miracle of empowerment in Israel, the innocence of the Jewish people and the redemptive aspects of Israel. What is important in Wiesel's work is his ability to articulate these themes in a preideological and pretheological manner, appealing to the emotive aspects of the experience of the Jewish people and gathering all Jews, regardless of their individual stories, into a collective history. Eichmann and Jerusalem become vantage points from which a perspective on Jewish singularity and continuity can form, and the historical mission of the Jewish people become articulate. Beyond this, Wiesel's genius is that this preideological and pretheological terrain is less definable as a political or religious program than formative as a platform from which Jewish thought and action emanates. Thus the dialectical tension allows Jewish suffering to point to the miracle of Israel's victory, yet not be consumed by it; the redemptive aspects of Israel continually evoke Jewish innocence because of the absolutely unjustified suffering of Jews in Europe. In a sense, Wiesel recreates the rhythms of contemporary Jewish life—almost as a liturgy—and suggests avenues of Jewish commitment within those rhythms. In Wiesel's world, and by extension in the Jewish world, Jews remain in the throes of suffering even as they are empowered, an innocent people haunted by isolation and abandonment even as redemption seems near.

Left on its own, Wiesel's poetic style would have helped Jews articulate the rhythms of Jewish life but hardly focus that articulation in a theological movement. This achievement was left to Emil Fackenheim, survivor of the Sachsenhausen concentration camps and later professor of philosophy at the University of Toronto.

In March 1967, just three months before the Six-Day War, Fackenheim participated in a symposium entitled "Values in the Post-Holocaust Future." Within the context of his own experience of suffering and the work of Elie Wiesel, Fackenheim had begun to see the crisis of contemporary Judaism as one of epic proportions, unique and unprecedented, to be faced by all Jews, religious and secular. For Fackenheim contemporary Jewish existence is permeated by three main contradictions. The first involves the Jew of today thriving as a universalist in pluralist societies (such as America), yet living in a time of the resurrection of Jewish particularism, in the rebirth of a Jewish nation. The second contradiction involves Jewish commitment to secularism, as both the Jewish believer and nonbeliever participate in secular society and are protected by it, while at the same time the future survival of Jewish life depends on past religious resources. As Fackenheim analyzes it, "Even the most Orthodox Jew of today is a secularist insofar as, and to the extent that, he participates in the political and social processes of society. And even the most secularist Jew is religious insofar as, and to the extent that, he must fall back on the religious past in his struggle for a Jewish future." The third and most radical contradiction, one that in Fackenheim's mind threatens to engulf the other two, has to do with the contradictory experience of Jews in modernity. On the one hand, the Jew in America and Israel has found freedom and autonomy in the modern world. On the other hand, Jews alive today are only decades removed from the greatest catastrophe in Jewish history—a catastrophe that in Fackenheim's understanding is distinctively modern in nature.[17]

Fackenheim is certain that authentic responses to these contradictions will come in time, but two responses have already occurred in the form of commitment to Jewish survival and to Jewish unity. Though in the past having been highly critical of Jewish philosophies that seemed to advocate survival for survival's sake, Fackenheim now believed that in this "present, unbelievable age" a collective commitment to Jewish group survival for its own sake is a momentous response. "I am convinced," Fackenheim writes, "that future historians will understand it, not as our present detractors would have it, as the tribal response-mechanism of a fossil, but rather as a profound, albeit as yet fragmentary, act of faith, in an age of crisis, to which the response might well have been either flight in total disarray or complete despair." Commitment to survival issues into a Jewish unity that, though incomplete, is also a reality. Though Fackenheim was originally indifferent to Zionism, today indifference or, worse, hostility to Zionism is for Fackenheim an anachronism. Whether aware of it or not, Jews have made a collective decision to endure the contradictions of present Jewish existence; they have rejected the option of leaving the Jewish community altogether or of avoiding the contradictions so as to diminish the authentic struggle of contemporary Jewish life.[18]

Is it possible to move beyond such a fragmentary commitment? Can we confront the Holocaust and not despair? Fackenheim offers a new commandment that complements Wiesel's evocative reporting, one revealed in the midst of total catastrophe: "The authentic Jew of today is forbidden to hand Hitler yet another, posthumous victory." The implications of such a commandment are momentous:

> If the 614th commandment is binding upon the authentic Jew, then we are, first, commanded to survive as Jews, lest the Jewish people perish. We are commanded, second, to remember in our very guts and bones the

martyrs of the Holocaust, lest their memory perish. We are forbidden, thirdly, to deny or despair of God, however much we may have to contend with him or with belief in him, lest Judaism perish. We are forbidden, finally, to despair of the world as the place which is to become the kingdom of God, lest we help make it a meaningless place in which God is dead or irrelevant and everything is permitted. To abandon any of these imperatives, in response to Hitler's victory at Auschwitz, would be to hand him yet other, posthumous victories.[19]

For Fackenheim, the response to this commandment was vividly illustrated several months later as Israel proclaimed victory in the Six-Day War and entered Jerusalem. By refusing to "lie down and be slaughtered" Jewish Israelis responded to what Fackenheim called the commanding voice of Auschwitz. In a series of lectures delivered in 1968 and published under the title *God's Presence in History*, Fackenheim defined the command.

Jews are forbidden to hand Hitler posthumous victories. They are commanded to survive as Jews, lest the Jewish people perish. They are commanded to remember the victims of Auschwitz lest their memory perish. They are forbidden to despair of man and his world, and to escape into either cynicism or otherworldliness, lest they cooperate in delivering the world over to the forces of Auschwitz. Finally, they are forbidden to despair of the God of Israel, lest Judaism perish. A secularist Jew cannot make himself believe by a mere act of will, nor can he be commanded to do so. And a religious Jew who has stayed with his God may be forced into new, possibly revolutionary relationships with Him. One possibility, however, is wholly unthinkable. A Jew may not respond to Hitler's attempt to destroy Judaism by himself cooperating in its destruction. In ancient times, the unthinkable Jewish sin was idolatry. Today, it is to respond to Hitler by doing his work.[20]

What Fackenheim declared in 1968 was the end of Jewish martyrdom as a religious commandment and the upbuilding of Jewish life in Israel as a sacred task in response to Auschwitz, themes already announced in poetic language by Elie Wiesel. The themes of innocence and redemption are present as well, though shadowed (as they are for Wiesel) with the possibility of destruction. In the span of a decade, beginning with the trial of Eichmann and ending with reflection on the incredible Israeli victory, Jewish theology takes on a character that would have been impossible to predict just a few years earlier. In the wake of the 1967 war, both Wiesel and Fackenheim realize that the epochal events of our century, the Holocaust and the birth of a Jewish nation, are the stuff of Jewish reflection and theology, and that there has been a response to the massive Jewish suffering of the Holocaust in the military, but more important in the moral and religious victory of Israel. These events—Holocaust and Israel—are now irrevocably tied together in the survival and creative future of the Jewish people.[21]

The events of Holocaust and Israel are also tied to the question of God's presence in Jewish history, and both Wiesel and Fackenheim address this difficulty with a courage rare among theologians. In a sense both refuse to abandon God, even if both entertain the possibility that God abandoned the Jewish people in the death camps. Typically Wiesel is evocative in this regard, especially in his autobiographical work *Night*. Fackenheim, as a philosopher, is more systematic in his *God's Presence in History* and a later work *To Mend the World*. What they agree on is that in the dialectical tension of suffering and empowerment, innocence and redemption, the question of God remains. For Wiesel and Fackenheim, and for all subsequent Holocaust theology, it is this historical reality that must be preserved in fidelity to those who have died. Ultimately Holocaust theology, then, is seen as an act of fidelity to the dead by the living who refuse to answer the questions that the dead and the dying could not.[22]

The Third Era of Jewish History

With the publication in 1977 of Rabbi Irving Greenberg's lengthy essay "Cloud of Smoke, Pillar of Fire: Judaism, Christianity and Modernity After the Holocaust," the main outlines of Holocaust theology were complete. Greenberg synthesizes the positions of Wiesel and Fackenheim, while at the same time providing new emphasis. For example, Greenberg perceives the Jewish Holocaust both as an indictment of modernity, because of modernity's false universalism and the evil perpetuated under its reign, and as a critique of the Jewish and Christian religions, because they contributed to powerlessness and hatred. Both modernity and religion have not only contributed to the Holocaust, they have essentially passed over its challenge in silence. The message of the victims—to halt the carnage and to reevaluate the dynamics of social and religious life—has fallen on deaf ears.[23]

Greenberg also sees the recovery of the story and of the meaning of Holocaust as essential to the redirection of modern life. However, this redirection can occur only if the brokenness is acknowledged. If in the past two centuries an allegiance has been transferred from the God of History to the God of Science and Humanism, the experience of the death camps asks whether this new God is worthy of ultimate loyalty. "The victims ask that we not jump to a conclusion that retrospectively makes the covenant they lived an illusion and their death a gigantic travesty." At the same time, nothing in the record of secular culture justifies its claim to authority, especially insofar as it provided the setting for mass death. According to Greenberg, the victims ask us above anything else "not to allow the creation of another matrix of values that might sustain another attempt at genocide." The experience of the past and the possibility of the future urges resistance to the absolutization of the secular.[24]

To refuse to absolutize the secular does not, however, allow one to escape into the religious sphere—here Greenberg echoes Wiesel and Fackenheim. After Auschwitz, we can speak only of "moment faiths," instants when a vision of redemption is present, interspersed with the "flames and smoke of burning children," in which faith is absent. Greenberg describes these "moment faiths" as the end of the easy dichotomy of atheist/theist and of the unquestioned equation of faith with doctrine. After the Holocaust, the difference between the skeptic and the believer is frequency of faith, not certitude of position. The rejection of the unbeliever by the believer is literally the denial or attempted suppression of what is within oneself. To live with moment faiths is to live with pluralism and without the superficial certainties that empty religion of its complexity and often make it a source of distrust for the other.[25]

For Greenberg, the dialectic of faith is illustrated in contemporary Jewish experience by the establishment of the state of Israel; Israel, like the Holocaust, takes on aspects of a formative experience as well. "The whole Jewish people is caught between immersion in nihilism and immersion in redemption," Greenberg suggests, and fidelity in the present means to remain within the dialectic of Auschwitz (the experience of nothingness) and Jerusalem (the political empowerment of a suffering community). If the experience of Auschwitz symbolizes alienation from God and from hope, the experience of Jerusalem symbolizes the presence of God and the continuation of the people. Burning children speak of the absence of all human and divine values, but the survial of Holocaust victims in Israel speaks of the reclamation of human dignity and value. "If Treblinka makes human hope an illusion, then the Western Wall asserts that human dreams are more real than force and facts. Israel's faith in the God of History demands that an unprecedented event of destruction be matched by an unprecedented act of redemption, and this has happened."[26]

Like Fackenheim, Greenberg understands that the victims of history are now called to refuse victimhood as meaning fidelity to the dead, although he adds the proviso that to remember suffering propels the community to refuse to create other victims.

> The Holocaust cannot be used for triumphalism. Its moral challenge must also be applied to Jews. Those Jews who feel no guilt for the Holocaust are also tempted to moral apathy. Religious Jews who use the Holocaust to morally impugn every other religious group but their own are the ones who are tempted thereby into indifference at the Holocaust of others (cf. the general policy of the American Orthodox rabbinate on United States Vietnam policy). Those Israelis who place as much distance as possible between the weak, passive Diaspora victims and the "mighty Sabras" are tempted to use Israeli strength indiscriminately (i.e., beyond what is absolutely inescapable for self-defense and survival), which is to risk turning other people into victims of the Jews. Neither faith nor morality can function without serious twisting of perspective, even to the point of becoming demonic, unless they are illuminated by the fires of Auschwitz and Treblinka.[27]

As we can see, within Greenberg's theological perspective the dialectic of Holocaust and political empowerment is crucial: the former expressed in Auschwitz, symbol of nothingness, the latter in Jerusalem, portent of redemption. But Greenberg's dialectic is broader and more nuanced. The experience of the death camps is a critique of false religion and of theological language as well as of political and technological developments within the modern secular world. It enjoins us to do acts of loving-kindness and to refuse that matrix of values and institutions that support genocide. Israel, as a manifestation of political empowerment, is a symbol of fidelity to those who perished. The counterpoint is the possibility that Israeli values and power may undermine that very sign Israel seeks to be to the Jewish community and the world. If for Greenberg the dialectic of Holocaust and political empowerment is the foundation of the struggle to be faithful, both poles of the dialectic are shadowed by the haunting possibility of betrayal.

A shift, almost unnoticeable at the time, begins to take place. In light of Greenberg's later works it was perhaps inevitable that Wiesel's and Fackenheim's theological positions were formulated at the time of the 1967 war, and it is the reunification of Jerusalem that crystallizes their understanding of the Holocaust. Israel becomes a response, perhaps *the* response, to the shattered witness of the Jewish people—the solitary figure of Eichmann, the commanding voice of Auschwitz, calls for empowerment. But in a general sense both Wiesel and Fackenheim remain within the notion of Jerusalem as a hope. Their main theme is in reality the death camps. The Yom Kippur War in 1973, the Israeli invasion of Lebanon in 1982, the massacre in the Palestinian refugee camps of Sabra and Shatila, the two decades of occupation on the West Bank and the Gaza Strip, and finally, the Palestinian uprising occasion little comment and less analysis from these two. What is offered by them is from the past. Elie Wiesel's statement upon learning of the massacre of Palestinians by Lebanese Christian militiamen in the West Beirut Shatila and Sabra refugee camps, while Israeli troops were in the area, is fueled by sadness, as if a dream that must survive is also capable of becoming a nightmare. The statement exemplifies both the starkness and the limitations of Wiesel's analysis: "Since the end of World War II, this has been the worst and darkest Rosh Hashanah for me. It is not that I accuse or indict anyone, and surely not the people of Israel, but I felt sadness, incommensurate sadness, almost disarmed. In a strange way, I felt responsible. Perhaps if we had told the story more convincingly, if we had prevented the trivialization and the cheapening of what was and remains a unique catastrophe, things would not have happened this way. I believe now that a gesture is needed on our part. Perhaps we ought to proclaim a day of fasting, surely a day of taking stock."[28]

Greenberg's task is to chart a path beyond the innocence of powerlessness and within the reality of Jewish empowerment, a path that represents yet another change in Jewish consciousness. While Wiesel and Fackenheim continue to speak of Jewish life as emerging from the death camps on the verge of empowerment, Greenberg begins to analyze Jewish empowerment as a reality, and to discuss its consequent ethical demands on the Jewish people. For Wiesel, especially, empowerment is a miracle tinged with sadness, for the dream is one of purity, though reality is more complex. For Greenberg the reality of empowerment is the end of innocence, and it is only by analyzing the demands of empowerment that the Jewish people can move forward in a responsible way. With this Greenberg adds a third dialectical theme to the evolving Holocaust theology: that of specialness and normalization. This is the burden of Greenberg's work, which begins in the early 1980s with his analysis of the third era in Jewish history and ends as the decade comes to a close with the Israeli response to the Palestinian uprising.

For Greenberg, the third era of Jewish history commences with the Holocaust and the crisis of faith and meaning that follows. The covenant of redemption is shattered, and the individual and communal response to that, especially in the formation of the state of Israel, is shaping the third era. The third era starts with a series of questions: "Does the Holocaust disprove the classic teaching of redemption? Does Israel validate it [the classic teaching of redemption]? Does mass murder over-whelm divine concern? How should we understand the covenant after such a devastating and isolating experience?" For Greenberg, the answer lies in activities that heal the brokenness of the Jewish people rather than in a spoken theology. Jews are called to a "new secular effort to recreate the infinite value of the human being" and, in this effort, to testify to the hope that a hidden relationship to God's presence still exists. Ultimately it is a call to a new level of covenantal responsibility.

> If God did not stop the murder and the torture, then what was the statement made by the infinitely suffering Divine Presence in Auschwitz? It was a cry for action, a call to humans to stop the Holocaust, a call to the people Israel to rise to a new, unprecedented level of covenantal responsi-bility. It was as if God said: "Enough, stop it, never again, bring redemp-tion!" The world did not heed that call and stop the Holocaust. European Jews were unable to respond. World Jewry did not respond adequately. But the response finally did come with the creation of the State of Israel. The Jews took on enough power and responsibility to act. And this call was answered as much by so-called secular Jews as by the so-called religious. Even as God was in Treblinka, so God went up with Israel to Jerusalem.[29]

To be sure, the new covenantal mandate challenges more traditional understandings of Jewish faith, for the rabbinic world of synagogue and prayer is no longer adequate. The move from powerlessness to power represents a decisive change in the Jewish condition. The resources, energy, and spirit necessary to create a Jewish state flow in a novel direction. Building the earthly Jerusalem comes first, and the "litmus test of the classic religious ideas becomes whether they work in real life and whether a society can be shaped by them."[30]

For Greenberg, the movement toward power is historically inescapa-ble in the face of the Holocaust. Jewish powerlessness is immoral, for it is no longer compatible with Jewish survival. Because the power needed for survival in the contemporary world is available only to sovereign states, achieving power in Israel reaches the level of sacred principle. Thus, according to Greenberg, "Any principle that is generated by the Holocaust and to which Israel responds . . . becomes overwhelmingly normative for the Jewish people." Arguing about how power is used is acceptable if the argument does not threaten the Jewish possession of power. How to use power is the critical point, but endangering the power is the unforgivable sin. In an era oriented by the Holocaust and Israel, a denial of Israel's legitimacy is the "equivalent of the excommunicable sins of earlier eras: denying the Exodus and the God who worked it in the

Biblical age or denying the Rabbis and separating from Jewish fate in the Rabbinic era."[31]

At the same time, Greenberg understands that power, being pragmatic and result-oriented, will test the ability of the tradition to advance values and community. Can Jewish ideals be actualized in the world, or are they empty spiritual generalities? Pragmatism rather than the prophetic, compromise rather than perfection, will be the norm in the third era. For Greenberg, this shift to pragmatism and compromise signals the end of the traditional Jewish presence on the radical end of the political spectrum, a presence that reflected not only the community's humanitarian concerns but also its lack of power. The use of power involves compromise and conservation as well as reform and perfection. Guilt and partial failures are inevitable. Despite the fact that power corrupts, it nonetheless must be appropriated. For Greenberg, then, the test of morality is a relative reduction of evil and improved mechanisms of self-criticism, correction, and repentance. "There is a danger that those who have not grasped the full significance of the shift in the Jewish condition will judge Israel by the ideal standards of the state of powerlessness, thereby not only misjudging but unintentionally collaborating with attempted genocide. Ideal moral stances applied unchanged to real situations often come out with the opposite of the intended result."[32]

Here Greenberg is again moving beyond Wiesel and Fackenheim, spelling out the political implications of empowerment. With Greenberg we see a shift in the religious legitimation already in motion in the Jewish community, a redefinition of the Jewish liberal agenda toward a neoconservative stance. If for Wiesel and Fackenheim Western civilizataion is, from the standpoint of Holocaust, bereft of promise, Greenberg understands the politics of that loss: self-defense, shifting alliances, trust only with constant verification. The engine of Jewish life is Israel, and all commitments are evaluated through that prism. With Greenberg, Jews embark, for the first time in two thousand years, on the development of a state theology, with its corollary meaning in the United States of a state-supporting theology. Israel as focal point redirects Jewish energy and concern toward and for Israel. American Jews play a crucial role here that Greenberg again articulates. Securing economic and military aid for Israel is a prime objective of the Jewish community in America; thus the Jewish prophetic voice vis-à-vis Israel in America can be dangerous. For Holocaust theologians, America is a haven for Jews and a harbor for Israel, which, because of United States support, will now no longer be challenged at its foundation. In short, for Greenberg, in the third era of Jewish history covenantal responsibility means state building and state supporting as a bulwark against a world still, and sometimes increasingly, hostile to Jewish interests. The mechanisms of limited self-criticism and correction are to replace the utopian vision of previous Jewish reformers, both in Israel and in America.

It is here also that Greenberg enunciates another theme of Holocaust theology already seen in embryonic form in the work of Wiesel and Fackenheim, that of the new anti-Semitism. Again the shifting of focus to Israel is crucial, because the new anti-Semitism, unlike the old, comes within the empowerment of the Jewish community. The new anti-Semitism is that which threatens the empowerment of the Jewish people, especially as embodied in the state of Israel. Though anti-Jewish attitudes of individuals are reprehensible, they pale before the significance of groups, movements, nations, and international bodies that are critical of Israel. At the time Wiesel and Fackenheim made their major contribution to Holocaust theology, there was a decidedly pro-Israel bias in Europe and America. By the late 1970s and early 1980s, though, criticism of Israel had increased dramatically. Thus Greenberg begins to confront a different climate, one in which entities of liberal background such as the National Council of Churches and the United Nations are perceived as harboring increasingly anti-Israel perspectives. An underlying fear in Greenberg's work is that the prophetic and the new anti-Semitism may join forces in a way that undermines the empowerment of Israel.[33]

Whereas Wiesel and Fackenheim were in their early writings clearly on the offensive, confronting the world with the horror of Jewish suffering and the need for empowerment, in Greenberg we see a more defensive tone as a critical posture toward Israel is adopted in the international and the American arenas and even by Jews themselves. The death camps and the miracle of Israel begin to fade into the past, and the reality of Israel asserts itself with a force unanticipated by early Holocaust theology. The importance of Israel to the Jewish community has already been explained, but as the second decade of occupation comes to a close, Greenberg's defense is just beginning. Now that defense is external and internal, for the unity engendered by the trial of Eichmann and the miracle of Jerusalem is dissipating quickly in the face of perceived Israeli arrogance and brutality. The collective awakening of the Jewish people articulated by Wiesel is moving toward an uprising within the Jewish community against Israeli state policy. In short, by the fortieth anniversary of the founding of the state of Israel, Holocaust theology is being forced to take a more critical posture while maintaining absolute loyalty, speaking less about the special qualities of Jewish power than about coming to grips with the normalization of the Jewish people.

The Ethics of Jewish Power

By March 1988 Greenberg was writing with a renewed urgency. The occupation of the West Bank and Gaza was now entering its third decade. The Palestinian uprising was in its fourth month. In a long essay, *The Ethics of Jewish Power*, which can be seen as a continuation of earlier reflections in both its seriousness and its importance, Greenberg begins with his most serious challenge:

> Many people are devastated when they see Jewish hands dirtied with the inescapable blood and guilt of operating in the world. The classic Jewish self-image—the innocent, sinned-against sufferer—is being shattered. The traditional Jewish conviction of being morally superior which has sustained our self-respect throughout centuries of persecution is being tested. Who imagined the day that to reestablish order, Jewish soldiers would deliberately beat Arabs on the hands? Or smash arms and legs of some civilians, not just terrorists? Who anticipated that such a policy would be morally superior to the alternative in which clashes led to shootings with live ammunition and to deaths? Some recoil and wish Israel away; some lash out and blame particular leaders. Many yearn for an alternative to regain lost innocence. The truth is more painful and must be faced.[34]

For Greenberg, the truth is clear: after almost two thousand years Jews have assumed power and therefore responsibility for themselves and for others. The costs have been high, in Greenberg's words staggeringly high, in both military casualties and difficult moral decisions. The unity of the Jewish people has made these costs bearable, but increasingly over the last decades the morally compromising situations into which Israel has entered endangers this unity. Here Greenberg alludes to Israel's historic ties to South Africa and Somocistas in Central America and to the war in Lebanon. Moral questioning of the legitimacy of Israeli actions has grown in certain circles. Citing the outcry surrounding the Sabra and Shatila massacres, and the appearance that Israel may have instigated them, Greenberg records his own reactions. "My personal reaction was: I do not believe that Israel would do such a thing. But let us assume the worst—what if it had organized the massacre (God forbid). The action should be condemned unequivocally. However, the United States of America was made possible in part by a systematic genocide of the Indians, pursued over the course of centuries. This was shameful and deeply regrettable, but did anybody suggest that the cost was too high and it were better that there had never been a United States? The Soviet Union has enslaved hundreds of millions, has persecuted Jews, has engaged in a genocidal invasion of Afghanistan. Does anyone seriously propose that it has lost its legitimacy as a state?"[35]

Yet beyond Greenberg's protest there is a fear that without the context of a Jewish ethic of power, the Jewish community may lose its moral bearings. This ethic will guide the Jewish people in avoiding what Greenberg calls the dangerous alternatives: "Undermining Israel or abandoning it through excessive criticism and faulty judgments—or betraying Israel by giving it a moral blank check and uncritical love."[36]

As in his earlier essays, Greenberg sees the beginning of ethical wisdom in the recognition that the world is unredeemed and that power can be exercised to protect and advance good. Yet power is not self-validating, and therefore power must be judged by a morality that seeks the perfection of the world and the triumph of life. Still, any exercise of power, no matter the standards to which it is held, will have "inescapable immoral side effects." The truly moral do not avoid using power because of its ambiguity; rather, they act only when necessary and seek to keep suffering caused by their actions to a minimum. The moral principle is thus in place. Accepting as given that evil cannot be avoided, there is still an ideal way of exercising power. This ideal rests in the ability to "reconcile prophetic demands with the compromising arts of governance and real policies." As Greenberg relates it, "Show me a people whose hands are not dirty and I will show you a people which has not been responsible. Show me a people which has stopped washing its hands and admitting its guilt, and I will show you a people which is arrogant and dying morally."[37]

Having outlined some general themes of this ethic of Jewish power, Greenberg turns to case studies, each presenting a different challenge to Jewish ethics and self-understanding. The first revolves around the rise of Meir Kahane, the angry and bellicose champion of the Greater Israel. Though some Jews are shocked by Kahane's racism and his call for the expulsion of Palestinians from Israel and the occupied territories, and disturbed by his small but vocal following, Greenberg is not. To be shocked is to assent to an underlying genetic fallacy, the belief that Jews are "intrinsically morally pure." For Greenberg, Jews are as capable of racism as any other people. The task is to correct the underlying problems that lead to Kahane's support, not to predict the end of Israeli democracy. "What all this attention to Kahane really proves is that 'covert chosenness'—the conviction of unreal Jewish exceptionalism—is alive and well in American Jewry, American media and Israel." This expectation leads to excessive harshness in judging Israeli behavior and a propensity to believe the worst about the decline of Jewish ethics. But for

Greenberg what it proves is that Jews are a normal people with hatred- and violence-prone members—that is, like all other groups of people. "Once the reality of Jewish normality is grasped, and the contextual nature of special moral behavior is admitted, then Israel—and Jewish power—will obtain a fair judgment."[38]

Greenberg continues with a discussion of the war in Lebanon, the first of Israel's wars to have aroused significant opposition within the Jewish community. Because the first four major wars were all, in Greenberg's view, preceded by Arab assaults, "combined with unvar- nished threats to wipe out Israel," there existed a one-sided moral am- bience focusing on Israeli suffering, heroics, and ethical self-restraint. Greenberg cites the classic quote of Golda Meir as the essence of the pre-Lebanon period. Said Meir, "Some day we will forgive the Arabs for killing our boys but we can never forgive them for turning our boys into killers." Yet for Greenberg that quote wraps a romantic haze around the Israeli reality, obscuring rather than dealing with the feelings of bereaved parents. The Arabs exist as highlights for Israeli heroism, not as flesh- and-blood casualties. Though Israeli soldiers are "killers," they are not really killers.[39]

For Greenberg, the pretense of the Lebanese war, to thwart the building of a Palestinian infrastructure in Lebanon as a threat to Israel's security, turned out to be waged on a gross misjudgment. On the one hand, Israel could not rearrange the balance of power in Lebanon as it had hoped. On the other hand, Israel did inflict civilian casualties with shellings and bombings, causing the death of innocent people. Still, as Greenberg sees it, Israel refused to bomb residential buildings where Palestine Liberation Organization guerrillas were situated, thus ac- cepting more casualties in order to spare civilians. Greenberg evaluates the war as follows: "In historical situations where sovereign, force- wielding nations wage wars, wars like the Lebanon invasion are likely, almost inevitable. In the Israel context, the war was bitterly criticized and opposed. This is a tribute to a higher standard of morality being applied by the Jewish people—the opposite of the standard interpretation of- fered by the media and others. The Lebanon War is often described as a complete breakdown of Israeli morality and democracy—which is a trib- ute to the excessive judgments bred by the continuing influence of the ethic of powerlessness. The war was wrong but well within the parame- ters of error and breakdown which characterize normal, healthy moral democracies."[40]

Finally, Greenberg turns his attention to the Palestinian uprising on the West Bank and Gaza as a classic example of the new moral situation facing the Jewish people. The uprising contains for Greenberg the contemporary Jewish dilemmas: trying to use restraint in the exercise of force, the inevitability of guilt, and the necessity of exerting moral control over power. For Greenberg, Israel drifted into a long-term occupation and was ill prepared for what in retrospect was inevitable: the desire of Palestinians to live freely. The initial Israeli response to the uprising, the policy in January 1988 of force and beatings announced by Defense Minister Rabin, was, to be sure, ethically preferable to shootings. But beatings introduced an element of "harshness and cold blood" heretofore absent. For Greenberg, Rabin's words were an invitation to excess in an already explosive situation. It stiffened Palestinian resolve even as it brought back memories of Jewish suffering through the ages. At the same time, the beatings policy constituted a drastic step beyond due process of the law—conviction without trial and use of corporal punishment, a method of punishment not accepted in Israeli law. Though in the past abuses were the outcome of individual breakdowns or deviations from the norms of military ethics, this policy framework meant that it was "likely that some officers or groups of soldiers—in the heat of daily clashes or in the cold blood of rage released—would seize Arabs, guilty of rioting or not, and beat them after arrest and beyond any security concern. This also raised the question whether such a policy of breach of legal norms can exist side by side with a democratic political and legal system without undermining it."[41]

Yet from Greenberg's perspective the basic fact is that the Palestinians are waging war. Though clearly Israel has superior military strength and the methods of Palestinian resistance physically endanger few Israelis, the situation is warlike insofar as the goals of the uprising are the destruction of Israel by "attacking its legitimacy, its support, its capacity to defend itself." And in the Middle East loss of Israel's sovereignty means the annihilation of the Jewish population in Israel. According to Greenberg, Israel is thus faced with moral choices that are problematic even in the best of situations. On the one hand, if the alternative is survival, Greenberg is clear: suppress the uprising and extend the occupation indefinitely. On the other hand, a policy driven by illusions of the Greater Israel will face the strength of Palestinian self-determination and the probability of increasing moral abuses by Jewish Israelis. Both will weaken the fabric of Israeli society and weaken support, Jewish and non-Jewish, for the state of Israel. In this scenario the cost of occupation is horrendous. "The creation of multiple Beiruts, unrelenting and brutalizing use of force, radical polarization within Israeli-Jewish society, a risk of alienating the loyalty of the Arabs inside the green line whose cooperation has made Israeli life infinitely more liveable in the past four decades. This path will likely lead down the road to Kahanism and moral perdition—even if unintended." Greenberg concludes that though there is something deeply moving about a people that reconnects with its roots after two millennia of absence, the ethical costs of militarily occupying the West Bank is too high: "Historical memories cannot justify suppression of another people's need for dignity and political self-realization."[42]

For Greenberg, the case studies of Jewish power and ethics point to the growing normalization of the Jewish condition as an inevitable and important part of group empowerment. To take responsibility in history is to accept normality with its possibilities and limitations. Yet for a people who have lived so long without power, the adjustment to normalcy is difficult. The difficulty arises out of Jewish self-perception and the perception of others vis-à-vis the Jewish people, and these two are addressed by Greenberg in the closing section of his essay.

Greenberg continues his analysis with questions that Jews often pose to themselves: Is not the Jewish covenant a covenant that imposes special expectations on the Jew? Did not the prophets hold Israel to this higher standard? Did not the Torah make it clear that failure to live up to the covenant will lead to expulsion from the land of Israel? To all those questions the answer is yes. But, for Greenberg, prophetic demands operate in a covenantal context in which ethics are rooted in the relationship and behavior of the covenantal partners. If in the biblical period the prophet could assure Israel of God's protection if they obeyed, and expulsion from the land if they disobeyed, the same cannot be said of the post-Holocaust period.

> The Divine decision not to intervene to save the righteous morally invalidates any Divine right to expel a people that does not live up to the covenant fully. There are people whose religious fervor leads them to disregard reality considerations in their actions—including calculation of the balance of power and the effects of policies. There are people who in the name of God or covenant, make absolute moral judgments on Israel—while ignoring the pragmatics of ethical standards or the impact of their words on support for Israel. In the light of the Holocaust, both types are guilty of irresponsibility and of deafness to divine instruction. Repeating the prophetic dicta that make possession of the land conditional on obedience and a pre-set standard of perfection constitutes not upholding Divine authority but an attempt to hold God to an earlier stage of relationship.[43]

For Greenberg, after the Holocaust, neither humanity nor God can require Israel to justify its existence by a perfect morality.[44]

Here the question of anti-Jewishness comes into play. Greenberg insists that with the assumption of power Jews resist the easy tendency to invoke anti-Jewishness as an explanation for people who have legitimate differences with specific policies and decisions. Citing Ronald Reagan's visit to Bitburg in 1985 and Pope John Paul's meeting with Kurt Waldheim in 1987 as errors in judgment rather than anti-Jewishness, Greenberg seeks a presumption of innocence unless proven otherwise. "Premature or excessive invocation of the specter of anti-Semitism can cripple Jews' capacity to see their own inevitable errors or pretensions and deaden their sensitivity to inflicting pain on others." It can also alienate those who are innocent of the charge and, as importantly, make it more difficult for the opponents of today to become supporters at a future date.[45]

Still, there are those who are anti-Jewish, and for Greenberg, their hatred may be masked as anti-Zionism. Though it is difficult to separate legitimate opposition to certain policies of a Jewish state and anti-Jewishness per se, Greenberg draws the line: "Blanket condemnation of Zionism as against specific Zionist policies is *ipso facto* anti-Semitic. Generic anti-Zionism opposes the Jewish right to national self-determination in contrast to the treatment of other nationalisms where people condemn specific acts or policies but do not deny the basic right to peoplehood and sovereign dignity." Those who insist that Israel live by absolute morality are anti-Jewish as well by demanding a standard of the Jewish state that can only lead to its own destruction. This applies to Jews and non-Jews alike. "If you insist that Israel's right to exist *depends* on its being perfect or if your self-image as a Jew demands that Israel *never* be morally compromised, in whatever way, then you are an anti-Semite. This judgment is true whether the individual making those absolute judgments is a sworn enemy of the Jewish people or a devoted and spiritual Jew who cannot abide the limits of the flesh. The taint of anti-Semitism is the 'punishment' for imposing absolute messianic demands on flesh-and-blood people in an unredeemed world." Why is this moral absolutism in Greenberg's mind anti-Jewish rather than simply immoral? Because for Greenberg this insistence discriminates against Jews when Israel is the only nation that is expected to live by the highest standards. Because it is impossible to survive with these standards, Israel must inevitably be condemned as a guilty nation with its right to exist denied. What makes this all so insidious for Greenberg is that some individuals who profess a love for Israel, as well as some committed Jews, push these standards, as do overt anti-Semites. The sponsorship of moralists and Jews makes the judgments harder to resist. Still, for Greenberg, "those

who weaken respect for Israel through judgments based on these standards of perfection are, *de facto,* collaborating with those who seek to
destroy Israel for less noble motives. Noble fellow-travelling with anti-
Semitism may be more dangerous than ignoble anti-Semitism because it
is more persuasive. By making total demands, moral absolutists destroy
the partial good that is possible. The ultimate immorality is to obliterate
the difference between the righteous-but-flawed and the wicked, and by
moral exaggeration, pave the way for the destruction of the righteous."[46]

Like Wiesel and Fackenheim before him, Greenberg concludes his
thoughts with the logic of Jewish unity as a willingness to bear the same
destiny. But he has also moved beyond them in that this shared destiny
includes the price of Jewish power. Citing the challenges to moral purity
that he has enunciated and the recent upsurge in anti-Jewish incidents
around the world, Greenberg thinks that the dividing line will be drawn
less by Israel's behavior, or agreement on that behavior, than by a simple
principle: whether one is prepared to pay the costs of Jewish destiny. To
a Jew who has embraced Jewish destiny, Israel remains the central the-
ater of collective Jewish action. Thus Greenberg's conclusion: "Israel is
the place where Jewish religion and Jewish morality is put to the test
because there a Jewish majority decides policy. The results can neither be
evaded nor denied, nor can responsibility be divided and diluted. Nothing can separate me from Israel. It is my people's statement of life and
vehicle to the future of a world perfected. I will be active to assure its
safety and will intervene to help it perform as morally and humanely as
possible. . . . Let there be a covenantal partnership between all Jews—
and all people who care—to assure that the power is exercised for life and
with full respect for the lives of others."[47]

With Greenberg the creative, even monumental, task of birthing a
new theology comes to an end. In less than a decade, Holocaust theologians like Wiesel and Fackenheim articulated the central dialectic facing
the Jewish community: suffering and the need for empowerment. By the
following decade Greenberg articulates both the end of innocence and
the end of the miracle as a challenge to the Jewish people. For Wiesel and
Fackenheim, Jerusalem is the fragile symbol of the unexpected survival.
For Greenberg, Jerusalem represents that survival and the assumption of
power that signifies a normalization of condition and the consequent loss
of innocence. Can Jews carry on, for the long haul, as it were, beyond the
moral simplicity of innocence and the immediacy of miracle?

There is little question that Holocaust theologians achieved to a startling degree the essential task of Jewish theology: to nurture the questions Jews need to ask about the history they are creating. In so doing,

perhaps without desiring it and certainly without planning it, Holocaust theologians helped to articulate a monumental shift in Jewish self-understanding and expression. Though there are other theologies that have been written during this period, they came into being and remain in the shadow of the questions Holocaust theology raises. Could we say that no theology in the history of Judaism has so expressed the feelings and longings of the Jewish people since the creation of rabbinic theology after the destruction of the Temple? And that like rabbinic theology, Holocaust theology arose within the Jewish catastrophe yet posed a great hope—the continuation of the people as an exercise in faith?

This is the power of Holocaust theology and its achievement. Yet like rabbinic theology, which emerged from destruction and through its articulation of Jewish survival and witness became normative for the Jewish people around the world, Holocaust theology proposes a certain orthodoxy that when unchallenged limits the new questions Jews need to ask about the history they are creating. To be sure, as the 1990s come upon us, the parameters of dissent, though expanding in the present, remain rigidly defined. It is not too much to say that the very passion of Holocaust theology poses challenges and limitations to Jewish thought and activity.

Every theology represents an argument, a series of choices of where one begins historically, what understandings and movements one includes, and thus decisions of who is within or outside the argument. To this, Holocaust theology is no exception. In relation to Jewish history, for example, the Holocaust and Israel are the formative events through which Jewish history is observed; everything is subsumed within these events. Even here, selection takes place precisely because of the angle of vision employed. If it is true, for example, that Holocaust and Israel are the crucial events of Jewish history, are they necessarily linked, as Holocaust theologians argue? Is empowerment in the state of Israel the necessary, almost exclusive, complement to the statement "Never again!"? When Holocaust becomes more and more the *raison d'être* of Jewish empowerment rather than a critical question about the forms of power Jews can with conscience employ, is this necessarily concomitant to the normalization of the Jewish condition, thus something Jews should welcome as well as struggle with? Is it true that dissenting Jews represent a prophetic element that is often unrealistic or damaging, perhaps even to the point of helping create the context for another holocaust? Is it helpful or even accurate to see the renewal of Jewish presence in the Middle East as a growing and organized community (which began at the close of the nineteenth century) simply within the context of the Holocaust? Can

Jews be certain that the countervailing pressures of assertion and adjustment, which Greenberg cites in theory and case studies as the essence of the Jewish ethics of power, are in fact operative from the view of those who experience that power as a form of oppression? Would Jews accept a Palestinian or, even more to the point, a German ethic of power that speaks of a similar corrective mechanism in their relation to Jews?

Holocaust theology, like almost any community theology, revolves around the community to which it is addressed. But recognizing self-interest and self-expression as givens, Holocaust theology seems to encourage self-absorption, almost to the exclusion of others. For example, Christians are present in Holocaust theology in reference to the events of Holocaust and Israel. Judgment on Christian faith and activity involves their resistance to, passivity in, or active complicity with the Holocaust and their support or nonsupport of Israel. Palestinians hardly exist at all; if they do exist, it is as a mass of people threatening the survival of the Jewish people. Though Palestinians, for the most part, are unmentioned, they become identifiable insofar as they operate within the parameters the Jewish people set for them. And even within the Jewish community there are many who remain unidentified, especially those who break with the empowerment of the Jewish community as Holocaust theologians envision it, as if anonymity could excommunicate them from Jewish life.[48]

Finally, the question revolves around the history of Jewish suffering. For Holocaust theologians, that meaning is clear and unequivocal: memory, survival, empowerment. In fact, that is the base, the historical material, out of which contemporary Jewish theology is fashioned. Few would quarrel with this. Still, each of these three elements remains open to interpretation, and often the passion of argument exhibited by Holocaust theologians perhaps masks doubts about the direction the community is taking. For in Wiesel there is often a somber quality, in Fackenheim anger, and in Greenberg perhaps too much insistence. Is it true that because of our history of suffering and struggle the accusation that Jews have also become oppressors is outrageous? Can we really argue that a history of suffering and struggle has brought Jews to a normalization that includes what Holocaust theologians rarely mention, expropriation of Palestinian land and labor, massive detentions without trial and continuous deportations, humiliation of a people, and torture? Does Holocaust theology, despite Greenberg's case study, critically deal with the realities of the formation of the state of Israel and its policies, past and present? What does the intrinsic and unequivocal link with Israel do to Jewish politics on issues other than Israel? Does not the price of normalization also lay the groundwork for neoconservative politics in America as well? Have Jews returned to history only to become powerful in Israel and in the United States? Or does Jewish empowerment make more complex and urgent the prophetic call of the Jewish people?

CHAPTER 2

Memory as Burden and Possibility: Alternative Views of Holocaust and Israel

There is little question that the Holocaust and the birth of the state of Israel represent the two formative events of the Jewish people in the twentieth century. But how Jews understand these events today, and how Jews understood these events as they were occurring, is more diverse than Holocaust theologians often observe. In fact, Holocaust theologians even differ in their analyses. What is crucial for the future of the Jewish people is to recover diversity of opinion and interpretation, past and present, so that Jews are not overwhelmed by grief, by the miraculous, or by entry into the process of normalization. If Jews are overwhelmed by their history, is it not too easy to use Jewish suffering and power as a blunt instrument rather than as a humble path of justice and compassion? And the need for total agreement is less than the need for airing of different views: the plurality of Jewish life may represent the breakthrough to deeper reflection on the crisis that Holocaust theologians have outlined so vividly.

Holocaust as Burden

In a recent essay Phillip Lopate, a Jewish essayist and novelist, reopens what for Jews is an extremely emotional subject. He begins with a most provocative title: "Resistance to the Holocaust." Lopate's intention is less to speak of the atrocities of the Nazi era, which are to his mind "enormous and unforgivable," than to address the cultural, political, and religious uses to which the disaster has since been put. Born after World War II, but before the term *Holocaust* had become commonplace, Lopate as a child heard "concentration camp; gas chambers; six million Jews; what the Nazis did." Some might see it as an improvement to use a single designation for the event. Yet for Lopate placing a label on such suffering serves to tame the experience. As use of the term *Holocaust* became more common in the mid-sixties, Lopate found it to have a self-important, almost vulgar, tone: "Then, too, one instantly saw that the term was part of a polemic and that it sounded more comfortable in certain speakers' mouths than in others; the Holocaustians used it like a club to smash back their opponents. . . . In my own mind I continue to distinguish, ever so slightly, between the disaster visited on the Jews and the 'Holocaust.' Sometimes it almost seems that 'the Holocaust' is a corporation headed by Elie Wiesel, who defends his patents with articles in the Arts and Leisure section of the Sunday *Times*."[1]

Taken in a certain context Lopate's words seem almost too easy. Yet it is clear throughout that he is participating in the most ancient of Jewish practices: refusing idolatry insofar as the Holocaust, or the use of it, becomes crystallized, untouchable, almost a God. What suffers, of course, when everything is reduced to the Holocaust or analogous to the Holocaust, is the ability to think through the issues that confront the Jewish people. As Lopate notes: "The Hitler/Holocaust analogy dead-ends all intelligent discourse by intruding a stridently shrill note that forces the mind to withdraw. To challenge the demagogic minefield of pure self-righteousness from an ironic distance almost ensures being misunderstood. The image of the Holocaust is too overbearing, too hot to tolerate distinctions. In its life as a rhetorical figure, the Holocaust is a bully."[2]

The Holocaust as a bully can also become Holocaust as kitsch. The Israeli author Avishai Margalit explores this theme in an essay titled "The Kitsch of Israel." According to Margalit, kitsch is based on an easy identification of the represented object; the emotion evoked in the spectator comes simply from a reference to the object. Although genuine art always maintains a distance from the represented object, thus involving the spectator in interpretation and allowing a variety of perspectives to emerge, the idea of kitsch is to arouse a strong emotion from the spectator's relation to the original object. Thus in the Jewish context a glimpse of Masada, or the Wall, or the Temple Mount is enough to move the "Jewish heart," and the marketing of Israel takes full advantage of these images. Kitsch can also be politicized and become, in Margalit's terms,

part of a state ideology whose "emblem is total innocence." The image of
the Israeli soldier and the Wailing Wall are two such items of kitsch,
evoking easy emotional identification with the important secondary understanding of a beleaguered nation. Of course, as Margalit points out,
the opposite of total innocence is total evil: "The innocent and pure with
whom we sympathize have to be relentlessly protected from those plot-
ting their destruction."[3]

For Margalit, however, the place that should be furthest from such
easy emotion, Yad Vashem, the Holocaust memorial in Israel, has, paradoxically, become an element of state kitsch. He cites a recently dedicated
children's room, pitch dark with tape-recorded voices of children crying
out for their mothers in Yiddish. As Margalit remarks, this kind of kitsch
even a "kitschman of genius" like Elie Wiesel would find hard to surpass:
"The real significance of this room is not its commemoration of the single
most horrible event in the history of mankind—the systematic murder of
two million children, Jewish and Gypsies, for being what they were and
not for anything they had done. The children's room, rather, is meant to
deliver a message to the visiting foreign statesman, who is rushed to Yad
Vashem even before he has had time to leave off his luggage at his hotel,
that all of us here in Israel are these children and that Hitler-Arafat is after
us. This is the message for internal consumption as well. Talking of the
P.L.O. in the same tone as one talks of Auschwitz is an important
element in turning the Holocaust into kitsch."[4]

Margalit reports that with the outbreak of the Palestinian uprising,
when criticism from within and outside Israel has reached its peak, the
increased invoking of Holocaust memories is noticeable. Included is a
Holocaust quiz show, shot in Poland, on which young Jews are asked
questions relating to the massacre of the Jews in Europe. For each correct
answer two points are awarded. Applause is forbidden as being in bad
taste. Margalit's conclusion: "Against the weapon of the Holocaust, the
Palestinians are amateurs. True, some of them have adopted their own
version of Holocaust kitsch, based on the revolting equation of the Israelis with Nazis and of themselves with Nazis' victims; but as soon as
operation 'Holocaust Memory' is put into high gear by the Israeli authori-
ties, with full-fledged sound-and-color production, the Palestinians cannot compete. The absence of the main actor and the stage queen, Begin
and Golda, is certainly a loss for political kitsch, but a new star has risen,
Benjamin Netanyahu ('Arafat is worse than Hitler'), and prospects are
now bright—nothing will make us cut the kitsch.' "[5]

Increasingly in Israel, the Holocaust is seen in a similar light, as an
event that is consciously manipulated by the state and its leadership.

This is the theme of Boas Evron, an Israeli writer and commentator, in his essay "The Holocaust: Learning the Wrong Lessons." For Evron, two terrible things happened to the Jewish people over the last half-century: the Holocaust and the lessons learned from it. The ahistorical interpretations of the Holocaust made deliberately or out of ignorance have become in Evron's mind a danger both to the Jewish people and to the state of Israel for the following reasons: The term *Holocaust* is rhetorical and ambiguous; it exists without historical reference and thus has become indefinite and movable, almost exempting one from understanding it. "The murder of the Jews in Europe," though not as galvanizing, more accurately reflects and locates a historical event in which there were murderers and those who were murdered. Such an event becomes worthy of historical investigation and is lifted from the mystical and pseudoreligious. By analyzing the historical context, Evron finds different lessons to be drawn from the event than Holocaust theologians do. For example, Evron points to the basic assumption that the Nazi policy of mass murder was directed almost exclusively against Jews. The facts speak differently: Gypsies and three million non-Jewish Poles were murdered, and millions of Russian prisoners of war and forced laborers were murdered as well. The enslavement and extermination of the Slav people was also a possibility for the Nazis. For Evron, anti-Semitism served as a "catalyst, as the focal point of the extermination system" that was destined to become a central and permanent institution of the Third Reich.[6]

Thus the Nazi murder of the Jews was unique only in preparing the world for the institutionalization of extermination. The argument presented as a corollary, that the Jews of Palestine were saved by Zionism, is also false: they were saved by the defeat of the Nazis at El Alamein and Stalingrad, which prevented the Nazis from conquering Palestine and exterminating the Jewish population. The lesson of the Holocaust is therefore different: "The true guarantee against ideologically-based extermination is not military power and sovereignty but the eradication of ideologies which remove any human group from the family of humanity." For Evron, the solution lies in a common struggle aimed at overcoming national differences and barriers rather than increasing and heightening them, as strong trends within Israel and the Zionist movement demand.[7]

There were many reasons why the historical presentation of the murder of the Jews in Europe was rejected for an ahistorical view summarized in the word *Holocaust*. According to Evron the Germans were interested in this because it limited, in a sense, their liability. Instead of focusing on the systemic and expanding possibilities of a system of extermination, a focus that might have kept alive the feelings of fear and suspicion after the war in Germany's neighbors, limiting the memory to the Jews and the Holocaust enabled Germany to more easily reintegrate itself into the world of nations. The Western powers were also interested in this insofar as it allowed them to wipe the slate clean and begin to rebuild Germany as a barrier to Soviet expansion.[8]

The "Jewish monopolization" of the Nazi experience was also welcomed by Jewish leadership in Israel and in the Diaspora, as a way of strengthening German guilt consciousness, thus continuing and increasing the amount of compensation payments for survivors, and as a way of mobilizing world support, moral, political, military, and financial, for the Jewish state. For Evron, this new and creative policy of inducing moral guilt was a prime reason for the Eichmann trial. It shifted the policy of Germany as well as that of other countries; it lifted the tragedy out of the past and made it a basis for future preferential relationships. And as importantly, this policy became a blueprint for relations with most Western Christian states, especially the United States; they were to support Israel on the basis of guilt rather than self-interest.[9]

Evron sees the ramifications of this policy to be enormous. In the first place it contravened an aim of the Zionist movement to normalize the status of the Jewish people and reduced Israel to the "level of an eternal beggar." Henceforth Israel survives on the "six million credit" instead of, like any other country, on developing and marketing its energy and skills. Living off its past, Israel exists, like the Holocaust, in an ahistorical context, thus avoiding economic and political confrontation in the real world. Paradoxically a renewed feeling of isolation grows as the adulation of the survivor Israel increases. The policy also generates what Evron considers a moral blindness: because the world is out to get Israel in the present and in the future, any links with oppressive governments and any oppression of non-Jews within and around Israel can be justified.[10]

The Holocaust can also be used as a powerful tool by Israeli and Jewish leadership in the United States to organize and police the Jewish community. Diaspora Jews, for example, are made to feel guilty for not having done enough to prevent the Holocaust; at the same time the message is conveyed that Israel is threatened with annihilation. The message is clear: unequivocal support for Israel to prevent a second holocaust. Evron sees the image of Holocaust past as Holocaust future as so important to Israel and American Jewry that the reality of Israel's strength is submerged in myth:

When you try to explain to American Jews that we are not, in fact, in danger of annihilation, that for many years to come we will be stronger than any possible combination, that Israel has not, in fact, been in danger of physical annihilation since the first cease-fire of the War of Independence in 1948, and that the average human and cultural level of Israeli society, even in its current deteriorated state, is still much higher than that of the surrounding Arab societies, and that this level rather than the quantity and sophistication of our arms constitutes our military advantage—you face resistance and outrage. And then you realize another fact: this image is needed by many American Jews in order for them to free themselves of their guilt regarding the Holocaust. Moreover, supporting Israel is necessary because of the loss of any other focal point to their Jewish identity. Thus, many of them resist the suggestion that the appropriate aim for Israel is to liberate itself from any dependency on outside elements, even Jewish ones. They need to feel needed. They also need the "Israeli hero" as a social and emotional compensation in a society in which the Jew is not usually perceived as embodying the characteristics of the tough, manly fighter. Thus, the Israeli provides the American Jew with a double, contradictory image—the virile superman, and the potential Holocaust victim—both of whose components are far from reality.[11]

The equation of Arab hatred of Israel with the Nazi hatred of Jews, for Evron, arises logically out of the ahistorical quality of the Holocaust. The Nazis, who created an irrational hatred of the Jews so as to justify their system of mass extermination, are likened to the Arabs, who, according to Evron, have a quite rational reason for opposing Israel as a powerful enemy that has expelled and displaced over a million of their compatriots. The difference between an illiterate Palestinian refugee and a highly trained SS trooper is blurred beyond distinction, and the defense of the country in the Six-Day War and the Yom Kippur War becomes less an integral part of sovereign political existence than a stage on which the destiny of the Jewish people is played out. Identifying Palestinians with Nazis, as the continuous reminder of the Holocaust does, leads to hysterical responses rather than reasoned policy. These parallels have serious moral consequences as well. Because the choices presented to Israel are not realistic—only holocaust or victory—Israel becomes free of any moral restrictions, because any nation that is in danger of annihilation feels exempted from moral considerations that might restrict its efforts to save itself. For Evron, this is the rationale of people who argue that everything is permitted because the world wants Israel's destruction. "They do not hesitate to recommend the most drastic steps against the non-Jewish population in Israel. Although it is a serious comparison to make, it is worth remembering that the basic Nazi claim justifying the slaughter of Jews was the 'Jewish conspiracy' to destroy the German nation." Evron concludes that Israeli and Jewish leadership, caught up in an ahistorical world, threaten to become victims of their own propaganda. They draw on a bank account continuously reduced by withdrawals. As the world moves on there are fewer who remember the Holocaust, and those who do, including the Jews, become tired of it as a nuisance and a reflection of a reality that does not exist: "Thus the leadership, too, operates in the world of myths and monsters created by its own hands. It has created this world in order to maintain and perpetuate its rule. It is, however, no longer able to understand what is happening in the real world, and what are the historical processes in which the state is caught. Such a leadership, in the unstable political and economic situation of Israel today, itself constitutes a danger to the very existence of the state."[12]

But to challenge the orthodoxy of Holocaust theology is not without penalty. Richard Rubenstein, for example, who helped initiate the discussion of the Holocaust in 1966 with the publication of his book *After Auschwitz: Radical Theology and Contemporary Judaism*, was for years ostracized from the Jewish community, in part for his probing of Jewish suffering in the Holocaust as a failure of internal Jewish leadership, for his understanding of the attempted annihilation of the Jews as partly an example of economic displacement and surplus population reduction, and finally for his envisioning of the Jewish experience of Holocaust as both unique *and* paradigmatic for other sufferings in the twentieth century. In fact, his book, *The Cunning of History: Mass Death and the American Future*, published in 1975, was written partially in response to the unwillingness of the organizers of the Holocaust convocation at Saint John the Divine Cathedral in New York City to extend an invitation for him to speak. This was the convocation, later published under the title *Auschwitz: Beginning of a New Era?*, that represented the height of the influence of Holocaust theology and included, among many others, Elie Wiesel, Emil Fackenheim, and Irving Greenberg.

In *The Cunning of History* Rubenstein approaches the most difficult of questions: Did Jews, in effect, no matter how involuntarily, cooperate in their own undoing? For Rubenstein the charge of desecrating the memory of the dead or even excusing their murderers cannot replace the objectivity of political reflection. "Regrettably, those who avoid objective reflection on the Jewish response add to the confusion concerning what took place. Every assault requires at least two actors. . . . Even the most innocent victim is part of the process of his own undoing by virtue of the fact that he did not or could not take protective measures."[13]

For Rubenstein, two factors were initially critical for the Nazis to carry out the mass murder of Jews: the cultural conditioning of two thousand years of rabbinic Judaism that counseled Jews to submit and endure rather than resist and the Germans' ability to utilize the existing leadership and organizations of the Jewish community wherever the extermination process was implemented. Rubenstein boldly asserts that the process of transforming Jewish communal bureaucracies into components of the extermination was one of the organizational triumphs of the Nazis. Most Jews instinctively relied on their own communal organizations to defend their interests wherever possible. Yet, according to Rubenstein, these organizations of self-governance were transformed into subsidiaries of the German police and state democracies. "Thus, the official agency of German Jews led by the most distinguished German rabbi of the twentieth century, a man in whose memory an important rabbinical seminary has been named (London's Leo Baeck College), undertook such tasks as selecting those who were to be deported, notifying the families and, finally, of sending the Jewish police to round up the victims. In the Warsaw Ghetto and in Lodz, Poland, the Jewish council, or *Judenrat*, did not resist German directives even when the Germans demanded the 'selection' of 10,000 Jews a day for deportation. Jewish bureaucrats made the selection, Jewish police rounded up the victims." In a provocative conclusion Rubenstein states that Germany "demonstrated that a modern state can successfully organize an entire people for its own extermination."[14]

Still the fate of the Jews was sealed earlier than the Nazi period with the active promulgation of Christian anti-Jewishness as well as economic and demographic changes relating to the capitalist revolution in Europe. For Rubenstein, from the moment of the Christian triumph in Europe, Jews were in an inherently dangerous position, and here Rubenstein simply reiterates the sense of other religious writers on the anti-Jewish aspects of the Holocaust. But Rubenstein raises a further question: Why with almost two millennia of hatred did Jews survive Christendom? Why did the activities of Christendom toward Jews, conversion and isolation, become in the twentieth century the pursuit of the final solution? According to Rubenstein the reason for the survival of Jews and Judaism in the harsh Christian ethos was that in premodern times the consequences of religious conflict were moderated by Europe's precapitalist economy, in which Jews played a necessary, though often despised, role. Like the ethnic Chinese of Southeast Asia, the Ibos of Nigeria, and the Armenians of the Ottoman Empire, Jews functioned as an elite minority filling certain commercial and professional roles that were not being filled by the dominant majority.[15]

As the urbanized middle class arose within the capitalist revolution, Jews ceased to play a complementary role and became highly visible competitors of a more powerful and rooted group, the rising Christian bourgeoisie. Thus already in the sixteenth century European Jews were being forced out of these elite though dangerous positions and entered marginal roles as peddlers of secondhand goods and pawnbrokers. Eventually the majority of the Jews were closed out of viable economic activity and were forced to migrate from western to eastern Europe, precisely because the latter remained feudal and agrarian. In the nine- teenth century this process of capitalist development took place in east- ern Europe, which reversed migration back to the west. In a great, though tragic, irony, Jews in these various migrations became identified with the general trends of disorientation and displacement of the native populations of east and west, and as competing with them for scarce resources, and therefore with the triumph of a capitalist, anonymous, uprooting society. For Rubenstein, Jews, in religious terms but also now in economic and social reality, became pariahs in the ultimate sense, unwanted and unneeded, thus superfluous. From that moment on, segregation into ghettos and the policy of extermination were policies that only awaited a certain configuration of events.[16]

Though the complexities of Rubenstein's argument for bureaucratic self-destruction and transformation of Europe's economic order are many and controversial, they point to his major contribution: broadening the understanding of the Holocaust. Rubenstein affirms that the Jewish experience of suffering is unique and tied to a long history of anti- Jewishness, but something happened in the capitalist revolution, culmi- nating in the twentieth century, that allowed the transformation of contempt into mass death. Yet the mass death of Jews involves and moves beyond the experience of the Jewish people, in effect binding Jewish suffering with others, past and present. In fact, Jewish suffering must take its place alongside other examples of mass death that help define the twentieth century.

> The mass death that took place in the West during World War I was prelude to the carnage that took place in the Russian sphere as a result of revolution, civil war, demographic violence, and large-scale famine. Exact figures are unavailable, but an estimated two to three million died as a

result of hard violence and six to eight million as a result of long-term privation. According to Gil Eliot, the foundations of twentieth-century military slaughter on a mass scale were laid during World War I; the foundations of mass civilian slaughter were laid immediately thereafter, especially in Central and Eastern Europe, the very area in which the Jews were to perish during the Second World War. Nor ought we to neglect to mention the Turkish massacre of about one million Armenians during World War I, perhaps the first full-fledged attempt by a modern state to practice disciplined, methodically organized genocide. The list of victims of twentieth-century mass slaughter also includes those who perished in the Sino-Japanese War and the Spanish Civil War; the millions who were killed in the various Stalinist purges, as well as those who died in the man-made famines which resulted from Stalin's slaughter of peasants who resisted collectivization between 1929 and 1933; the Russian and Polish prisoners of war exterminated by the Germans; the Russian prisoners of war who escaped death at the hands of the Germans only to be murdered when they returned home; those who perished at Hiroshima and Nagasaki, and the victims of the wars and revolutions of Southeast Asia.[17]

For Rubenstein, rather than an exception or a unique event, the Jewish Holocaust becomes a paradigm, "an expression of some of the most significant political, moral, religious and demographic tendencies of Western civilization in the twentieth century." Rubenstein concludes his analysis with a prophetic warning:

> Perhaps it was no accident that the most highly urbanized people in the Western world, the Jews, were the first to perish in the ultimate city of Western civilization, Necropolis, the new city of the dead that the Germans built and maintained at Auschwitz. Auschwitz was perhaps the terminal expression of an urban culture that first arose when an ancient protobourgeoisie liberated its work life from the haphazard, unpredictable, and seasonable character of agriculture and sustained itself by work which was, in the words of Max Weber, "continuous and rational." In the beginning, removed from immediate involvement in "the vital realities of nature," the city was the habitat of the potter, the weaver, the carpenter, and the scribe; in the end, it houses the police bureaucrat and his corporate counterpart coldly and methodically presiding over the city of the dead.[18]

There are, of course, many other ways of looking at the Holocaust, but the themes surfaced by Lopate, Margalit, Evron, and Rubenstein— the Holocaust as block to creative and emphatic thought, as kitsch, as open to political, economic, and sociological interpretation, as paradigmatic rather than unique—forces Jews to continually be open to history rather than be determined by it.

Dissenters in Zion

All this suggests further questioning of still another almost sacred assumption, that of the relationship of the Holocaust to the state of Israel. So often is the connection presumed without a second thought that one may be startled by such a question. Yet historically the Zionist movement predated the Nazi period by at least four decades and the death camps by five. The assumed link between Holocaust and Israel and the way the two are discussed, especially since the 1967 war, in a sense cuts off much of the most principled and interesting dissent that Jews have provided over the last century, and thus makes it more difficult to gauge the limits of dissent in the present. It is as if Zionism, and thus the state of Israel, has no history. Of course, without history there is no accountability. Would it be so horrible, for instance, to know that many of the most interesting and important Jews at the formative period of Zionism actually opposed the creation of Israel as a state? And that despite its existence there always has been and still remains systematic and sustained opposition to many of Israel's most fundamental policies and outlooks? In fact, one might say that there is now a tradition of dissent vis-à-vis Israel that is largely unmentioned by Holocaust theologians and unspoken—perhaps unknown—within the Jewish community at large.

There is little question that Zionism represented a revolutionary force in Jewish life at the end of the nineteenth century. Although because of Holocaust theology we often think of Zionism almost exclusively in relation to anti-Jewishness, it is important to see it as well within the framework of the forces unleashed by the Enlightenment and the French Revolution. This is the point made by Shlomo Avineri in his book *The Making of Modern Zionism: The Intellectual Origins of the Jewish State.* For Avineri, those Jews who were seeking mere survival and economic security, those who were suffering pogroms and pauperization, tended to emigrate to America. Those who went to Palestine, then within the Ottoman Empire, where living conditions were similar or worse, went seeking a liberation announced within post-1789 European culture—self-determination, identity, the fulfillment of a newly awakened self-consciousness.[19]

Hence early Zionism was less a response to anti-Jewishness (or even religious sentiment, though both were surely present) than to the challenge of liberalism and nationalism. This is why the anti-Jewishness of the previous millennium occasioned only sporadic and individual returns to the land—and almost always within the framework of religious orthodoxy. According to Avineri, Zionism was the fundamental revolution in Jewish life (possible only in the post-1789 European culture) precisely because it substituted a secular self-identity of the Jews as a nation for the traditional and orthodox self-identity in religious terms, and because it changed a passive, quietistic, and pious hope of the return to Zion into an effective social force, moving millions of people to Israel. Finally, it transformed Hebrew from a language of mostly liturgical use into the modern, secular language of a nation. Clearly, as Avineri sees it, the rise of Zionism and ultimately the state of Israel is a completely modern phenomenon—in fact, a response to the challenge of modernity.

Of course, this journey of a dispersed people to a modern state was fraught with puzzling dilemmas and contradictions. If Zionism was a modern secular phenomenon, how did it relate to Jewish tradition? If Zionism was a revolution in Jewish consciousness and activity, how did it transform a minority movement among Jews into a majority? What was a Jewish nation, and what would it represent? Was the task of Zionism to normalize the Jewish condition, that is, to form a nation like all others? Or was the gathering of Jews in Palestine to represent a rebirth of a special calling to be a light among the nations?

From the beginning of the Zionist movement there were fundamental divisions relating to these questions and many others. What is of interest here is the initial division between political Zionism and cultural Zionism. Political Zionism, represented by Theodore Herzl, saw the main task of Zionism as founding and creating a functioning Jewish state. Cultural Zionism was championed by Asher Ginsburg (1852–1927), who wrote under the pseudonym of Ahad Ha'am "one of the people"; it saw the gathering of Jews in Palestine as critical to the cultural and spiritual renewal of Judaism and the Jewish people, and thus the essential task of the Zionist movement.[20]

For Ahad Ha'am, who was born into a Russian Hasidic family but, like many Jews of his generation, participated in the secular, emancipatory atmosphere of Odessa, Zionism needed to address the two faces of Jewry, those in western Europe faced with the failure of nineteenth-century Europe to provide an adequate answer to the individual quest for Jewish identity in the modern world and those in eastern Europe who found themselves faced with the collective difficulty of finding a place in emerging national cultures. For western European Jews a Jewish state would mean an ideal and an opportunity:

If a Jewish state were re-established [in Palestine], a state arranged and organised exactly after the pattern of other states, then he [the western European Jew] could live a full, complete life among his own people, and find at home all that he now sees outside, dangled before his eyes, but out of reach. Of course, not all the Jews will be able to take wing and go to their state, but the very existence of the Jewish state will raise the prestige of those who remain in exile, and their fellow citizens will no more despise them and keep them at arm's length as though they were ignoble slaves, dependent entirely on the hospitality of others. As [the western European Jew] contemplates this fascinating vision, it suddenly dawns on his inner consciousness that even now, before the Jewish state is established, the mere idea of it gives him almost complete relief. He has an opportunity for organised work, for political excitement, he finds a suitable field of activity without having to become subservient to non-Jews, and he feels that thanks to this ideal he stands once more spiritually erect, and has regained human dignity, without overmuch trouble and without external aid. So he devotes himself to the ideal with all the ardor of which he is capable, he gives rein to his fancy, and he lets it soar as it will, up above reality and the limitations of human power. For it is not the attainment of the ideal that he needs: its pursuit alone is sufficient to cure him of his moral sickness, which is the consciousness of inferiority; and the higher and more distant the ideal, the greater its power of exaltation.[21]

For eastern European Jews a Jewish state would forge a new focus of identity:

So it [Judaism] seeks to return to its historic center, in order to live there a life of natural development, to bring its powers into play in every department of human culture, to develop and perfect those national possessions which it has acquired up to now, and thus to contribute to the common stock of humanity, in the future as in the past, a great national culture, the fruit of the unhampered activity of a people living according to its own spirit. For this purpose Judaism needs at present but little. It needs not an independent state, but only the creation in its native land of conditions favorable to its development: a good-sized settlement of Jews working without hindrance in every branch of culture, from agriculture and handicrafts to science and literature. This Jewish settlement, which will be a gradual growth, will become in course of time the center of the nation, wherein its spirit will find pure expression and develop in all its aspects up to the highest degree of perfection of which it is capable. Then from this center the spirit of Judaism will go forth to the great circumference, to all the communities of the Diaspora, and will breathe new life into them and preserve their unity, and when our national culture in Palestine has attained that level, we may be confident that it will produce men in the country who will be able, on a favorable opportunity, to establish a state which will be truly a Jewish state, and not merely a state of Jews.[22]

The challenge of bringing culture and spirit together is primary for Ahad Ha'am and hardly new to Jewish history. He uses the conflict of the Sadducees, who saw the very existence of the Jewish state as the essence of national life, and the Pharisees, who saw the spiritual context as the mainstay of Jewish existence, as the dialectical tension worthy of consideration in the contemporary Zionist discussion. For Ahad Ha'am, the Pharisees represent the true synthesis of the spiritual and the material, holding a dialectical defense of political power that views power as a tool rather than an end in itself. Thus they were faced with a twofold battle: "On the one hand, they opposed the political materialists from within, for then the State was only a body without an essential spirit; and, on the other side, they fought together with these opponents against the enemy without, in order to save the State from destruction." When Rome defeated and destroyed the Jewish nation, the Pharisees held out the possibility for the continuation of the people.

> The political materialists, for whom the existence of the state was everything, had nothing to live for after the political catastrophe [the destruction of the Temple by the Romans]; and so they fought desperately, and did not budge until they fell dead among the ruins that they loved. But the Pharisees remembered, even in that awful moment, that the political body had a claim on their affections only because of the national spirit which found expression in it, and needed its help. Hence they never entertained the strange idea that the destruction of the state involved the death of the people, and that life was no longer worth living. On the contrary, now they felt it absolutely necessary to find some temporary means of preserving the nation and its spirit even without a state, until such time as God should have mercy on His people and restore it to its land and freedom. So the bond was broken: the political Zealots remained sword in hand on the walls of Jerusalem, while the Pharisees took the scroll of the Law and went to Jabneh.[23]

For Ahad Ha'am, the work of the Pharisees bore fruit in preserving the Hebrew national spirit, in organizing a cultural and spiritual life for a scattered and despised people, and in preparing diaspora communities for a "single aim and perfect union in the future."[24]

Ahad Ha'am's initial visit to Jewish settlements in Palestine in 1890 occasioned an essay, "Thoughts from the Land of Israel," in which he recognized the complexities of realizing the Zionist vision. Already he is dealing with the myths of Palestine as a relatively empty place and the Arabs as backward people. "We tend to believe abroad that Palestine is nowadays almost completely deserted, a noncultivated wilderness, and anyone can come there and buy as much land as his heart desires. But in reality this is not the case. It is difficult to find anywhere in the country

Arab land which lies fallow; the only areas which are not cultivated are sand dunes or stony mountains, which can be only planted with trees, and even this only after much labor and capital would be invested in clearance and preparation." Ahad Ha'am also warns against use of violence and humiliation toward the Arab population:

> One thing we certainly should have learned from our past and present history, and that is not to create anger among the local population against us. . . . We have to treat the local population with love and respect, justly and rightly. And what do our brethren in the Land of Israel do? Exactly the opposite! Slaves they were in their country of exile, and suddenly they find themselves in a boundless and anarchic freedom, as is always the case with a slave that has become king, and they behave toward the Arabs with hostility and cruelty, infringe upon their boundaries, hit them shamefully without reason, and even brag about it. Our brethren are right when they say that the Arab honours only those who show valour and fortitude, but this is the case only when he feels that the other side has justice on his side. It is very different in a case when [the Arab] thinks that his opponent's actions are iniquitous and unlawful, in that case he may keep his anger to himself for a long time, but it will dwell in his heart and in the long run he will prove himself to be vengeful and full of retribution.[25]

By 1912 he wrote protesting the boycott of Arab labor as a strategy to conquer the land: "Apart from the political danger, I can't put up with the idea that our brethren are morally capable of behaving in such a way to humans of another people, and unwittingly the thought comes to my mind: if it is so now, what will be our relation to the others if in truth we shall achieve at the end of times power in Eretz Israel? And if this be the 'Messiah': I do not wish to see his coming."[26]

At his death in 1927 in Tel Aviv, Ahad Ha'am was brokenhearted, outraged by what he considered to be a cycle of violence almost impossible to break. "My god is *this* the end? . . . Is this the dream of our return to Zion, that we come to Zion and stain its soil with innocent blood? It has been an axiom in my eyes that the people will sacrifice its money for the sake of a state, but never its prophets."[27]

Prophetic Warnings

Another early critical Zionist was Judah Magnes (1877–1948), a Reform rabbi born in America who emigrated to Palestine in 1923, where he became chancellor of Hebrew University. As chancellor, Magnes became a symbol of hope for Zionists who believed in the progressive endeavors

of the Jewish return to the land. He became closely tied to such lumi-
naries as Martin Buber and Hans Kohn. He also challenged some of the
most important and powerful Jewish leaders of his time, Louis D. Bran-
deis, Stephen S. Wise, Chaim Weitzman, and David Ben-Gurion. In
Magnes we find American pragmatism and Jewish faith, a crusader's zeal
and a deep commitment to the renewal of his people. And like Ahad
Ha'am, Magnes realized both the possiblities of Zionism for renewal of
Jewish culture and spirit and the limitations of a Zionism that ignored the
Arab/Palestinian population or, worse, sought to subjugate them in or
outside a Jewish state.[28]

In a 1924 journal entry, written just after his arrival in Jerusalem,
Magnes outlined one of his basic themes in relation to Zionism, the
possibility that through Jewish nationalism, nationalism itself would be
transcended by an internationalism worthy of the Jewish spirit. For
Magnes, it is only after being rooted in a nation that nationalism can be
overcome. Being rooted in a nation allows one to transcend the nation
without fear of assimilation and the loss of self that results. A freedom
ensues that Magnes compares to the technique of a musician that is so
perfect it ceases to be of concern. What concerns the musician is the
higher things, those of the spirit.[29]

This is not easy for a Jew. Though many things predispose Jews to
universalism—including the historical experience of wandering and the
prophets—Magnes believes Jews have a much harder job overcoming
their nationalism. Only Jews who feel themselves firmly rooted in the
Jewish nation, for whom there is not the slightest possibility of being
anything other than a Jew, can overcome this difficulty. This is precisely
where, for Magnes, the universalist doctrine of Reform Judaism—of the
merging of nations, races, and peoples into a spiritual synthesis of
prophetic human solidarity—fails. By uprooting themselves from
their nationality Jews lack roots in "Jewish earth." While preaching the
doctrine of universalism, they are trying to escape from Judaism and
their Jewish selves, only through the care of which a true internationalism can grow. In essence, for Magnes, two kinds of Jews can become
universalists:

> The Jew who knows and thinks so little of himself as a Jew that he can in
> very truth say he is no Jew but an internationalist, universalist (e.g.,
> Trotsky), and the Jew who has so thoroughly grounded himself in his
> Judaism that his universalism becomes the development and crown of his
> Judaism.
>
> Many a Jew of the latter type is himself predisposed to his higher
> attitude, but he is afraid that his people is not strong enough nationally to

bear this development. The question is really fundamental, and my answer is that the Jews are a strong, vital people and not a weak one—and
this despite pogroms and wanderings. They are mighty and vital physically. They seem incapable of being annihilated, and give Jewish children
a chance in fresh air and with good food and see how they blossom. His
spiritual forces are equally great. See how he maintains himself and grows
with the Diaspora, and how he is embedding himself in Eretz Israel. This
very experiment must give every one of us courage. It shows that the Jew
can and will live apart and at the same time render homage to the highest
of human ideals—witness his communistic settlements.[30]

Thus for Magnes—and this is often forgotten today—Zionism was a
movement that emerged from the strength rather than the weakness of
the Jewish people. The renewal of the Jewish community in Palestine
needed and was possible only within the context of a strong and vibrant
Diaspora. Magnes concludes his journal entry with a general rule to act
from Jewish strength, as if Zion were already rebuilt: "Therefore let us
seek our brethren of all peoples. Fear for the Jews or fear of others cannot
be our guiding force, only confidence in Jewish strength and belief in
great human ideals."[31]

By 1929 Magnes's sense of nationalism and universalism was under-
going a rigorous refinement in the context of new agitation over the
possibility of the establishment of a Jewish state in Palestine. In a letter to
Chaim Weitzman, a leading advocate of such a development, Magnes
outlined the two possibilities before the Jewish people and the consequences of those choices: statehood, which would base Jewish life in
Palestine on militarism and imperialism or a "pacific" policy that focused
less on a Jewish state than on the development of a Jewish educational,
moral, and religious center in Palestine. For Magnes, the first policy
would involve politics, governments, and armaments and deal only
secondarily with Jews and lastly with Arabs. The pacific policy would
deal first of all with the Jews, then the Arabs, and only incidentally with
all the rest. "The imperialist, military and political policy is based upon
mass immigration of Jews and the creation (forcible if necessary) of a
Jewish majority, no matter how much this oppresses the Arabs mean-
while, or deprives them of their rights. In this kind of policy the end
always justifies the means. The policy, on the other hand, of developing
a Jewish spiritual center does not depend upon mass immigration, a
Jewish majority, a Jewish state, or upon depriving the Arabs (or the Jews)
of their political rights for a generation or a day but on the contrary, is
desirous of having Palestine become a country of two nations and three
religions, all of them having equal rights and none of them having special

privileges; a country where nationalism is but the basis of internationalism, where the population is pacifistic and disarmed—in short, the Holy Land."[32]

Magnes posed the critical question to Weitzman of whether Jews would genuinely desire to conquer Palestine as in the time of Joshua or take into account the religious developments of Judaism since Joshua— the prophets, psalmists, and rabbis—and thus be in harmony with the words "not by right, and not by violence, but by my spirit, saith the Lord." Just five years after Magnes's entry into Palestine that question was as much addressed to himself as to Weitzman. Was it possible to enter any country—no less the Holy Land—and build it up pacifistically? "If we cannot (and I do not say that we can rise to these heights), I for my part have lost half my interest in the enterprise. If we cannot even attempt this, I should much rather see this eternal people without such a 'National Home,' with the wanderer's staff in hand and forming new ghettos among the peoples of the world." One week later, in a letter to Felix Warburg, a New York financier and philanthropist, Magnes wrote even more directly:

> Palestine does not belong to the Jews and it does not belong to the Arabs, nor to Judaism or Christianity or Islam. It belongs to all of them together; it is the Holy Land. If the Arabs want an Arab national state in Palestine, it is as much or as little to be defended as if the Jews want a Jewish national state there. We must once and for all give up the idea of a "Jewish Palestine" in the sense that a Jewish Palestine is to exclude and do away with an Arab Palestine. This is the historic fact, and Palestine is nothing if it is not history. If a Jewish national home in Palestine is compatible with an Arab national home there, well and good, but if it is not, the name makes very little difference. The fact is that nothing there is possible unless Jews and Arabs work together in peace for the benefit of their common Holy Land. It must be our endeavor first to convince ourselves and then to convince others that Jews and Arabs, Moslems, Christians and Jews have each as much right there, no more and no less, than the other: equal rights and equal privileges and equal duties. That is practically quite sufficient for all purposes of the Jewish religion, and it is the sole ethical basis for our claims there. Judaism did not begin with Zionism, and if Zionism is ethically not in accord with Judaism, so much the worse for Zionism.[33]

In 1930 Magnes published a pamphlet with the provocative title "Like All the Nations?" and prefaced with the biblical quotation "a unique nation" (2 Samuel 7:23). Here Magnes begins with the startling admission that if the evolving definition of Zionism takes hold—that is, creating a Jewish state by force if necessary, including the subjugation of the Palestinian Arabs and the massive immigration of the Jews in the Diaspora—then, though living in Zion, Magnes defines himself no longer a Zionist but rather the traditional *hibbat Zion*, the lover of Zion. For Magnes, it is increasingly clear that despite the central emerging theme of Zionist ideology, Palestine cannot solve the so-called Jewish problem of the Jewish people. The Diaspora will neither disappear nor be subsumed by Jewish life in Palestine. On the contrary, Magnes feels the Jewish people to be growing stronger, as they should, for Palestine without communities in the Diaspora would lose much of its significance as a spiritual center for Judaism.[34]

Because of this confusion in Zionist ideology, Magnes felt it necessary to redefine the three chief elements of Jewish life in order of their importance: the living Jewish people around the world; the Torah seen in its broadest sense of the documents, history, and ethical ideals of the Jewish people; and the land of Israel, where the people and the Torah "can exist and be creative as they have existed and have been creative without the Land." The importance of the land for Magnes was that it was one of the chief means of "deepening the People and the Torah." Because the living Jewish people is primary, as the carrier and vessel of Judaism and the Jewish spirit, the Diaspora has spread light and learning throughout the world. "Palestine can help this people to understand itself, to give an account of itself, to an intensification of its culture, a deepening of its philosophy, a renewal of its religion." But it is also a testing ground, a dangerous frontier land for the lovers of peace in Judaism. For Magnes, much of the theory of Zionism had been concerned with making the Jews into a "normal" nation in Palestine like the Gentiles of the lands and the families of the earth. "The desire for power and conquest seems to be normal to many human beings and groups, and we being the ruled everywhere must here rule; being the minority everywhere, we must here be in the majority. There is the *Wille zur Macht*, the State, the army, the frontiers. We have been in Exile; now we are to be master in our own Home. We are to have a Fatherland, and we are to encourage the feelings of pride, honour, glory that are part of the paraphernalia of the ordinary nationalistic patriotism. In the face of such danger one thinks of the dignity and originality of that passage in the liturgy which praises the Lord of all things that our portion is not like theirs and our lot not like all their multitude."[35]

In 1943, in the midst of the Jewish Holocaust, Magnes continued his argument for a Jewish presence in Palestine alongside of and in harmony with the Palestinian Arabs with an essay *Toward Peace in Palestine*, published in *Foreign Affairs*. To those who sought the accommodation of millions of persecuted Jews in Palestine and the establishment of a Jewish state, Magnes welcomed the idea if only Palestine were large and empty. The fact of the matter was that Palestine was neither; another people had been in possession of the land for centuries. The concept of a Jewish state in Palestine would quite properly be regarded by the Palestinian Arabs as "equivalent to a declaration of war against them." Thus in the first place there was a need to distinguish between messianic expectation and hard reality. The growth of Palestinian Arab nationalism also created a new problem: the desire for a Palestinian Arab state at the price of Jewish subjugation.[36]

Though each side's argument for statehood assured the others of full and equal rights, there was already ominous discussion of transferring populations. Magnes cites a Jewish commentator who assured the Palestinian Arabs of Jewish support for independence if they recognized Palestine as a Jewish state. As for the transferring Arabs, the commentator added, "The question of the exchange of populations is likely to become pressing in our days. I believe this question to be essential for us and also for them." At the same time, a spokesperson for the Arabs sought the establishment of a Palestinian Arab state: "No other solution seems practicable, except possibly at the cost of an unpredictable holocaust of Arab, Jewish and British lives. . . . No code of morals can justify the persecution of one people in an attempt to relieve the persecution of another. The cure for the eviction of Jews from Germany is not to be sought in the eviction of the Arabs from their homeland; and the relief of Jewish distress may not be accomplished at the cost of inflicting a corresponding distress upon an innocent and peaceful population." Magnes instead offered a compromise he called "Union for Palestine," which included a union between Jews and Arabs within a binational Palestine, a union of Palestine, Transjordan, Syria, and Lebanon in an economic and political federation, and finally a union of this federation with an Anglo-American union that would work together in a post–World War II reconstruction. In Magnes's plan, Palestine as a binational state would provide for equal political rights and duties for both the Jewish and Arab nations regardless of which was the majority and which the minority, and the larger federation would allow increased immigration of homeless Jews without altering the balance of power in the union. Jerusalem might become the federal headquarters or capital and thus would flourish again as a center of spiritual and intellectual exchange.[37]

Magnes spent the years until his death in 1948 arguing for his understanding of a binational state. The last months of his life found him in

Washington lobbying the State Department against the United Nations resolution of 1947 partitioning Palestine into Jewish and Arab states, which he understood intuitively and correctly would lead to imminent war and a cycle of violence continuing for generations. In the last few months of his life Magnes met and worked with the as yet relatively unknown Hannah Arendt, who continued Magnes's work after his death. Arendt, who became known for her monumental study on European anti-Semitism and the rise of fascism, *The Origins of Totalitarianism* (1951), was a German philosopher who emigrated to France after Hitler's rise to power in 1933 and then emigrated to the United States in 1941. By the 1940s she was, like Magnes, actively and perceptively engaged in a Zionism that supported a renewed Jewish presence in Palestine but opposed the establishment of a Jewish state.[38]

After Magnes's death, just months after the partition of Palestine and the establishment of a Jewish state in 1948, Arendt wrote a perceptive and troubling essay "To Save the Jewish Homeland: There Is Still Time." According to Arendt, the declaration of statehood had polarized positions on both sides, as non-Zionist Jews were now diehard enthusiasts and moderate Palestinian Arabs were being forced to choose sides. Palestinian Jews and American Jews were essentially in agreement on the following propositions, propositions Arendt felt were detrimental to the possibility of peace:

> The moment has now come to get everything or nothing, victory or death; Arab and Jewish claims are irreconcilable and only a military decision can settle the issue; the Arabs—all Arabs—are our enemies and we accept this fact; only outmoded liberals believe in compromises, only philistines believe in justice, and only schlemiels prefer truth and negotiation to propaganda and machine guns; Jewish experience in the last decades—or over the last centuries, or over the last two thousand years—has finally awakened us and taught us to look out for ourselves; this alone is reality, everything else is stupid sentimentality; everybody is against us, Great Britain is anti-Semitic, the United States is imperialist—but Russia might be our ally for a certain period because her interests happen to coincide with ours; yet in the final analysis we count upon nobody except ourselves; in sum—we are ready to go down fighting, and we will consider anybody who stands in our way a traitor and anything done to hinder us a stab in the back.[39]

Arendt saw this unanimity of opinion as ominous, though characteristic of our modern mass age. It tended to limit discussion and reduce social relationships to those of an "ant heap": "A unanimous public opinion tends to eliminate bodily those who differ, for mass unanimity is not the result of agreement, but an expression of fanaticism and hysteria. In contrast to agreement, unanimity does not stop at certain well-defined objects, but spreads like an infection into every related issue." The loyal opposition, so important to critical thought and politics, was in the process of being eliminated. For Arendt, the two great contributions of Jewish settlement, the kibbutz movement and Hebrew University, as well as the great precedent of cooperation between a European and a colonized people, were in danger of collapse. The advantage of the Jewish people in having no imperialist past to live down was also threatened; thus their ability to act as a vanguard in international relations on a "small but valid scale" was being lost. Even if the Jews won the war and affirmed their claim to statehood, the unique possibilities and achievements of Zionism in Palestine would be destroyed:

> The land that would come into being would be something quite other than the dream of world Jewry, Zionist and non-Zionist. The victorious Jews would live surrounded by an entirely hostile Arab population, secluded inside ever-threatened borders, absorbed with hysterical self-defense to a degree that would submerge all other interests and activities. The growth of a Jewish culture would cease to be the concern of the whole people; social experiments would have to be discarded as impractical luxuries; political thought would center around military strategy; economic development would be determined exclusively by the needs of war. And all this would be the fate of a nation that—no matter how many immigrants it could still absorb and how far it extended its boundaries (the whole of Palestine and Transjordan is the insane Revisionist demand)—would still remain a very small people greatly outnumbered by hostile neighbors.[40]

The ends of such an endeavor were clear to Arendt: degeneration into a warrior state with the political initiative in terrorist hands. The Jewish state could only be erected at the price of a Jewish homeland.[41]

Arendt closed her essay with the following propositions and hopes:

1. The real goal of the Jews in Palestine is the building up of a Jewish homeland. This goal must never be sacrificed to the pseudo-sovereignty of a Jewish state.

2. The independence of Palestine can be achieved only on a solid basis of Jewish-Arab cooperation. As long as Jewish and Arab leaders both claim that there is "no bridge" between Jews and Arabs (as Moshe Shertok has just put it), the territory cannot be left to the political wisdom of its own inhabitants.

3. Elimination of all terrorist groups (and not agreements with them) and swift punishment of all terrorist deeds (and not merely protests

against them) will be the only valid proof that the Jewish people in Palestine has recovered its sense of political reality and that Zionist leadership is again responsible enough to be trusted with the destinies of the Yishuv.

4. Immigration to Palestine, limited in numbers and in time, is the only "irreducible minimum" in Jewish politics.

5. Local self-government and mixed Jewish-Arab municipal and rural councils, on' a small scale and as numerous as possible, are the only realistic political measures that can eventually lead to the political emancipation of Palestine. It is still not too late.[42]

Two years later Arendt wrote of the nonnationalist tradition in Zionism and of the danger of nationalism for small nations as lying in military and economic dependency. To continue support from abroad Israel might find itself in the "unenviable position of being forced to create emergencies, that is, forced into a policy of aggressiveness and expansion." Arendt concluded, "The birth of a nation in the midst of our century may be a great event; it certainly is a dangerous event."[43]

In Ahad Ha'am, Magnes, and Arendt we have an analysis of the situation in Palestine that is both committed and generous. The desire of a minority of the Jewish people for return to the land is bound more to culture and education and less to nationality and statehood. The Nazi years, which Magnes observed from Palestine, and Arendt within Europe, intensified rather than diminished their desire to be connected with international politics, culture, and religion, with the Palestinian Arabs, and, indeed, with the Arab world. From their perspective Jews were not usurping the land or colonizing if equality with Palestinian Arabs was offered, struggled for, and achieved. They feared, a fear to some extent realized today, that the achievement of a Jewish state would isolate the Jews of Palestine in a ghettoized reality and mentality and thus lead to a fortress Israel. If this happened the hopes and dreams of the Jewish return would dissipate into endless violence. Instead of a final break with the ghetto, Israel would become a ghetto in continuity with the ghettos of Europe.

What relevance does this have today, especially to the Holocaust theology under whose influence Jews interpret much of contemporary reality? That these ideas of a cultural and spiritual Zionism, of honest equality with Palestinian Arabs, of a Jewish presence as part and parcel of the Middle East—and the names identified with these ideas—are rarely invoked by those who support or demur from Israeli policy shows how narrow the contemporary discussion has become. We might say that Israeli policy since the foundation of the state has perforce narrowed the limits of discussion and dissent lest a contemporary disaster overtake it, which is precisely what the early dissenters in Zion predicted. Thus Jewish spokespersons like Wiesel, Fackenheim, and Greenberg have lost the vocabulary of such ideas, at least publicly. These ideas are in their truest sense unmentionable. But what if it is precisely this vocabulary from the past that can open Jews to a future beyond isolation and war, and thus beyond policies and understandings that are difficult, if not impossible, to defend? Could it be that once again Jews can reclaim clear reasoning on the issues that constrain them—clarity often exhibited by Ahad Ha'am, Magnes, and Arendt—rather than the labored, sometimes tortuous connections and justifications offered today in the name of the Holocaust and the state of Israel? Is there any possibility of committed thought beyond the categories of innocence and redemption? The idea that Jews must at this point begin clarifying the issues of Holocaust and Israel is daunting. Fortunately, it need not be. In fact, a framework already exists for linking the early dissenters within the Zionist movement with those who oppose certain Israeli policies in the present; it only needs to be rediscovered. As we shall see, dissent hardly ended with the creation of Israel, and the lessons of the Holocaust were intimately related to that dissent. If it is true that Jews have inherited the formative events of Holocaust and Israel, it is also true that a difficult and often painful dissent has accompanied these events and awaits a renewed hearing.

CHAPTER 3

A Tradition of Dissent

The idea of a Jewish homeland seems today, when considered at all, a faded memory of a distant utopian vision, given the reality of a Jewish state. Yet as a symbol of dissent, as a cornerstone of a tradition of disparate voices, its power is formidable. The nonnationalistic tradition of the Jewish people as Hannah Arendt wrote of it in 1948 remains alive today, though transformed in language and outlook in response to more than four decades of Israeli statehood. The title of Arendt's 1948 essay "To Save the Jewish Homeland: There Is Still Time" seems at first glance almost archaic until compared with the title and vision of Roberta Strauss Feuerlicht's 1983 book *The Fate of the Jews: A People Torn Between Israeli Power and Jewish Ethics*. Feuerlicht ends her first chapter with the following words that Arendt, and perhaps Ahad Ha'am and Magnes as well, would applaud: "The heritage of the Jews is not power but ethics. Whether Jews are a religion, a people, a civilization, a historical process, or an anomaly, whether they are Hasidim or heretics, what binds all Jews from antiquity to the present is not statehood but the burden they placed upon themselves and posterity when they internalized morality and gave the world the ethical imperative." Yet Feuerlicht's title, emphasizing the military power of Israel, and her conclusion, reclaiming the ethical within this power, also reveals the distance traveled since the birth of the state of Israel and the challenge of dissent. "Judaism as an ideal is infinite; Judaism as a state is finite. Judaism survived centuries of persecution without a state; it must now learn how to survive despite a state." For Feuerlicht, the state of Israel has become what many of the early dissenters feared: a danger to the Jewish people rather than a center of creativity and spirit.[1]

Many of those who have spoken of Israel's reversal from beacon to burden over forty years of statehood have been ostracized from the

Jewish community, excommunicated, as it were, as heretics. Non-Zionist and even anti-Zionist Jews, who were certainly a majority of the Jewish people earlier this century and have a significant following today, have been stricken from Jewish history, erased from our inheritance. Yet many of their ideas are now found without attribution in contemporary Jewish dissent. To recall the vision of those ostracized and excommunicated, as well as their limitations, provides a line of continuity for dissent and perhaps a depth lacking in the discussion today.

The Internal Conflict over Zionism, 1937–1967

One of the major struggles over the adoption of Zionism as normative for the Jewish people can be found in the divisive debate within the Reform movement that took place in the 1940s and continued after the war with the development of the American Council for Judaism. In his book *Turning Point: Zionism and Reform Judaism*, Howard Greenstein traces the historical struggle for the acceptance of Zionism and a Jewish state within a movement that was founded in the nineteenth century as explicitly universalist in orientation. Formed in the post–French Revolution era of liberalism and universalism, as was Zionism, the Reform movement took a different path: it sought to divest Judaism of its parochial features and emphasize the moral principles around which all people could unite. As Greenstein portrays them, the early leaders of Reform Judaism in Germany and later in America were not only liberals intellectually, they boldly proclaimed the brotherhood and sisterhood of all men and women. "They joined their political liberalism to their spiritual liberalism and declared that Reform Judaism was not only a religion for the liberated mind of the new day, but it was now and forever anti-nationalist. Whereas traditional Judaism had temporarily suspended all laws depending upon residence in Israel for their fulfillment, Reform Judaism completely abrogated them. It rejected all laws pertaining to the priests and Levites and declared instead that all Jews were a 'kingdom of priests and a holy people' and that the obligations for moral purity applied to every Jew with equal responsibility."[2]

To accomplish this goal Reform leaders eliminated all references to the exilic condition of the Jewish people or to a messiah who would restore world Jewry to the land of Israel. The nationalist period of Jewish life was regarded as a stage in the evolutionary development of Judaism preparatory for the more universalistic mission among all peoples. Thus the essence of Reform Judaism was that Jews constituted a religious community seeking to advance with others universal understanding and goodwill. Reform Jews were to be at home among the nations wherever they lived.

In tracing the conflict between Zionism and Reform Judaism, it is important to recognize the degrees and kinds of opposition and support within the debate. For example, few Reform Jews objected to Jews going to Palestine to live as a creative embrace of Jewish language and culture. The overwhelming opposition was related to the establishment of an independent political Jewish state in Palestine. In the main, Reform Jews saw no need to create a Jewish home, as they were at home in America, a home fueled with the promise of democracy and prosperity. As Greenstein articulates it, the clash was substantial:

> Zionism was the antithesis of every principle that was sacred to the majority of early Reformers. Those who drafted the Pittsburgh Platform of 1885 had anticipated a new world of justice and freedom in which Jews would enjoy equal rights and privileges with all other citizens wherever they lived. Zionism, however, had declared that Jews would be strangers everywhere until they could reclaim their own homeland. Reform Judaism had regarded nationalism as the cause of Jewish suffering, but for Zionism it was a solution. For Zionists the essence of Jewish existence was the concept of peoplehood, and everything else depended on that premise, whereas for Reform Jews the essence of Jewish existence was faith, especially the conviction that creative survival depended upon recognition of a universal "mission" through which Jews would labor to achieve ideals of justice, brotherhood and peace among all men. Finally, Zionism emphasized the ethnic bonds that united all Jews and did not require any specific spiritual commitments; but in Reform Judaism the priorities were exactly the reverse: the spiritual ties transcended whatever other differences existed among Jews, and ethnic distinctions were among the least important or meaningful of all those differences. All Jews, in their view, were primarily "Americans of Mosaic persuasion."[3]

The ideological antithesis issued into a sustained political controversy, perhaps the most significant in the history of the Reform movement. It caused a crisis in the three major bodies of the movement—its seminary, the Hebrew Union College; its lay organization, the Union of American Hebrew Congregations; and its rabbinic arm, the Central Conference of American Rabbis (CCAR). The controversy threatened to split and undermine the movement itself. But more than that, Zionism challenged Reform Judaism to reexamine its most basic suppositions: its optimism about the world in the face of two world wars and in relation to the Jewish people and the rise of Nazi Germany.[4]

What brought the controversy to a head was the passing of a platform, in an afternoon session with many rabbis absent, at the 1937 annual convention of the Central Conference of American Rabbis in Columbus, Ohio. Henceforth it was known as the Columbus Platform and included the following:

> Judaism is the soul of which Israel is the body. Living in all parts of the world, Israel has been held together by the ties of a common history, and above all, by the heritage of faith. Though we recognize in the group-loyalty of Jews who have become estranged from our religious tradition, a bond which still unites them with us, we maintain that it is by its religion and for its religion that the Jewish people has lived. The non-Jew who accepts our faith is welcome as a full member of the Jewish community.
>
> In all lands where our people live, they assume and seek to share loyally the full duties and responsibilities of citizenship and to create seats of Jewish knowledge and religion. In the rehabilitation of Palestine, the land hallowed by memories and hopes, we behold the promise of renewed life for many of our brethren. We affirm the obligation of all Jewry to aid in its upbuilding as a Jewish homeland by endeavoring to make it not only a haven of refuge for the oppressed but also a center of Jewish culture and spiritual life.[5]

Though by today's standards innocuous, this platform statement touched off bitter invective and political maneuvering. Coupled with the platform adopted in the 1942 convention of the CCAR in Cincinnati supporting the creation of a Jewish army in Palestine, this act was the turning point in the Reform movement and led to a particularly interesting confrontation when Congregation Beth Israel of Houston, Texas, passed a restatement of its own principles relating to membership the following year. The formation of the American Council of Judaism, which remained for years the longest standing identifiable anti-Zionist movement in America, arose out of the same controversy and subscribed to a similar position. In what is perhaps the last statement of classical Reform Judaism, Congregation Beth Israel promulgated in 1943 the following as principles for membership in their synagogue:

> We believe in the mission of Israel which is to witness to the Unity of God throughout the world and to pray and work for the establishment of the kingdom of truth, justice and peace among all men. Our watchword is "Hear, O Israel, The Lord Our God, the Lord is One." We accept it as our sacred duty to worship and to serve Him through prayer, righteous conduct and the study of our Holy Scriptures and glorious history.
>
> We are Jews by virtue of our acceptance of Judaism. We consider ourselves no longer a nation. We are a religious community, and neither pray for nor anticipate a return to Palestine nor a restoration of any of the

laws concerning the Jewish state. We stand unequivocally for the separation of Church and State. Our religion is Judaism. Our nation is the United States of America. Our nationality is American. Our flag is the "Stars and Stripes." Our race is Caucasian. With regard to the Jewish settlement in Palestine we consider it our sacred privilege to promote the spiritual, cultural and social welfare of our co-religionists there.

We believe in the coming of a Messianic Age and not in a personal Messiah. We recognize that it is our hallowed duty to speed the coming of the Brotherhood of Man under the Fatherhood of God, which is the Messianic ideal for which the righteous of all people work and pray.[6]

Just three years later in 1945 Rabbi Elmer Berger outlined in proposition form a similar platform, the essence of the anti-Zionist position he maintains to this day:

> There is no political entity that can be called with any realistic accuracy, "a Jewish people."
>
> It is mere romanticism and sentimentality to speak of "righting historic wrongs done to Jews" or of "the homelessness of Israel" or of "a solution to the problem of the Jewish people."
>
> The great majority of the Jews who will survive the war are at home in nations where there may be a certain amount of social anti-Semitism and economic anti-Semitism, but where they need no radical, revolutionary treatment. "The Jewish problem" needs nothing more than extending a condition of equality to all Jews, everywhere, and a continued move in the direction of emancipation which will see the gradual elimination of even these social and economic discriminations.
>
> The so-called "Jewish problem" about which people are urgently concerned in working out the peace, has nothing to do therefore with "a Jewish people." It has to do with, at the very most, five million Jews, practically all of whom lived in the vestigial feudalism of Central and Eastern Europe. Of these, we do not know how many will survive the Nazi policy of extermination.
>
> About the several categories of refugees and the oppressed Jews, we know only one thing: Upon the basis of their own past and experiences of other Jews elsewhere they want only peace, security and opportunity for happiness as free human beings. Some will wish to return to their homelands. Some will wish to become citizens of other countries that gave them refuge. Others will want to go to Palestine, or elsewhere.
>
> Freedom and happiness have been achieved, for Jews, and the so-called "Jewish problem" has progressed nearer and nearer a solution, where Jews have had the opportunity to integrate their lives and to weld their destiny, not as a separate group, but as different and separate individuals, to the destiny of the nations that have been their homes and of which they are a part.

This process of integration or emancipation has been enhanced where Jews are considered people different only in their devotion to their religion—Judaism. The process of integration and emancipation has been retarded or completely stultified where the concept of a separate and different nationality status has prevailed for Jews. It is an accurate observation that to designate Jews as a religious group is a part of the heritage and tradition of liberalism and democracy in the Western World. To designate them as a national group is a vestige of the past. Enlightened states always refer to Jews as citizens of Jewish faith. Therefore as nations emerge from absolutism and oligarchy and join the march of freedom into representative government, Jews slowly get out from under the concept of a restrictive, separate nationality group. This process of transition has been witnessed in our own time in Russia, Czechoslovakia and Yugoslavia.[7]

By the 1950s the voices of Jewish dissent were quieted. The Reform movement made its peace with the fledgling state of Israel. The postwar reconstruction of Europe and the emerging cold war diverted much of the intellectual and ideological energy of the community. Holocaust consciousness, so to speak, at least as articulated publicly, lay in the future. Yet dissent continued with the *Jewish Newsletter*, which began publication in 1948 and was guided by William Zukerman (1885–1961), who was born in Russia and emigrated to the United States in 1909. His editorial board included, among others, distinguished Jews and non-Jews such as Roger Baldwin, Abraham Cronbach, Erich Fromm, Norman Thomas, Dwight MacDonald, and David Riesman.

In October 1949 Zukerman, in an essay entitled "Jews as Conquerors," began a series of editorials relating to the new Jewish condition of statehood and its effects on Jews in Israel and around the world. Zukerman refers to an essay by the Yiddish-American dramatist and story writer, David Pinsky. Now living in Israel, surrounded by Jewish settlers who had taken over Palestinian Arab villages, homes, gardens, orchards, and fields, Pinsky asks the question of how Jews, after two thousand years of wandering and subjugation, comport themselves as victors and conquerors. According to Pinsky, most of the Jewish refugees occupy former Arab homes and villages "with the laughter of victors," regretting only the condition in which many of the former occupants left their homes. Yet some, especially former refugees from Nazi Europe, felt uncomfortable, remembering their own experience of homelessness. Pinsky relates the story of one such refugee who occupied a home of a formerly well-to-do Arab family. When one day the children discovered a closet full of toys and began to play with them, the mother was suddenly struck by the thought that the children whose toys these were now were themselves exiled and homeless. Ordering the children to put the toys back in the closet, she began to brood. "What right had she and her family to occupy a house which does not belong to her? To use a garden and field which were taken by force from other people who ran away in a panic of war and are not permitted to return? Are she and her family not living on goods robbed from others? Is she not doing to the Arabs what the Nazis did to her and her family?"[8]

Two years later Zukerman describes the visit of Joseph Shlossberg, a veteran American Jewish labor leader, to the Arab city of Midgal Gad occupied by the Israelis. Finding the Arabs confined to a "ghetto," Shlossberg writes that it is difficult to believe and make peace with this reality. "Jews who are now in Israel were just now in a ghetto themselves. In Eastern countries they are still segregated in ghettos. How can these ghetto people of yesterday introduce ghettos themselves?" Zukerman also records the words of the Jewish Israeli Nathan Chofshi:

> The point that is usually overlooked [in reports that glorify Israel] is the tragedy of the Arab refugees. Whatever the political and other causes which have brought about the mass psychosis of an entire people and made them run naked and barefoot from their homes, gardens and fields, the fact is that hundreds of thousands of people are now in want and suffer hunger, cold and disease. Among them are children—small, inno-cent children who live in tents, in cold and heat, and do not even know why they are suffering. Among them are also old Arabs—grandfathers and grandmothers—and simple folk in general who never participated in the war on Israel and want only to be permitted to return to work their fields and workshops. How can one remain indifferent in the face of such an awful tragedy? Have we no conscience? What did we use to say to non-Jews who remained indifferent to similar tragedies of the Jews?[9]

Contemplating a call among some in Israel to transfer the Palestinian Arabs remaining in Israel to other Arab countries, Zukerman wrote:

> For nothing could be more outrageous morally and more disastrous politically for Israel and for the Jewish people outside it, than such a shabby attempt on the part of Israel to get rid of its small Arab minority by a maneuver of "exchange" after having eliminated the majority through a common accident of war. Can any sane person reasonably believe that Israel could ever have real peace with her Arab neighbors after such an "exchange"? And what would be the position of Jewish minorities all over the world after an act of this kind? For two thousand years the Jewish people have lived among others as a minority, and by their very existence repudiated the lie that a country must consist only of one people. Now

that they have established a state of their own, are they to create their own minority not only as second-class citizens but attempt to eliminate it altogether? Would not that be an open invitation to other states which, for one reason or another, do not want Jews in their midst, to follow the example set by Israel? And what about the morality of it all? In what way does an "Arab-rein" state differ from a "Juden-rein" state? It is terrible to contemplate the depths of moral degradation to which nationalism can lead even liberal-minded people in our age.[10]

In 1953 Zukerman wrote two essays concerning a recent Israeli reprisal attack in the Jordanian town of Quibya, which took the lives of more than sixty Arabs. Zukerman compared the massacre to the one in Deir Yassin in 1948, in which two hundred fifty Arabs were massacred in the early phase of the Arab-Israeli war; the fear of such events led in large part to the Arab exodus. Clearly there was a line of continuity both in forcing the Arabs to flee and in keeping them from returning. But there was also a great difference. The Deir Yassin massacre was carried out by Irgunist extremists, and a "cry of protest and pain arose from every Jewish heart in Israel." The government at that time dissociated itself from the crime and denounced it. Five years later a similar crime was committed by the Israeli army. This time the government took "semiofficial" responsibility for it rather than repudiate or express moral outrage against it. For Zukerman, the horror of the incident was the "alarming moral deterioration" in Israel; it showed how far Israel "had advanced on the road to militarization and reaction." What Israel needed now was humility, not a false moral superiority; repentance not self-righteousness. The massacre at Quibya reenforced Zuckerman's understanding of the changes in Jewish character:

> The truth which a good many Jews have deliberately avoided facing is that the rise of nationalism has had the same effect on Jews as on most other people of our age. Together with the normal emotions of love for wronged and persecuted people, it has awakened also the feeling of group selfishness and chauvinism and has unleashed the latent forces of cruelty from which the Jews are not exempt. It has transformed the entire character of the people. Nor is this a new manifestation. It began with the upsurge of nationalistic Zionism in the thirties. It came dramatically into the open before and during the Second World War, when the Irgunist terrorist movement sprang up in Palestine and was glorified and supported by American Jews. It was an American Jew who said: "Every time a British Tommy is killed in Palestine, there is a holiday in the hearts of New York Jews and dancing in New York streets," and thousands of militant Zionists and even non-Zionists applauded these sentiments.

Later, when the British ceased to be enemies and the Arabs took their place, the hatred was transferred to the Arabs, although American Jews as such have as little cause for hatred of the Arabs now as they had for rejoicing in the death of British soldiers then.[11]

Five years later, in 1958, in an editorial "The Arab Refugees: Summary of a Tragedy," Zukerman wrote in angry tones:

To this observer, nothing demonstrates more sharply the uncanny power of modern propaganda to control minds, sway emotions and brutalize people than the Zionist propaganda on the Arab refugees during the last decade. It literally succeeded in turning black into white, a blatant lie into a truth, a grave social injustice into an act of justice glorified by thousands. It has turned clever people with more than average intelligence into starry-eyed fools, believing everything they are told, and has converted kindly and gentle men and women with a strong sense of mercy into fanatics, insensible to the suffering of any people except their own. In no other way can this writer explain the many paradoxes which the Arab refugee problem has created in Jewish life.[12]

Victory and Occupation, 1967–1987

With the Israeli victory in the 1967 war, the possibilities and limitations of dissent shifted radically. The euphoria with which many Jews greeted the defeat of the Arab countries and the reunification of Jerusalem helped to create a consensus surrounding Israeli power and initiative, at the same time birthing a theology that saw empowerment as *the* response to Jewish suffering. For many who were indifferent to the state or even opposed it, the 1967 war represented a conversion experience. At the same time institutions that had arisen in the 1940s and 1950s to support Israel assumed a new power and authority. Dissenters in the previous decades (for example, those who argued for a binational state and the spiritual elements of education and culture), though often attacked by political Zionists, had a constituency from which to operate. The debate also took place among public intellectuals, in print and at organizational conventions. After the 1967 war, however, the concept of Jewish statehood achieved a significance for Jewish leaders and the mass of Jews hitherto unknown. The institutional framework for promoting Israel began to operate with a power, an almost irrational power, that raised the cost of dissent to its highest level.

Though chastened, dissent continued. Just days after the conclusion of the 1967 war I. F. Stone, social critic and political activist, wrote of the dangers of the complacency of military victory. In 1970 Michael Selzer, educator and political scientist, edited a book of essays titled *Zionism Reconsidered: The Rejection of Jewish Normalcy* that included a historical survey of dissent relating to the state of Israel and had it published by a major publishing house. One year earlier Noam Chomsky, professor of linguistics at MIT who was to become a much-vilified Jewish intellectual, published what in retrospect can be seen as a highly balanced account of the tension and possibilities existing in the Middle East after the 1967 war.[13]

Chomsky argued that both Palestinians and Jews can make their case with a high degree of plausibility and persuasiveness. The Palestinian case is based on the premise that the "great powers imposed a European migration, a national home for the Jews, and finally a Jewish state, in cynical disregard of the wishes of the overwhelming majority of the population, innocent of any charge." The result: hundreds of thousands of Palestinian refugees in exile, while the "law of return" of the Jewish state confers citizenship, automatically, on any Jew who chooses to settle in their former homes. The Zionist case relies on the "aspirations of a people who suffered two millennia of exile and savage persecution culminating in the most fantastic outburst of collective insanity in human history, on the natural belief that a normal human existence will be possible only in a national home in the land to which they had never lost their ties, and on the extraordinary creativity and courage of those who made the desert bloom." For Chomsky the conflict between these claims is obvious, especially when raised to the level of a demand for survival, in that sense becoming an absolute demand. Each side sees itself as a genuine national liberation movement. To the Israelis, the 1948 war is the war of liberation. To the Palestinians, it is the war of conquest. This formulation leads to an unresolvable conflict. And more, the exilic condition of the Palestinians is likely to take on the characteristics of the Zionist movement itself. For Chomsky, each Israeli victory, especially the victory in the 1967 war, is likely to strengthen Palestinian nationalism. Both Jews and Palestinians are locked into a "suicidal policy" with the ante constantly being pushed higher. In Chomsky's view the only way out is to create a democratic, socialist Palestine that preserves, for Jew and Palestinian, some degree of communal autonomy and national self-government, and where each people will have the right to participate in self-governing national institutions. Individuals will be free to live where they want, free from religious control, and free to define themselves as Jews, Palestinians, or something else, and to live accordingly. "People will be united by bonds other than their identification as Jews or Arabs (or lack of any such identification). This society in former Palestine should permit all Palestinians the right to return, along with Jews who wish to find their place in the national homeland. All oppressive or discriminatory practices should be condemned rather than reinforced. The society will not be a Jewish state or an Arab state, but rather a democratic multinational state."[14]

By 1983 in the second decade of Israeli occupation of the West Bank and Gaza, Chomsky was less optimistic than he had been in 1969. His book *The Fateful Triangle: The United States, Israel and the Palestinians*, written just after Israel's invasion of Lebanon, details the policies of occupation and the war in Lebanon in vivid and exhaustive detail. As in his earlier work, Chomsky begins with the framework "that Israeli Jews and Palestinian Arabs are human beings with human rights, equal rights; more specifically, they have essentially equal rights within the territory of former Palestine. Each group has a valid right to national self-determination in this territory. Furthermore, I will assume that the state of Israel within its pre-June 1967 borders had, and retains, whatever one regards as the valid rights of any state within the existing international system." For Chomsky, those parties who accept these principles seek accommodation; those who do not accept these principles should be labeled rejectionists. The standard use of the term *rejectionism* for the position of those who deny the right of the state of Israel to exist and as the term is applied to Palestinians, the Arab states, and critics (Jewish and non-Jewish) on the left needs now to be broadened. In Chomsky's words, "Unless we adopt the racist assumption that Jews have certain intrinsic rights that Arabs lack, the term 'rejectionism' should be extended beyond its standard usage to include also the position of those who deny the right of national self-determination to Palestinian Arabs, the community that constituted nine-tenths of the population at the time of the First World War, when Great Britain committed itself to the establishment of a 'national home for the Jewish people.' " For Chomsky, the international consensus that emerged after the 1967 war seeks accommodation; the main barriers are not, as Israeli supporters suppose, the Palestinians and the Arab states but Israel itself, backed by the United States. In Chomsky's view, U.S.-Israeli rejectionism has blocked the achievement of a viable and comprehensive settlement. With the occupation in its second decade and the development of settlements in the West Bank and Gaza expanding, the discussion is urgent. If accommodationist policies do not replace the rejectionist policies of Israel and the United States, the struggle will move to a new phase to forestall the "expulsion of a substantial part of the Arab population on some pretext, and conversion of Israel into a society on the South Africa model with some form of Bantustans, committed to regional disruption, etc."[15]

In the case of Israel, Chomsky finds the two major political parties in Israel, Labor and Likud, to be in fundamental agreement regarding the occupied territories: both are rejectionist as to any expression of Palestinian national rights west of the Jordan. The problem stated by both Labor and Likud is one of security, though as Chomsky points out the Palestinians have already "suffered the catastrophe that Israelis justly fear," that is, denial of the legitimacy of national rights and displacement. But, for Chomsky, the motives of Israeli rejectionism are much deeper: the occupation of the West Bank and Gaza provides Israel with a substantial unorganized, cheap labor force, a controlled market for Israeli goods, and badly needed water. This accounts for the so-called Allon plan adopted in 1970, a plan that envisions the annexation of 30–40 percent of the West Bank, with the centers of dense Arab settlement to be excluded. Those areas are to remain under Jordanian control or stateless to avoid the "demographic problem" of absorbing too many non-Jews into a Jewish state. For Chomsky the Allon plan is designed to "enable Israel to maintain the advantages of the occupation while avoiding the problem of dealing with the domestic population." However, the Allon plan, submitted by the Labor minister Yigal Allon, is complemented by the Likud policy of extending sovereignty into the occupied territories as "a more subtle device, which allows Israel to take what it wants while containing the Arab population to even narrow ghettoes, seeking ways to remove at least the leadership and possibly much of the population, apart from those needed as the beasts of burden for Israeli society. Outright annexation would raise the problem of citizenship for the Arabs, while extension of sovereignty, while achieving the purposes of annexation, will not, as long as liberal opinion in the West is willing to tolerate the fraud."[16]

As described by Chomsky, the war in Lebanon was also a part of this rejectionism; its purpose was to continue the Israeli policy of dispersing Palestinian refugees and destroying Palestinian nationalism. Destruction of the P.L.O. would help suppress meaningful forms of Palestinian self-expression in the occupied territories and end Palestinian opposition to Israel's power in the international arena. This action was in accordance with Ariel Sharon's assumption that peace on the West Bank requires the destruction of the P.L.O. in Lebanon, and it would also further Israel's policy of rejecting accommodation, a position that was becoming more and more difficult to uphold in the international arena.[17]

The propaganda for and casualties of the Lebanese war were and continue to be enormous. After the first months it became increasingly clear that no matter what interpretation one gave to past Israeli-Arab wars, this one was less a defensive war than a bold act of aggression.

Chomsky systematically debunks the myths of Israel's hesitant invasion and desire to avoid civilian casualties. Israel's "Peace for Galilee" was a war of precision bombing organized against an unarmed civilian population. The official Lebanese government casualty figures of nineteen thousand dead and over thirty thousand injured were to Chomsky's mind both horrific and too low.[18]

The most horrible symbol of the Lebanese war was the September 1982 massacre in the Palestinian refugee camps of Sabra and Shatila. Though actually carried out by Christian Phalange troops, it became clear that they operated under the close supervision and with the permission of the Israel Defense Forces (IDF). Chomsky again goes into fine detail, and his case study analysis differs greatly from Irving Greenberg's analysis, as explained in chapter 1. From Chomsky's point of view, Israel was culpable in the massacre, which may have left as many as two thousand dead. He analyzed the massacre in continuity with Deir Yassin and Quibya, the former atrocity involving Menachem Begin, the latter led by Ariel Sharon, the two architects and leading proponents of the Lebanese war. Chomsky concludes:

> The picture that emerges from the Kahan Commission Report is therefore quite clear. The higher political and military echelons, in their entirety, expected that Phalangists would carry out massacres if they were admitted into Palestinian camps. Furthermore, they knew that these camps were undefended, so they were willing to send in approximately 150 Phalangists known for their unwillingness to engage in any conflict with armed men. Within 1–2 hours after the Phalangists had entered on Thursday at 6 P.M., clear evidence reached the command post 200 meters away from the camps and overlooking them that massacres were taking place, and that there was no serious resistance. At the command post, the IDF and Phalange commanders and their staffs, including intelligence and liaison, were present and in constant contact. The IDF then provided illumination, and the next day, after receiving further corroboratory evidence that massacres were in process and that there was no resistance, sent the Phalange back into the camps, with tractors, which the IDF knew were being used to bury bodies in the mass grave which they could observe (the latter fact is ignored by the Commission). The Phalange were selected for this operation because, as the Chief of Staff stated, "we could give them orders whereas it was impossible to give orders to the Lebanese army." And in fact, the IDF did give the Phalange orders, from the moment they sent them into the camps to conduct their murderous operations, to the time when they were sent back in on Friday afternoon to complete them, to Saturday morning when they were withdrawn because of American pressure, at which time the IDF began rounding up

those who had escaped and sending them to Israeli concentration camps (again, this fact is not discussed by the Commission). That is the story as it emerges from the Commission Report (with the exceptions noted). What will a rational person deduce from this record?[19]

By 1983 Chomsky, as a prime carrier of the tradition of dissent between the miracle of 1967 and the horror of Sabra and Shatila, is joined by others who are both outraged by Israeli violence in Lebanon and surprised by it. Roberta Strauss Feuerlicht's book, Earl Shorris's *Jews Without Mercy: A Lament,* and Jacobo Timerman's *The Longest War* discuss from different vantage points the theme that Chomsky emphasizes and for which he in the past was so vilified: Jews are no longer innocent. And by this time the intuitive linkage of Nazi Germany and Israeli power, found in the editorials of William Zukerman in the 1950s, reappears. As Timerman, who was the victim of anti-Jewishness in Argentina and upon his release from prison left for Israel, writes in regard to the Lebanese war, "In these past months I have left behind many illusions, some fantasies, several obsessions. But none of my convictions. Among all these things, there is one that shatters me beyond consolation. I have discovered in Jews a capacity for cruelty that I never believed possible." "A man walks among those ruins, carrying in his arms a child of ten. A group of men, women and children with their arms raised are under guard, and the expression on their faces, what their eyes say, is easily understood by almost any Jew. Yet we are forbidden to equate today's victims with yesterday's, for if this were permitted, the almost unavoidable conclusion would be that yesterday's crimes are today's."[20]

The arrest and conviction of the American Jew Jonathan Pollard in 1987 for spying for the Israeli government rekindled a discussion that Holocaust theologians had almost buried: the question of dual loyalty and the possibility that U.S. and Israeli foreign policy interests might at some points diverge or even be in opposition. Like the Bitburg affair to be discussed in chapter 4, the Pollard spy scandal tended to focus the energy of Jews in the United States, and indeed around the world, and crystallized trends in Jewish dissent.

At the time of the Pollard affair, Jacob Neusner, professor of Judaic studies at Brown University, perhaps the best known non-Zionist in America, wrote a startling series of commentaries titled "The Real Promised Land Is America" and "It Isn't Light to the Gentiles or Even Bright for Most Jews." Originally published in the *Washington Post,* the pieces were also republished in the *International Herald Tribune.* In these articles Neusner analyzed the achieved promise of America compared with the unrealized goals of Zionism. He begins his article with a provocative statement: "It is time to say that America is a better place to be a Jew than Jerusalem. If ever there was a Promised Land, Jewish Americans are living in it. In the United States, Jews have flourished, not alone in politics and the economy but in matters of art, culture and learning. Jews feel safe and secure in ways that they do not and cannot in the state of Israel. And they have found an authentically Jewish voice—their own voice—for their vision of themselves."[21]

The warnings of Israelis that Jews will disappear in the Diaspora through assimilation or have to leave for Israel because of anti-Jewishness are for Neusner contradicted by the experience of Jews in America. On the contrary, Jewish commitment in America is flourishing, and anti-Jewishness is on the wane. But what is behind the fears that Israelis express is even more problematic than the sociological mistake: that a free and open environment is destructive to Jewish culture and that Jews can maintain themselves only in segregated circumstances. "What I hear in the odd turning of ideology is that Jews cannot live in a free and open society, that Judaism requires the ghetto, and that freedom—an absolute good for everyone else—is bad for the Jews. What a remarkable judgment upon the human meaning of Judaism!"[22]

Neusner then reverses the question to inquire about the quality of Jewish life in Israel. If America has kept its promise to the Jews in America, has Israel kept its promises to Jews in Israel and around the world? The answer for Neusner is clearly that it has not, either as a spiritual and educational center or even in the matter of Jewish independence and security. As to the former, Neusner exposes the "poorly kept secret" that Israeli scholarship is dull and boring and that since Martin Buber and Gershom Scholem (both born in Germany) Israel has not produced a single scholar in theology, philosophy, or history who is important outside of Israel. Further, Israel is a client state dependent economically and militarily on the United States. Neusner concludes: "So much for being a Jew in the state of Israel. Here in the Diaspora we can be what we want, when we want—from nothing to everything, all the time or once in a while. Freedom is nice, too. And the United States really has become a free country for us Jews. For American Jews—Jewish Americans—the American dream has come true. I wonder how many Israelis think the Zionist one has come true, too."[23]

With this statement we have come full circle in the activity and literature of dissent and have discerned what might be termed a tradition of dissent, the themes of which are important to identify. From the beginning of this tradition the question of Jewish interest has been foremost. Even the pioneers of a Jewish homeland were to some degree paternalistic toward Palestinian Arabs, an attitude perhaps inherent in what was at least partially a Western and colonialist adventure. And in fact, it was precisely within this framework that people like Ahad Ha'am, Magnes, Arendt, and others understood the challenge of cultural and spiritual Zionism, that is, to spark a rebirth of Jewish culture and creativity without being seen, and without consciously wanting to, participate in the history of Western colonialism and imperialism. Though this could not be avoided completely, from the Jewish perspective the intention was crucial to the project involved. The early critics of Zionism understood that a repetition of Western history vis-à-vis the Palestinian Arabs would place the Jews in that framework as well, either again as victims or this time as conquerors. Power and nationality for its own sake was a blind alley that Jews had suffered within and sought to escape.[24]

If the early dissenters were idealists whose vision was overcome by Palestinian Arab intransigence and violence, as many claim today, they saw themselves as practical observers trying to implement that vision. In their collective wisdom the Jewish people could not sustain or, over the long run, sponsor a revival of Jewish culture and spirituality built on the oppression of others. They recognized Palestinian rights (within a strategic framework as some do today), and beyond that recognition they saw the possibility of peace with justice in the land. Though their main concern rested with the Jewish enterprise, they saw little possibility of or reason for separation of Jews and Arabs. To be sure, a measure of autonomy was crucial for both—and realizable within a framework of integration. The last thing that the early dissenters in Zion longed for was a reghettoization, with or without power to Jews.

The non-Zionist and anti-Zionist Jews belong to the dissenting tradition as well and contribute what is, even in today's climate, the unmentionable: most Jews were not and are not Zionists. As it turns out, the major discussion in Reform Judaism revolved less around Zionization, the issue of whether it was vital for Jewish people to live in Palestine (even the Columbus Platform upheld the legitimacy of Jews living in the Diaspora). Rather it concerns whether or not the Jewish people in the Diaspora will lend their hearts, religious belief, political strength, and financial resources to the growing Jewish community in Palestine. Although the decision cost the Reformers little—few then went or since have gone to Israel itself—the battle is seen as a significant turning point in Jewish consciousness and commitment. Those who supported and those who opposed Zionism in this struggle understood at some level the stakes involved, for it meant the reorientation of Jewish self-consciousness and spirituality, and ultimately the birth of a theology that undermined the essential tenets of Reform Judaism. This was also true in the Zionist struggle within Orthodox Judaism, a movement founded, like Reform Judaism, in the nineteenth century but that harkened to the witness and learning of the rabbis after the destruction of the Temple and loss of nationhood. Here again, the triumph of Zionism shifted the fundamental basis of Orthodox Judaism, which, like Reform Judaism, was non- or even antinationalistic.[25]

Though the stakes were high, the argument in the early 1940s and to some extent in the 1950s revolved around potentialities rather than established history. The rise of Nazi Germany, the refugee problem that it generated, and the discovery after the war of the extent of mass death in the Holocaust provided the Zionist argument, however its objectives and methods are interpreted, with a fuel difficult to suppress. Thus the level of naïveté about the actual events in Palestine and later the state of Israel was almost equal to the genuine horror of the atrocities that preceded it in Europe. Still, as shown by our following of Zukerman's editorials and the literature he uses to sustain his commentary, this naïveté was less widely shared or even accepted than one might expect. However, at this stage already the level of argument is sinking, and charges of anti-Jewishness and Jewish self-hatred are increasing. Invective rather than critical thought is triumphing.

With the trial of Eichmann and the Israeli victory of 1967, the consensus was formed and a new orthodoxy promulgated. Israel leaves its position on the periphery and moves to the center as the defining point of Jewish identification and faith. The innocence of Israel, Israel as redemptive, concepts that previously existed on the periphery of Jewish consciousness are now beyond contention. Or so it seems. In the assertiveness of Holocaust theology and in the anger vented on those who dissent, one sees more and more a defensive posture, as if to preempt the inevitable questions and suspicion. And here the question of Israel, which up until the 1967 war to some extent remained an internal discussion within the Jewish community, becomes a prominent public discussion involving the call for unqualified U.S. support of Israel, a complete accounting for the theological components of Christian anti-Jewishness, and a projection of Jewish suffering as unique unto itself in scope and quality. Thus dissent comes to be treated in the public arena as having consequences that go to the heart of the evolving American-Israeli alliance, the evolving ecumenical dialogue between Christians and Jews, and the interpretation (and the lesson) of the history of the twentieth century.

Nevertheless, it is inevitable that dissent also finds a public voice. As the public arena for Holocaust theology expanded so too did the arena of public dissent. In a sense the triumph of Holocaust theology, which was articulated in theological language (albeit leaving unmentioned these two most disturbing qualities of occupation and unlimited power), establishes a new orthodoxy whose foundations lie in innocence and redemption. Yet Holocaust theology carries within itself the seeds of its own demise, as it becomes less and less possible to leave unmentioned or to defend the soon-to-be-challenged triumphant power of Israel. In retrospect the heyday of Israel's power and the power of Holocaust theology is in the years 1967–82.

The dissent that emerged at the time of the Lebanese war brings many themes of the pre-1967 critique forward even as it reaches a new level of strength and outrage. It is as if the dream of an empowered Israel has been fulfilled and turned into a nightmare. If Israel's other wars could be justified in terms of national defense, Lebanon could not. At the same time it had become clear that the occupation of the West Bank and Gaza was hardly a temporary reality but more and more an integral part of the daily ideological substance of Israeli life. By 1983 it could be stated unequivocally by dissenters that Israel, far from being innocent and beleaguered, was now an aggressor and a conqueror. The dire predictions of the early dissenters in Zion had been realized.

Jewish Responses to the Palestinian Uprising

On 23 January 1988, a little more than a month after the Palestinian uprising had begun, Alexander Schindler, president of the Union of American Hebrew Congregations, sent a telegram to Chaim Herzog, president of the state of Israel. The telegram protested the policy of force, might, and beatings announced by Defense Minister Yitzhak Rabin just weeks before. His message read in part, "I am deeply troubled and pained in sending you this message, but I cannot be silent. The indiscriminate beating of Arabs, enunciated and implemented as Israel's new policy to quell the riots in Judea, Samaria and Gaza, is an offense to the Jewish spirit. It violates every principle of human decency. And it betrays the Zionist dream." Two weeks before Schindler's telegram, Albert Vorspan, senior vice president of the Union, recorded these thoughts in his diary: "Beyond any issue in recent years, American Jews are traumatized by events in Israel. This is the downside of the euphoric mood after the Six-Day War, when we felt ten feet tall. Now, suffering under the shame and stress of pictures of Israeli brutality televised nightly, we want to crawl into a hole. This is the price we pay for having made of Israel an icon—a surrogate faith, surrogate synagogue, surrogate God. Israel could not withstand our romantic idealization. Israel never asked us to turn it into a kidney machine to pump some Jewish blood into our moribund lives."[26]

Over the next months the *New York Times* was inundated with messages of Jewish concern and anger published as op-ed pieces and paid for on that paper's advertising scale. In February 1988 four well-known Israeli writers—Yehuda Amichai, Amos Elon, Amos Oz, and A. B. Yehoshua—implored Jewish Americans to speak up against Israel's policy of occupation and its subsequent attempt to use military force to end an uprising whose only solution was political compromise. In March a half-page advertisement appeared, a statement signed by Jewish Israeli and American Jewish teachers, writers, and intellectuals under the heading "Israel Must End the Occupation." The statement reads:

> Out of deep concern for the character, the security and the future of the State of Israel, we, the undersigned, demand a reassessment of Israeli policy so that it may become possible to treat the fundamental causes of the recent violent unrest. It is impossible to ignore or deny the connection between the latest escalation in the expression of hostility between Arabs and Jews and the political stalemate that has existed for twenty years. There can be no solution to the problem in which Israel finds herself so long as rule by force is exercised by Israel over the Arab populations of the occupied territories. To present the problem as merely a matter of the necessary use of force to restore order is an evasion of the core of the issue, as is the placing of responsibility for finding a solution upon the shoulders of the army, diverted from its proper task of national defense in order to quell the disturbances. We cannot and must not tolerate situations in which our young soldiers find themselves forced to open fire upon demonstrations of civilians, many of them mere youths. The refusal of the government of Israel to face up to the root causes is both immoral and futile. We call upon the government of Israel to take immediate steps towards political negotiation before the rapidly changing situation gets completely out of hand.[27]

At the same time Arthur Hertzberg, former president of the American Jewish Congress and professor of religion at Dartmouth College, began writing a series of articles for the *New York Review of Books*, beginning with "The Uprising" and ending with "An Open Letter to Elie Wiesel." A main theme of these essays is the seemingly intractable quality of the Israel-Palestine conflict, the futility of Israel's military reaction to the uprising, the coming end of American Jewish innocence regarding Israel, and finally the illusion of Jewish unity regarding Israel. In his first essay, written in January 1988, Hertzberg concludes on a somber note: "Everyone with whom I have talked in the past few years about the Middle East—and, at various times, I have met with leaders of all the different camps—agrees that stalemate leads to disaster, but no one seems to have summoned up the political will to say that a settlement can no longer be postponed. After each visit to the Middle East, I return more pessimistic. Prophets of gloom rarely like the words they utter: they feel compelled to describe a despairing vision in the hope that someone will act to prove them wrong." Nine months later, in September, Hertzberg ends his essay with pleas for both sides to finally accept partition and, in furtherance thereof, the need for forgiveness:

> The time is now past for pragmatic politics. The majority in Israel cannot even persuade itself that it is in its pragmatic interest to do business with the P.L.O. even as a way of curbing the *intifada* and avoiding the Palestinian ultranationalists and Muslim fundamentalists—as it once did business with Abdullah to avoid the Palestinian question. The leaders of the P.L.O. will probably look for ways of adopting a position that will not drive their extremists out, and thus the P.L.O. may avoid the issue of Israel's legitimacy. The turning point that came with Hussein's speech of July 31, leaving the Palestinians and the Israelis to work out their relationship directly with each other, demands nothing less than confronting fundamental issues between Israelis and Palestinians. It is an old Middle Eastern tradition that enemies do not end their quarrels with lawyers' negotiations; they have a *Sulha*, a publicly staged act of forgiveness in which they wipe out past angers and begin anew in mutual acceptance. Such a *Sulha* must precede the negotiation for the final enactment of partition, for without it there will not be passion enough among the moderates of both camps to create the necessary majorities for such a settlement, and the result will be ceaseless conflict between two nations fought with more and more dangerous weapons.[28]

In June, after months of virtual silence, Elie Wiesel wrote an op-ed piece for the *New York Times*. Several months earlier he had written a short note commemorating the Warsaw Ghetto uprising. The following paragraph from that earlier piece contains a veiled reference to the current situation: "Little did we know that in our own lifetime, pseudo-scholars would write books to deny that the greatest of Jewish tragedies ever took place. And that the Jewishness of the Jewish victims would be watered down and cheapened. And that the uniqueness of the Holocaust would be questioned. And that anti-Semitism would be clothed in anti-Zionism. And that vicious minds would dare to compare the state of

Israel to Nazi Germany." However, his article "A Mideast Peace—Is It Impossible?" had a different tone. It was his first official statement on the uprising and told the story of his first trip to Israel since the uprising had begun.[29]

Wiesel records the Israeli military presence in Gaza and the "implacable plight of the tens of thousands of refugees who dwell in inhuman conditions nearby. Their suffering could be sensed everywhere, as if it had a life of its own." He spoke to Palestinians, whose aspirations were for a Palestinian state, and he spoke to Jewish Israeli soldiers about the possiblity of reconciling the needs of security with Judaism's concept of humanism. In the soldiers Wiesel finds determination and sadness, hatred and sorrow. The televised images of the beating of prisoners, breaking of bones, and demolition of houses have taken their toll, and in the world's eyes Israel is taking the place of "America during Vietnam, France during Algeria and the Soviet Union during the Gulag." Unfortunately, from Wiesel's perspective, many of these critics are being outdone by "some Jewish intellectuals who had never done anything for Israel but now shamelessly used their Jewishness to justify their attacks against Israel." Wiesel feels criticism is justified, but it often goes beyond the boundaries of the acceptable: "Israel is being presented as mostly blood-thirsty—and that is simply not true. In certain pro-Arab circles, the argument is even more vicious and ugly: Israel is being compared to Hitler's Germany, its policy to Nazism and the Palestinians of today to the Jews of yesterday. How are we to convince Israel's political adversaries that the Holocaust is beyond politics and beyond analogies?"[30]

Wiesel understands the anger of Palestinians who have been denied self-determination and laments the fact that the territories had been "imposed on Israel in war." Contrary to opinions expressed by others, Wiesel feels that Israel has not lost its soul and that its soldiers are not sadists, but a realistic solution—Israeli security and Palestinian self-determination—escapes him. Right-wing fanatics who speak of transferring Palestinians to Jordan are to Wiesel's mind a disgrace, but the liberals ready to give up all the territories immediately—to whom are they going to give them? "As long as the P.L.O. remains a terrorist organization, as long as it has not given up on its goal of destroying Israel, why should Israel negotiate with its leaders? But then, if the P.L.O. is not an interlocutor, who could be? There must be, and are, moderate Palestinians. But many have been assassinated—not by Israelis." Weisel concludes with a hope that harkens back to his visit to Jerusalem after the 1967 war, a six-day war that now has entered its third decade: "And yet, one must not lose hope. Somehow there must be a solution, acceptable to both sides, that would end a tragedy that generates such hatred. If extremists in both camps gain ground, all will suffer. I think of the Arab children whom I watched walking to school—and of the young Jewish soldiers with their tormented gaze. How long will joy be denied to all of them? More than ever, I would like to believe in miracles."[31]

Hertzberg's response to Wiesel's essay begins by recalling their initial meeting in the 1950s after the publication of their first books, Wiesel's *Night* and his own *The Zionist Idea*. They spoke Yiddish together, reminiscing about their respective childhoods in eastern Europe and their loss of family during the Holocaust. It is their common background that poses the first question: "We are, both of us, part of what is left of the Hasidic communities of your birthplace in Vishnitz and of mine in Lubaczow. What have we learned from the murder of our families? How must we live with their memory? You and I read and reread the Bible and Talmud: What do the sacred texts command us to think, to feel, and to do?"[32]

Hertzberg finds Wiesel, like many others, deeply troubled by the cycle of violence between Israelis and Palestinians, at the same time being sympathetic to Palestinian aspirations of self-determination. Hertzberg agrees with Wiesel's appeal to Palestinians to halt the throwing of stones and start negotiations. But Hertzberg is astonished that Wiesel does not accompany such an assertion with an appeal to the Israelis to do anything at all—in particular to move away from the policy of repression and toward negotiation. In the statements that Hertzberg has seen, Wiesel seems to have avoided saying anything about the content of Israel's policies.

> In a speech in Washington on March 13, after saying that American Jews behave "appropriately" when they question actions by Israel, you quickly added that "I am afraid of splitting the Jewish community with regard to Israel." How appropriate are the questioners, in your view, if their questions "split" the community and thus, so you clearly imply, do harm to Israel? You have reduced the political questions before Israel to all-or-nothing choices. You condemn the "right-wing Israeli fanatics" for the "disgraceful suggestion" of transferring all the Palestinians immediately to Jordan; you are equally critical of "some liberals who are ready to give up all the territories immediately," for there is, in your view, no one to whom to give them. Thus you are able to throw up your hands, as you have done repeatedly in interviews and statements since January, and say, "What are we to do?"[33]

For Hertzberg, the effect of what Wiesel is saying is to support the Likud line, that there are no options other than the present course. The discussion of Palestinian extremists, for example, so often cited by Likud and by Wiesel, ignores Jewish extremists like Meir Kahane who feel commanded to expel Muslims and Christians from Israel. "That a former chief of staff, Rafael Eitan, called the Palestinians 'drugged cockroaches' has, surely, not escaped your attention. I wonder whether you, and I, would have been silent if a Russian general had uttered a comparable slur about Jews demonstrating in Red Square. You know that the prime minister of Israel, Yitzhak Shamir, has been saying that he will not return a single inch of the West Bank to Arab sovereignty; he has thus stalled even the beginnings of negotiation." Jewish dissidents as well are placed within the dangerous category of disloyal Jews betraying their people and endangering their survival. Wiesel's predilection is to accuse Jewish dissenters of endangering Jewish support of Israel, of using their Jewishness to defame Israel:

> You have found no place, so far, in any of your writings or statements that I have seen to suggest that there are Jews in the world who have been devoted to Israel for many years and who have expressed outrage at such actions as dynamiting houses in the Arab village of Beta. Some of these villagers had tried to protect a group of Jewish teen-agers who were on a hike against stone throwers. In the melee a girl was shot by accident by one of the group's Jewish guards. The army then blew up fourteen houses in the village. According to accounts in the Israeli press, this was done not to punish anyone who was guilty but to appease the angry hard-line settlers in the West Bank. You were not among those who said anything in public after this and all too many other incidents. Are such figures in the diaspora as Sir Isaiah Berlin, Philip Klutznick, Henry Rosovsky, and the president of Yeshiva University, Rabbi Norman Lamm, and hundreds of others like them, who have spoken up in criticism of actions that they could not countenance, simply to be written off as people whose public statements endanger Jewish unity?[34]

To Wiesel's question of what Israel and the Jewish people are to do, Hertzberg's response is clear: accept the principle of partition and agree that Palestinians have a right to a territorial base for their national life. But to accept this principle and act upon it, Wiesel has to make a choice that represents an unequivocal break with the Likud party line and to accept the command to act justly, especially when "actions seem imprudent and embarrassing, and never to be silent, even to protect Jewish unity." In short, Hertzberg calls on Wiesel to reembrace the prophetic tradition with regard to Israel as he has so eloquently done with the Holocaust. To give aid to the "armed zealots" in Israel today, even through silence, is to lead to disaster as it has done in the past in Jewish history. Hertzberg concludes his letter with a plea to move beyond the illusion of Jewish unity and to speak prophetically:

> I keep thinking these days of the saying that both of us have quoted many times, and sometimes at each other, especially in those early years when we were closest. Menachem Mendel of Kotsk, the tortured Hasid of the last century, once said that when the Evil One wants to destroy us, he tempts us not through our wicked desires but through our most virtuous inclinations; we do good deeds at the wrong time, with the wrong intensity, and in a setting in which they do devastating harm. I fear that for all your love of Israel, you, in what you say, sometimes risk falling into the moral trap that Menachem Mendel described. You belong among those who speak the truth, even to Jewish power, and who do not look away because of real or invented Jewish weakness. We show the truest love of Israel and the Jewish people when we remind ourselves that, in strength or in weakness, we survive not by prudence and not by power, but through justice.[35]

Desecrating a Legacy

As the Jewish debate heated up in the *New York Times* and *New York Review of Books*, two established and respected venues of public opinion, a major new voice arose that claimed to represent the rebirth of progressive Jewish concern in America. This voice took the form of the journal *Tikkun*, with its editor, Michael Lerner, as its driving editorial force. Though publication began in 1986, with the uprising *Tikkun* clarified its position and found its place in the public debate. In the March/April issue, just four months after the beginning of the uprising, Michael Lerner wrote a lengthy editorial titled "The Occupation: Immoral and Stupid." Lerner begins the editorial with a passionate statement invoking Jewish memory of suffering as a command to halt the violence:

> The pain and sorrow many American Jews feel about Israel's policies on the West Bank and Gaza are rooted deep in our collective memory as a people. Israel's attempt to regain control of the refugee camps by denying food to hundreds of thousands of men, women and children, by raiding homes and dragging out their occupants in the middle of the night to stand for hours in the cold, by savagely beating a civilian population and breaking its bones—these activities are deplorable to any civilized human being. That they are done by a Jewish state is both tragic and inexcusable. We did not survive the gas chambers and crematoria so that we could become the oppressors of Gaza. The Israeli politicians who have led us into this morass are desecrating the legacy of Jewish history. If Jewish tradition has stood for anything, it has stood for the principle that justice

must triumph over violence. For that reason, we typically have sided with
the oppressed and have questioned the indiscriminate use of force. We,
who love Israel, who remain proud Zionists, are outraged at the betrayal
of this sacred legacy by small-minded Israeli politicians who feel more
comfortable with the politics of repression than with the search for
peace.[36]

The time for silence is over, and the truth must be stated in unequivocal
terms. Of the Israeli government Lerner demands: "Stop the beatings,
stop the breaking of bones, stop the late-night raids on people's homes,
stop the use of food as a weapon of war, stop pretending that you can
respond to an entire people's agony with guns and blows and power.
Publicly acknowledge that the Palestinians have the same right to national self-determination that we Jews have, and negotiate a solution
with representatives of the Palestinians!"[37]

Though Lerner is willing to express his anger in moral terms, he is
also willing to discuss the end of the occupation in terms of Israel's
survival and the survival of the Jewish people. In Lerner's understanding, the occupation is immoral and at the same time self-defeating for the
following reasons. First, the longer the occupation continues, the angrier
and more radical Palestinians become. As time goes on, Palestinians will
be less inclined to negotiate a two-state solution, as they will come to
regard a state on the West Bank and Gaza as a sellout of a fully liberated
Palestine. P.L.O. leadership, at this point willing to settle for such a state,
will, as time goes on, be seen as "betrayers of the struggle." A more
radical option relating to Islamic fundamentalism, which "makes it a sin
to live in peace in Israel," may then be embraced. Second, Palestinians
within the pre-1967 borders are being drawn into the struggle for the first
time since the creation of the state of Israel. Through participation in
general strikes and protest demonstrations, the situation within Israel
may come to resemble that in Beirut or Northern Ireland.[38]

Third, a logic of domination will take hold, and as the occupation
continues Israelis will necessarily become increasingly insensitive toward those they have so long dominated. Thus Israeli politics will continue to move to the right, and dissenters in Israel will swell the already
large emigration rate. Increasingly the people who leave—scientific,
technical, and professional personnel so important to the defense technology, economic strength, and intellectual creativity of the country—
will do so because they find the political and moral situation of Israel
unjustifiable. Fourth, because of the silence of much of American Jewish
leadership, the only voices articulating clear moral criticism have been
those of "Israel's enemies." According to Lerner, anti-Semites and anti-

Zionists now have a clear field of attack because Israel's current policies give "credibility to the worst lies about Judaism." And the Jewish people may also face criticism from those who are neither anti-Jewish nor anti-Zionists but who are justifiably indignant with a Jewish state that embodies a "viciousness and moral callousness" that they find abhorrent in other places of the world. Additionally, Lerner finds that the occupation threatens popular support for the state of Israel in the United States, within the American governmental and corporate structure as well as among individual citizens. As the United States is Israel's lifeline, politically, militarily, and financially, loss of support would be a disaster. The images of Israelis "beating, teargassing, shooting and starving a civilian population" erode U.S. support for Israel.[39]

Finally, the occupation threatens the survival of Judaism and the Jewish people in the Diaspora. Lerner cites the revival of interest in Judaism over the last two decades among Jewish Americans who find the values of American society lacking in depth and morally questionable. These Jews have turned to Judaism because of Judaism's emphasis on morality and transcendence, which stands in opposition to the logic of domination and empire that permeates American life. However, the occupation may reverse this trend as Jews dismiss this vision as pious moralizing without substance: "A Judaism that has lost its moral teeth and becomes an apologist for every Israeli policy, no matter what its moral context, is a Judaism that not only betrays the prophetic tradition, but also risks the adherence of the Jewish people."[40]

For Lerner, the moral and practical reasons for ending the occupation complement the religious reasons. The continuing occupation puts Jewish supporters of Israel in an agonizing dilemma: either reject its policy of occupation or reject the central teachings of Judaism. Here Lerner refers to the Exodus tradition, the commands relating to treatment of the stranger, and the wisdom of the Torah, which asks Jews to resist the pattern of oppressing others as Jews were once oppressed. Hence the period of wandering in the desert—to let the mentality of slavery die off and the acceptance of God's command of moral responsibility enter the land. According to Lerner, God's voice here is demanding: "There is no right to the Land of Israel if Jews oppress the *ger* (stranger), the widow, the orphan, or any other group that is powerless." The liberating message of Passover insists that the logic of domination can be broken, and therefore in the present we must resist the tendency to justify Israeli policy in relation to past Jewish suffering.[41]

Though Lerner cannot justify the Israeli occupation and the attendant violence, he also cannot ignore the aspects of Jewish history that may lead to the brutality of Israeli soldiers in the face of the Palestinian uprising.

> The rage that these soldiers exhibit when they beat civilians they suspect have been involved in rock-throwing may be understood, in part, as a response to the two thousand years during which the world systematically denied their right to exist as a people, a denial that culminated with extermination in gas chambers and crematoria. This oppression occurred not only in Europe; many Jews also had to flee Arab lands after hundreds of years of oppression and delegitimation. This same process of delegitimation has been further perpetuated by the Arab states in their refusal to relocate Palestinian refugees in 1948, in their insistence that these refugees stay in camps in Gaza and the West Bank, and in their failure to follow the lead of other countries that resettled much larger refugee populations, such as Pakistan's resettlement of nearly ten million Moslems after the struggle for Indian independence. This conduct by the Arab states was a loud proclamation: "You Jews don't really exist for us. Your presence here is temporary. We don't have to resettle the Palestinians or deal with this problem because you will soon be gone."

Thus Lerner has strong words for Palestinians as well: "So we say to the Palestinians: stop the rock-throwing, stop the talk of violently overthrowing Israel, reject the rejectionists, and publicly proclaim your willingness to live in peace with Israel. Begin to talk publicly about peaceful coexistence. You will not be granted genuine self-determination until you allay the legitimate fears of many Israelis that you are still committed to destroying Israel."[42]

What is the solution to the crisis of Israel and the Palestinians? For Lerner, it is a demilitarized and politically neutral Palestinian state in the West Bank and Gaza, guaranteed by the United States and the Soviet Union with Israel's right to intervene to prevent the introduction of tanks, heavy artillery, or airplanes. A unified force comprising the United States, the Soviet Union, and Israel will be established to protect the new Palestinian state from attack by foreign powers, be they Arab or others, and the United States and Israel will join in a collective security pact guaranteeing American support if Israel is attacked. Palestinians will police their own factions who seek to continue the struggle against Israel and renounce all claims to the rest of Palestine. After an agreed-upon period of peaceful coexistence, Israel and Palestine will enter into an economic confederation. Lerner ends with a call to action, for the crisis in Israel is a "moment of truth for all of us. It should be considered with the deepest seriousness and with the full understanding that the choices we make now may have consequences that reverberate for centuries to come."[43]

Beyond the writings of Diaspora Jews, Israel was experiencing its own new level of dissent. Simple demonstrations begun to protest the Lebanon War seemed less and less effective. In January 1988, a group calling itself the Twenty-first Year was established in Tel Aviv as an umbrella group of activists working in different sections of Israel "to confront the various elements of Israeli society and consciousness which allowed the continuation of the occupation." Its founding document, "Covenant for the Struggle Against Occupation," was signed by over one thousand Israelis, including writers Yoram Keriuk and David Schutz, poets Yosef Sharon and Harold Shimel, and academics Amos Funkenstein, Ruth Garrison, and Paul Mendes-Flohr.

The covenant calls for moving beyond protest to resistance and refusing any longer to "collaborate with the occupation." The occupation, existing for more than half of Israel's existence as a state, has infiltrated cultural and individual life and thus has to be rooted out bit by bit. If the presence of the occupation is total, the struggle against occupation has to be total as well:

> The occupation has become an insidious fact of our lives; its presence has not been confined to the occupied territories; it is, alas, among and within us and its destructive effects are in evidence in every aspect of our lives:
>
> The Israel Defense Forces and the conception of our national security are subordinated to the dictates of the occupation.
>
> The Israeli economy benefits from the blatant exploitation of Palestinian labor; it has developed a distorted colonialistic structure.
>
> The educational system is based on a double message: while promoting "democratic values,"it condones a repressive regime which controls the lives of disenfranchised subjects.
>
> By yielding to the authority of the Military Government in the occupied territories, the Supreme Court of the civilian judicial system tacitly condones the violation of the human rights of the Palestinians. The military judicial system unapologetically and brazenly subjects considerations of legal justice to the regnant needs of the occupation policy.
>
> Israeli culture is pervaded by a self-satisfied glorification of its tortured posture; its political involvement is by and large sterile.
>
> The Hebrew language has undergone a process of contamination. It has been harnessed to the imperatives of the occupation. It has been called upon to provide a misleadingly benign vocabulary to anesthetize the repression and flagrant violations of human rights.
>
> Israeli political thought is preoccupied and impoverished by the debate over the future of the occupied territories; it has locked itself into stereotypical conceptions of the Palestinian enemy and a demonological perception of its acts of resistance.[44]

Because the occupation came to encompass all aspects of Israeli life, resistance had to take the form of practical steps:

> We shall not abandon our national symbols to the distorting interpretation of the occupation. We shall not participate in any celebration, ceremony, or symbolic occasion held in the territories under occupation or in one which lends it legitimation in any way whatsoever.
>
> We shall not take excursions in the occupied territories uninvited by local Arab inhabitants. We shall not take advantage of the protection of the Israel Defense Forces and seek bargains and leisure in the occupied territories.
>
> We shall not allow our children to be exposed to the means by which the school system and its official curriculum promote and sanction the occupation.
>
> We shall not collaborate with the exploitation of Palestinian labor taking place under the sponsorship of the occupation. We shall publicize and boycott institutions, places of entertainment and the products of companies whose Palestinian employees are denied human dignity and decent working conditions.
>
> We shall not tolerate the willful ill-treatment of Palestinians which has become rampant within Israel proper. We shall act to stop such conduct; we shall expose each incident of this sort and take all legal measures to eradicate it.
>
> We shall not stand by while the Palestinians in the occupied territories are subjected to coercion, humiliation, and physical maltreatment through measures such as collective punishment, banishment, arrest without trial, torture, beatings and daily harassment. We shall not allow these ignoble deeds to be pushed from our consciousness; we shall not harden our hearts. We shall remain vigilant and accordingly protest such deeds in every possible way, including being physically present where and when they take place.
>
> We shall not buy goods produced by Israeli settlements in the occupied territories and shall avoid any economic ties with the settlers.
>
> We shall not condone the deliberate confusion of acts of protest and resistance by the Palestinians with Palestinian acts of terrorism.
>
> We shall not go along with the new vocabulary promoted by the reality of the occupation. We shall insist on using language true to the moral and political condition created by the occupation.
>
> We shall not obey any military command ordering us to take part in acts of repression or policing in the occupied territories.
>
> We shall not cease our quest for new strategies of critical inquiry and political action in the struggle against the occupation.[45]

At the same time that the Covenant was being signed, Israel Shahak, survivor of the Bergen-Belsen concentration camp and now professor of organic chemistry at the Hebrew University in Jerusalem as well as chairman of the Israeli League for Human and Civil Rights, began to translate eyewitness testimony and articles in the Hebrew press testifying to the brutality of the occupation. In his first collection, "Atrocities as a Method," Shahak compares the brutality of Israeli soldiers with that of the Nazis, whose butchery he himself experienced.

> It should be clear to everybody who reads this collection of testimonies, that the systematic use of the atrocities, which in their intensity and the special intention to humiliate *are* Nazi-like and *should* be compared to the analogous German Nazi methods, is intentional and in fact constitutes the Israeli method for ruling the Palestinians. There cannot be any doubt in my opinion that those Nazi-like methods, in whose effectiveness the stupid Israeli Army top command reposes a blind faith, have been devised by "experts," in this case by the Israeli "Arabists" (no doubt helped by some of their foreign colleagues) together with the military psychologists. There should be also no doubt that those Nazi-like horrors can and probably will become worse, if not stopped from outside, and their use can lead to actual genocide, whether by a "transfer" or by an extermination. Indeed this is one of my reasons for assembling this collection: to show that the actual genocide of the Palestinians in the territories is now possible, since those Israeli soldiers and officers who have committed the outrages recorded here are capable of anything and everything, and like the commander in Item No. 1 will consider that they are only carrying out their orders.[46]

The stories of torture and humiliation are many and include bringing naked prisoners to open fields for "death parades," tying suspects to electricity poles for hours and harassing them with guard dogs, use of the "banana method," in which a person's hands are caught from behind and tied to their feet, so that a person's body is contorted into the form of a banana, and the "current Jesus method" where prisoners are placed in the position of a cross, their hands tied up as to be stretched out to both sides, and finally the almost standard practice of beating fathers in the presence of their children. One soldier who testified at a hearing on the methods of containing the uprising said of a Palestinian they arrested and had beaten: "It was a beating for the hell of it. The man did not resist. We began to beat him at once. We hit his feet, his shoulders, and perhaps his head." The soldiers' commanding officer then spoke: "We were very nervous because of the incident. We found relief in beating him and in getting ecstatic about it. We kept beating him mindlessly."[47]

A victim of a second atrocity, a Palestinian who worked as a correspondent for the East Jerusalem–based *Al Fajr* daily, related the following story. "The Givati brigade soldiers forced me to stand on all fours, to bray, and to behave as if I were a donkey. This lasted half an hour, during which time they beat me all over my body with clubs and electric wires. . . . When I told them I was a journalist cooperating with Israeli journalists, they laughed and replied, 'That's nice, because beating journalists is what we particularly like.' At one point, one of the soldiers took away my eyeglasses, saying 'From now on you will be a blind donkey,' whereupon he smashed the eyeglasses with his feet. I begged for his mercy but he kept hitting me saying 'You understand nothing but force.' "[48]

It is this theme of humiliation that permeates almost the entire corpus of writing regarding the Israeli reaction to the uprising, and the humiliation of the Palestinian people reminds some Jews at least of their own humiliation at the hands of others, including the Nazis. Thus the Nazi analogy is being made by Jews intuitively, almost instinctively, and being made by those who because of their own previous suffering might be expected to avoid such comparisons. Coinciding with this theme of humiliation is the theme of refusal—the signatories to the Convenant, and the soldiers in Yesh Gvul who refuse out of conscience to serve duty on the West Bank and Gaza. And coinciding as well is the theme of solidarity, as if the destinies of Jews and Palestinians are tied together and that solidarity might represent the mutual liberation of both peoples. This solidarity includes Jews working against the occupation inside Israel's 1967 borders, like the Women in Black who every week gather in Jerusalem wearing mourners' clothes as a gesture of solidarity with the beaten and dead of the Palestinian community, and Jews working directly with Palestinians sharing legal skills, medical supplies, and other intellectual and physical materials needed by the Palestinian movement.[49]

A History of Oppression

But ultimately the challenge of Jewish dissent during this period is to see the uprising in historical perspective as a continuation of Palestinian suffering rather than something new and unprecedented. Thus the Palestinian uprising provides Jews the possibility for viewing the renewal of Jewish life in Palestine and Israel as a historical event a century in duration and therefore allowing fundamental judgments to be made concerning that history, judgments that can contribute to choices for the future.

Recent books reflecting other than the standard history, written by Jewish Israelis and published before the uprising, assume new importance within the context of the uprising. In a sense they help place the uprising in context as almost inevitable, or at least understandable within the framework of the birth of Israel. They challenge the myth of the state's origins and thus the myth of Israel's original innocence. To do this is to challenge the theory that Israel's present problems and methods of dealing with those problems are aberrational, simply to be corrected by self-adjustment. Rather, they point to a flawed beginning, to inherent contradictions that are manifested in the uprising today. Together with the outrage expressed by Schindler, Hertzberg, Lerner, Shahak, and others, these books make clear the implications, at least for now, of the tradition of dissent.

A polemical but essentially accurate framing of the issue, *The Birth of Israel: Myths and Realities*, was written by Simha Flapan, who was born in Poland and emigrated to Palestine in 1930. Flapan, who died in April 1987 just as his book was going to press, had a long and distinguished career as a writer, publisher, peace activist, and educator. From 1954 to 1981 he was national secretary of Israel's Mapam party and director of its Arab Affairs department.

In his previous book, *Zionism and the Palestinians, 1917–1947*, Flapan traced the evolution of the Jewish and Arab conflict as it developed in the prestate period. Flapan's next book, which turned out to be his last, was supposed to survey the next stage of the Israeli-Palestinian conflict, beginning with Israel's War of Independence in 1948 and ending with the 1967 war. But his concentration on the years 1948–52 as the formative years of Israeli statehood came about, strangely enough, because of Menachem Begin's challenge to massive antiwar protest during the Lebanese war.[50]

In defending the actions and aspirations surrounding the invasion of Lebanon, Begin claimed continuity with David Ben-Gurion's policies of 1948 as Israel's first prime minister. Among other things, Begin cited Ben-Gurion's plan to establish a homogeneous Jewish state by dividing Lebanon, setting up a Christian state north of the Litani River, and destroying Arab villages within the borders of Israel and expelling their inhabitants during the 1948 war. Because the 1948 war had never been a subject of controversy, and the difference between the "defensive" War of Independence and the offensive invasion of Lebanon was clear, and further because Ben-Gurion and Begin had always been enemies, and because, at least for most progressive Israelis, the Likud's policies and vision clearly represented a break with traditional Labor aspirations, Begin's claim of continuity came as quite a shock to Flapan and others. And it represented a challenge as well. For Begin was claiming to be carrying out in an open way what was there from the beginning; Ben-Gurion, and by implication the Labor party from then to the present, had resorted to subterfuge.[51]

For Flapan, the uncovering of the origins of the state to dispute or verify Begin's claims was essential to understanding the course of the Jewish-Palestinian conflict leading up to and including the Lebanon War—and surely now the Palestinian uprising, which erupted months after Flapan's death. The historical parallel of the War of Independence and the Lebanon War, and by extension the Palestinian uprising, raised for Flapan the following questions: "Was the policy of the Zionist leadership in 1948 and that of Israel's subsequent leaders actually aimed at attaining a homogeneous Jewish state in the whole or most of Palestine? If this was the case, then the attempted destruction and further dispersal of the Palestinian refugees in Lebanon appears to be a more advanced application of the same policy. Does this mean that the socialist leadership of the Jewish community in 1948 and their successors up until 1977—when Begin's party came to power—were no different from their hated Revisionist rivals on this issue? And even more frightening, to what extent does the growing support for the theocratic racist Rabbi Meir Kahane—who talks openly of deporting the Palestinians from Israel and the West Bank and Gaza—have its roots in the events of 1948?" Flapan continues:

> Like most Israelis, I had always been under the influence of certain myths that had become accepted as historical truth. And since myths are central to the creation of structures of thinking and propaganda, these myths had been of paramount importance in shaping Israeli policy for more than three and a half decades. Israel's myths are located at the core of the nation's self-perception. Even though Israel has the most sophisticated army in the region and possesses an advanced atomic capability, it continues to regard itself in terms of the Holocaust, as the victim of an unconquerable, bloodthirsty enemy. Thus whatever Israelis do, whatever means we employ to guard our gains or to increase them, we justify as last-ditch self-defense. We can, therefore, do no wrong. The myths of Israel forged during the formation of the state have hardened into this impenetrable, and dangerous, ideological shield. Yet what emerged from my reading was that while it was precisely during the period between 1948 and 1952 that most of these myths gained credence, the documents at hand not only failed to substantiate them, they openly contradicted them.[52]

For Flapan these were less abstract theories to be debated than a personal challenge to the naïveté and ignorance of a person committed to the Zionist ideal since his childhood in Poland in the post–World War I years.

Flapan's book traces several myths central to understanding the origins of Israel and the present predicament facing Israel. These myths are crucial to the entire premise of Holocaust theology: that Zionists accepted the United Nations partition plan of 1947 as a compromise by which the Jewish community abandoned the concept of a Jewish state in the whole of Palestine and accepted the right of the Palestinians to their own state; that Palestinian Arabs rejected partition and responded to a call for all-out war on the Jewish state, forcing Jews into a military conflict; that Israel as a "numerically inferior, poorly armed people in danger of being overrun" faced and defeated a military giant composed of the entire Arab world bent on destroying the embryonic state and expelling its inhabitants; and finally, that the flight of the Palestinians before and after the establishment of the state of Israel was prompted by Arab leadership as a temporary measure, that they were to return with the victorious Arab armies, and that despite those efforts, Jewish leaders tried to persuade the Palestinian Arabs to remain in Israel.[53]

Contrary to these assumptions, Flapan's research shows the reality to be either more complex or completely different. According to Flapan, from the beginning Israeli policy was to thwart the emergence of a Palestinian state through secret agreements with the leaders of Transjordan, who were interested in creating a Greater Syria. The majority of Arabs did not respond to the call for a holy war against Israel; instead, many Palestinians, at leadership and grass-roots levels, tried to find an accommodation with the new Israeli state, an effort that was undermined by the Israeli government's opposition to the creation of a similar Palestinian state. Arab states aimed to prevent the agreement that might lead to a Greater Syria rather than liquidate the Jewish state. Furthermore, Israel was on the defensive only for the first month of the war and for the remainder of it had superiority in weapons and armed forces. Finally, the flight of Palestinian Arabs was prompted by Israel's political and military leaders, who "believed that Zionist colonization and statehood necessitated the 'transfer' of Palestinian Arabs to Arab countries."[54]

From these understandings of the myths and realities of Israeli history, Flapan concludes that there is a clear line of continuity between Ben-Gurion and Begin, the War of Independence and the Lebanon War, and, by extension, the current prime minister, Yitzhak Shamir, and the uprising: the identification of Palestinians as the enemy, the Israeli army confronting not only soldiers but a civilian population, the subsequent dehumanization of the Israeli soldiers through brutality and violation of elementary human rights. Still, the end of this cycle, the brutalization of Israel's soldiers, cannot occur without dehumanizing of the enemy, and here the continuity is again clear. Ben-Gurion described the Palestinian Arabs as the "pupils and even the teachers of Hitler, who claim that there is only one way to solve the Jewish question—one way only: total anni-hilation." Begin described the P.L.O. fighters as "two-legged animals" and compared the bombings of Beirut, the stronghold of Yasser Arafat, with the bombings of Berlin, the last fortress of Adolph Hitler. The last element of this cycle, the philosophy of expulsion promulgated by Kahane and others today, was already in place in 1948, though expressed in the more benign terms necessary for the creation of a homogeneous Jewish state. Thus for Flapan, a fundamental contradiction exists from the beginning with Ben-Gurion and continues through Begin and Shamir, that is, the desire to build a democratic Jewish society in the whole, or in most, of Palestine.[55]

The strength of Flapan's work rests in his framing of the issues and their patterns of continuity. The details of the history, which in the main confirm Flapan, can be found in works of younger historians like Avi Shalim's *Collusion Across the Jordan*, Ilan Pappe's *Britain and the Arab-Israeli Conflict, 1948–1951*, Tom Segev's *1949: The First Israelis*, and Benny Mor-ris's *The Birth of the Palestinian Refugee Problem, 1947–1949.*[56]

The latter two books are crucial to undermining Jewish naïveté about the creation of the state of Israel, and they point to the continuity of policies faced by Jewish dissenters today. Morris's book, for example, outlines in great detail and complexity the mass movement of Pales-tinians, estimated between 600,000 and 760,000 people, from their homes, villages, and cities during the war and the creation of a refugee population as an unexpected but generally welcomed bonus for the new Jewish state. This exodus was initially instigated by some regular and irregular Jewish forces, through the massacre of Deir Yassin in 1948, for example, which carried a lesson to those Palestinian Arabs who stayed behind at the end of the war. There was also "Plan D," in which Jewish brigade- and battalion-level commanders were given "carte blanche to completely clear vital areas: it allowed the expulsion of hostile or poten-tially hostile Arab villages."[57]

During the early part of the war there was never any official decision to expel Palestinians; no plan or policy was articulated. But according to Morris it was "understood by all concerned that, militarily, in the strug-gle to survive, the fewer Arabs remaining behind and along the front lines, the better, and, politically, the fewer Arabs remaining in the Jewish state, the better. At each level of command and execution, Haganah officers 'understood' what the military and political exigencies of survival required."

By the second half of the war the readiness to expel grew, both because of the unforeseen possibility, as a result of the first waves of the Palestinian exodus, of an almost completely Jewish state and because of the length and bitterness of the war itself. Still, the reality of expulsion was not announced as policy: "Ben-Gurion clearly wanted as few Arabs as possible to remain in the Jewish state. He hoped to see them flee. He said as much to his colleagues and aides in meetings in August, September and October. But no expulsion policy was ever enunciated and Ben-Gurion always refrained from issuing clear or written expulsion orders; he preferred that his generals 'understand' what he wanted done. He wished to avoid going down in history as the 'great expeller' and he did not want the Israeli government to be implicated in a morally questionable policy. And he sought to preserve national unity in wartime." By the end of the war another as yet unannounced policy went into effect: except for a few notable exceptions, and despite tremendous international pressure, the Palestinians who left what became the state of Israel would not be allowed to return.[58]

Tom Segev provides an account of the human side of the creation of the Palestinian refugee population and the way Jews in power handled the question of expulsion. In a Ministerial Committee for Abandoned Property meeting of 7 July 1948, Segev cites the following dialogue between Eliezer Kaplan, minister of finance, and Behor Shalom Shitrit, head of the ministry for the minorities.

> E. Kaplan reported that the conquest of Lydda and Ramlah has now, for the first time, confronted us with the problem of possessing an area occupied by a very large number of Arabs. The total number of inhabitants in these two towns and the adjoining villages is estimated at several tens of thousands.
>
> B. Shitrit had "visited occupied Ramlah and observed the situation close up. The army proposed to capture all the men who are capable of bearing arms (except for those who signed the letter of surrender), take them as far as the Arab border and set them loose. Mr. Shitrit contacted the Foreign Minister and asked him to formulate a policy. The Foreign Minister's reply was that those inhabitants who wished to remain could do so, provided the State of Israel did not have to support them. Those who wished to leave could also do so."
>
> E. Kaplan: "Discussed the problem of the population of Ramlah and Lydda with the Minister of Defense [Ben-Gurion] and received an answer

which to a certain extent contradicts that of the Foreign Ministry. The Minister of Defense replied that the young men should be taken captive, the rest of the inhabitants ought to be encouraged to leave, but those who remain, Israel will have to provide for."[59]

Aharon Cizling, minister of agriculture, also made the following comments when informed of murderous acts and rape committed by Israeli soldiers:

> I've received a letter on the subject. I must say that I have known what things have been like for some time and I have raised the issue several times already here. However after reading this letter I couldn't sleep all night. I felt the things that were going on were hurting my soul, the soul of my family and all of us here. I could not imagine where we come from and to where we are going. . . . I often disagreed when the term Nazi was applied to the British. I wouldn't like to use the term, even though the British committed Nazi crimes. But now Jews too have behaved like Nazis and my entire being has been shaken. . . . Obviously we have to conceal these actions from the public, and I agree that we should not even reveal that we're investigating them. But they must be investigated.[60]

This history is relevant to the uprising and to Jewish dissent because the essential contradictions posed by the historical analysis are in essence posed today four decades after the creation of the state of Israel. Moreover, they were posed initially three decades before the state was established. This history is relevant also because it undermines the themes of innocence and redemption central to Holocaust theology and therefore can provide a bridge of understanding between Jews and Palestinians if its reality is recognized at any deep level. Perhaps the challenge that faces Jewish dissenters today is that of achieving that depth of understanding, which will also give rise to a call for repentance. But this history is particularly relevant because important sectors of the Jewish community refuse to understand the present situation. Alongside the progressive response to the Palestinian uprising has been a conservative and chilling defense of Israel's innocence, and this too can be seen in statements made in paid advertisements in the *New York Times*. Clearly, after the first months of the uprising these statements began to predominate, with their essential call to support Israel against its enemies, variously defined as Palestinians, the P.L.O. leadership, Yasser Arafat, the Arab states, the national network news anchors, and self-deluded Jews. As Michael Lerner wrote his lead editorial in March 1988, labeling the occupation immoral and stupid, a rally in support of Israel was publicized and a welcome message to Prime Minister Shamir on his visit to the United

States was included under the title "Territory for Peace—Bad Deal: International Conference—A Trap." Believing that Israel had a historically legal and moral right to "Judea, Samaria, Gaza and the Golan Heights," the signed message applauded "the dignified and principled manner in which you have performed your duties as leader of the Jewish state," and prayed for the success of Shamir's visit, assuring him that the American people were with him.[61]

Two months later, in May, a wealthy Jewish man born in Poland, Jack Mondlak, whose entire family perished in the Holocaust, wrote of his early life in Poland and the anti-Semitism in the "attacks, pogroms, humiliation and sense of terror that all Jews knew." Mondlak's concern was focused on the relation of the Holocaust to Israel when in the present crisis the existence of Israel was being debated and slandered in the press and when some Jews were attempting to undermine Israel by distortion and unjust charges:

> Shame on you "Concerned Jews"! You have added heavily to Israel's burden. You accuse Israel of having lost its soul because you have lost your nerve. You have maligned Israel but in so doing you have revealed the emptiness of your Jewish commitment. Israel, a nation that has made huge strides in medicine and science, deserves no rebuke from you. Israel, which has illuminated the Middle East with a spirit of democracy, needs no lesson from you who would stifle her voice. Israel, which has demonstrated unparalleled restraint in the face of those who would destroy her, should be a source of pride to every Jew—yes, even including you. I see again the shadows of the Holocaust which began with the assassination of character and ended with physical extermination. We should not take this threat lightly. We should not blind ourselves again.[62]

The themes that emerge in the tradition of dissent often assume a dialectical form. Jewish renewal is haunted by the prospect of creating new victims. Jews' own history of victimization is shadowed by the present reality of power, and fear of imperiling the Jewish community is confronted with the need to question Jewish power. The larger Jewish community suppresses the direction of dissent that seeks to revitalize the Jewish witness to the world. Dissent traditionally has been expressed in ethics and critical thought rather than statehood and political power. Too often the discussions framed by dissent are argued within the parameters set by Jewish institutions and the state of Israel itself. Thus the tradition of dissent continues even today, but can remain ineffectual. The fears expressed in reaction to dissent—often even by dissenters themselves—of recreating a climate of anti-Semitism, also continues, to circumscribe the ability to speak and act without equivocation.

In a sense the tradition of dissent has reached an impasse both in numbers and in its ability to develop thought and activity without fear. Thus the tradition can only move forward by listening and incorporating the voices and lives of those who live side by side with Jews: present enemies, Palestinians; and former enemies, Western Christians. The task of the following chapters is to explore the dynamics of listening and including Palestinian and Western Christian analysis, thus broadening and deepening a tradition of dissent Jews today inherit.

CHAPTER 4

Toward an Inclusive Liturgy of Destruction

In a fascinating and important book, *Against the Apocalypse: Responses to Catastrophe in Modern Jewish Culture*, David Roskies examines the history of the Jewish people through its various responses to destruction. What Roskies finds is a people with a remarkable ability to reclaim ancient Jewish archetypes and therefore create meaning within suffering and death. "The greater the catastrophe, the more the Jews have recalled the ancient archetypes," Roskies writes. This was true in the ghettos of eastern Europe where the archetypes of destruction came alive in the minds of the common people and intellectual alike: the burning of the Temple (the sacred center), the death of the martyr (the sacred person), and the pogrom (the destruction of the holy community). The walls and barbed wire that separated Jews from the non-Jewish population paradoxically helped to bring some of the internal boundaries down. "The elite were brought closer to the masses, the assimilated closer to the committed, the secular closer to the religious, Yiddish closer to Hebrew. The modernists became, despite their long battles against it, part of the literature of consolation. With the ghetto's intellectuals moving closer to the people, the writers could use the polylingualism of Jewish eastern Europe to restore conceptually and socially the idea of a Jewish nation that was the penultimate consolation for the ultimate destruction. And a literature that was for centuries retrospective (including 'prophecies after the fact') became increasingly prophetic—so that, in fact, analogies could be used at last not for consolation but for action, including uprisings."[1]

The scribes of the ghetto wrote as an act of faith and, in fact, participated in and transformed the "liturgy of destruction" that the Jewish people had articulated over the millennia. Though overwhelmingly secular in background and outlook, the ghetto writings continually referred to religious themes. Yitzhak Katzenelson, a secular poet, organized a public reading of the Bible on the day the Warsaw Ghetto was sealed, though this was to demonstrate a continuity of history as a people rather than belief in God. However when it came to the Psalms, Katzenelson rejected them as too placid a form of response to catastrophe. At the same time Hillel Zeitlin, for years a modern religious existentialist, began translating the Psalms into Yiddish, and when his ghetto tenement was blockaded, Zeitlin arrived at the roundup point for deportation dressed in prayer shawl and tefillin.[2]

We have here, in its most difficult articulation, memory as a form of resistance: the refusal to cut oneself off from one's own people while at the same time speaking to the world in cries of anguish. Roskies concludes that to understand the collective response of the Jewish people during the Holocaust one must look to the writers, "who because they shared the same fate and were intimately involved in all facets of the people's Armageddon, were able to transmute the screams into a new and terrible scripture."[3]

This power—the use of the archetypes of destruction in a time of crisis as a way of affirming Jewish commitment—continues after the Holocaust in the empowerment of the Jewish people. Some Jews relate directly to preserving the memory of the Holocaust as a day of liturgical remembrance, and to this end Yom Hashoah has gained a place in the official liturgical cycle of the Jewish people. In synagogues around the world, but also in special ceremonies of public and governmental remembrance in the United States and Israel, Yom Hashoah is the time to recall the untold sufferings of the Jewish people as a sign both of respect for those who perished and hope for the continuation of the people beyond the tragedy of the Holocaust. In the United States, for example, the chairperson of the U.S. Holocaust Memorial Council and often the president of the United States deliver speeches on the Holocaust, and at the state level governors and senators participate publicly as well. Ceremonies include survivors and clergy, both Jewish and non-Jewish, and the music of the ghettos and camps is often sung. In Israel, the president or prime minister participates in a nighttime ceremony at Yad Vashem as part of a national commemoration. During the day all work, traffic, and broadcasts cease at 11:00 A.M., when a long whistle blast is heard throughout Israel, heralding a moment of national silence. It is not surprising that two of the strongest and most articulate proponents of Yom Hashoah are Irving Greenberg and Elie Wiesel. Nor should it surprise us that, for both, the path of destruction points to the path of redemption in Israel; therefore, Greenberg suggests contributions to the United Jewish Appeal, the central fund-raiser for Israel, as an appropriate form of remembrance.[4]

Bitburg and the Messianic

The announcement of Ronald Reagan's proposed visit to the military cemetery in Bitburg, Germany, in the spring of 1985 and the consequent furor surrounding the visit exemplifies the public quality of this liturgy of destruction. Initially planned as a gesture of reconciliation between the American and German nations, whose armed forces opposed each other in World War II, and as a final act of normalization between countries who are now staunch allies, the event touched the nerves of American army veterans, U.S. political figures, and, of course, most specifically the Jewish community. The visit to Bitburg became even more controversial when it was discovered that along with ordinary German soldiers, members of the infamous Waffen SS were also buried there. This, coupled with Reagan's remarks, which seemed to equate the German soldiers and the victims of those soldiers, including the Jewish victims, as well as his initial decision not to visit the Dachau or Bergen-Belsen concentration camp sites, raised a gathering protest to a storm. President Reagan and Chancellor Kohl's desire to, in a sense, close the chapter on World War II did just the opposite, opening old wounds and spurring new divisions. And it became the most prominent, widespread, and, paradoxically perhaps, one of the last public displays of the Jewish liturgy of destruction.[5]

Prominent among the commentators on the event were Irving Greenberg and Elie Wiesel, Greenberg because of his place in the ongoing development of Holocaust theology, and Wiesel because of his national prominence and the coincidental timing of his acceptance of the Congressional Gold Medal of Achievement, awarded by Reagan at the White House in a ceremony televised nationally. Greenberg's writings and Wiesel's acceptance speech demonstrate both their depth of feeling and some of the complexities involved in criticizing in public a president who, while betraying a deeply held trust in relation to the memory of the dead, fervently supported Israel.

In an essay titled "Some Lessons from Bitburg," Greenberg began by reflecting, sometimes angrily, on the reception of Holocaust memorials in the Jewish community itself. Some weeks before Bitburg, the *Baltimore Jewish Times* ran a story taking issue with the emphasis given to the Holocaust in contemporary Jewish life, with one person quoted as find-

ing the hundred-million-dollar fund-raising campaign for a national Holocaust memorial to be an "obscenity." Greenberg cites the difficulties in
the 1950s and 1960s for thinkers like Wiesel and Fackenheim in establishing the Holocaust as central to Jewish life. Often they were attacked and
vilified. For Greenberg, to criticize commemoration of the Holocaust
today as excessive is to continue that denial and to accomplish what
Reagan's visit to Bitburg did: equate German soldiers and their victims,
make similar war and genocide. It also represents, in Greenberg's mind,
confusion about the reasons for a Holocaust memorial, "the fact that
Holocaust commemoration is not a focus on death but a goad and entry
into reaffirmation of life and ethics."[6]

For Greenberg, the primary message of the Holocaust com-
memorations is that true reconciliation comes through repentance and
remembrance and is necessary to prevent recurrence. "Repentance is the
key to overcoming the evils of the past. When people recognize injustice,
they can correct the wrongdoing and the conditions that lead to it.
Memory leads to higher levels of responsibility and morality and reduces
the anguish of the feeling that the dead may have died in vain. Repentance has liberated many Christians from past stereotyping and hatred of Jews, thus transforming Christianity into a true gospel of love—
which it seeks to be. Repentance has liberated many Germans from the
sins of the Nazi past. Those that resist are themselves implicated in the
past, or give aid and comfort to those who still identify with those days
and those evil forces in the German nation and soul."[7] Having disagreed
vehemently with Reagan's decision to visit Bitburg, and hoping that
Holocaust commemoration would one day through affiliation with a
United States agency become part of the ebb and flow of American public
life, Greenberg cautions against too harsh a judgment on Ronald Reagan.
Citing Reagan's record in commemorating the Holocaust in the White
House, his service as honorary chair of the campaign to create a national
Holocaust memorial, and his ongoing support of Israel—"the single
most powerful Jewish commitment that the Holocaust shall not recur"—
Greenberg pleads for American Jews not to falsify the overall record of
one who supports Jewish interests.[8]

In a nationally televised speech with Reagan sitting by his side, Elie
Wiesel accepted his congressional award with a somber realism. Forty
years earlier Wiesel, as a young man, had awakened "an orphan in an
orphaned world." The Jews were alone, and forty-two years before on
the same date as the speech he was giving, the Warsaw Ghetto had risen
in arms to fight the Nazis—and they too were alone. "The leaders of the
free world, Mr. President, knew everything and did so little, or at least

nothing specifically, to save Jewish children from death. . . . One million Jewish children perished. If I spent my entire life reciting their names, I would die before finishing the task." What had Wiesel learned over the past forty years? The perils of language and of silence; that neutrality, when human lives and dignity are at stake, is a sin; that the Holocaust was a "unique and uniquely Jewish event," albeit with universal implications, and that suffering confers no privileges. "And this is why survivors, of whom you spoke, Mr. President, have tried to teach their contemporaries how to build on ruins, how to invent hope in a world that offers none, how to proclaim faith to a generation that has seen it shamed and mutilated. And I believe, we believe, that memory is the answer, perhaps the only answer."[9]

Along with these lessons learned, Wiesel also expressed gratitude to America, whose army liberated the death camps, whose doors opened to survivors as haven and refuge, and whose support of Israel was ongoing. And Wiesel expressed gratitude for Israel: "We are eternally grateful to Israel for existing. We needed Israel in 1948 as we need it now." Then the conclusion, which becomes almost liturgical.

> May I, Mr. President, if it's possible at all, implore you to do something else, to find a way, to find another way, another site? That place, Mr. President, is not your place. Your place is with the victims of the SS.
>
> Oh, we know there are political and strategic reasons, but this issue, as all issues related to that awesome event, transcends politics and diplomacy.
>
> The issue here is not politics, but good and evil. And we must never confuse them.
>
> For I have seen the SS at work. And I have seen their victims. They were my friends. They were my parents.
>
> Mr. President, there was a degree of suffering and loneliness in the concentration camps that defies imagination. Cut off from the world with no refuge anywhere, sons watched helplessly their fathers being beaten to death. Mothers watched their children die of hunger. And then there was Mengele and his selections. Terror, fear, isolation, torture, gas chambers, flames, flames rising to the heavens.[10]

For Greenberg and Wiesel, the liturgy of destruction is retrospective and future oriented, representing the Holocaust and Israel. Here the ghetto pleas are placed before the public by affluent and honored men representing a community that has survived and now flourishes. But the memory, the internalized landscape of sufferings, remains, and Wiesel's words especially are meant to transport his listeners to another day and time. In fact, we see both Wiesel and Greenberg living in two worlds, one vanished, the other, the present world, interpreted within that frame-work. The liturgy is a Jewish one but with an invitation, almost a sum-mons, for non-Jews to enter as well. However, beneath the rhetoric is a haunting lament that the true sense of suffering is slipping away and that the platform for such liturgies will one day be gone. The pledge of loyalty to the United States and to Reagan is a symbol of a liturgy that can be publicly enacted and yet ultimately is beholden to those who are distant in history and faith.

The return to the land of Israel has similarly brought to contemporary consciousness ancient Jewish themes, and this can be most clearly seen in the various forms of religious renewal now commonplace. Janet Aviad, in her book *Return to Judaism: Religious Renewal in Israel,* docu-ments the return of secular Jews to Orthodox or neoorthodox Judaism, people known as *ba'alei-teshuvah,* or "those who return." Many of these Jews are from upper- and middle-class neighborhoods in the United States. Their feelings of loss and alienation lead them to search for new foundations upon which to build a life. Many find their way to Israel, study in Jewish houses of learning, and make their lives in a new reli-gious environment. Whether they remain in Israel or not, it is often the return to the ancient symbols and places of Judaism that lead to or help solidify their new commitment. Clearly Yad Vashem and the yeshivas of Jerusalem are main centers of Jewish renewal, functioning as visible reminders of membership in an ancient suffering and now empowered people.[11]

One can also see the revival of Jewish religious fundamentalism in Israel as stimulated both by the crisis of the Jewish people and by the recovery of ancient myths and texts, as well as renewed access to ancient Jewish sites. Thus Ian Lustick in his book *For the Land and the Lord: Jewish Fundamentalism in Israel* emphasizes Israel's military triumph in 1967 as a crisis point in Israeli history that has polarized sentiment and opinion on the most profound questions facing Israeli society, at the same time serving as a catalyst for the formation of religious fundamentalist move-ments such as Gush Emunim (Bloc of the Faithful). For Lustick, it is ironic that the transformation of Israel, known for its unity and intimacy, into a bitterly, perhaps irrevocably, divided society, can be traced to its light-ning victory in the Six-Day War. By opening questions of tremendous emotional and practical import the war has divided rather than united. The "religious and emotional fervor surrounding the renewal of contact between Jews and the historic heartland of ancient Judea" has intro-duced religious language that allows little room for nuance and com-promise. As Lustick describes it, after more than eighteen centuries of dormancy "the distinctive blend of messianic expectation, militant politi-cal action, intense parochialism, devotion to the land of Israel, and self-sacrifice that characterized the Jewish Zealots of Roman times caught the imagination of tens of thousands of young religious Israeli Jews and disillusioned but idealistic secular Zionists." Biblical references abound, exemplified in the following statement by a Jewish fundamentalist:

> The commandment that pounded in the heart of Joshua and the generation who captured Canaan, in the heart of David and Solomon, and their generation, the word of God in his Torah, is thus, as it was first purely stated, what motivates us. The source of our authority will be our volunteering for the holy because we only come to return Israel to its true purpose and destiny of Torah and Holiness . . . we are looking for the complete renewal of the true official authority—the Sanhedrin and the anointed from the House of David—we are those who nurse from the future, from which we gain our authority for the generations.[12]

As frightening is the conclusion of another fundamentalist.

> Even if 100% of the Jewish inhabitants of Israel should vote for [the West Bank and Gaza's] separation from the Land of Israel, that "hundred percent consensus" would not have any more validity than the "hundred percent consensus" that prevailed within the people of Israel when it danced around the golden calf. The fate of those dancers around the golden calf, and they represented a massive "democratic" majority, was branded as with a hot iron into the genetic code of the Jewish people. The same is true of the fate of the spies [sent by Moses into Canaan] who were ready to abandon the Land of Israel, ten of the twelve of them at any rate, a solid "consensus," the fate of whom is also deeply engraved on the historical consciousness of the people. The history of Israel is the history of the minority, of Joshua son of Nun and Caleb son of Yephunah, who said: "Let us arise and take it, we shall succeed." In the end the consen-sualist majority turned on its heels and died in the desert while these two did enter the Land.[13]

Lustick concludes that the influence of those movements on Israeli soci-ety and government far outweighs their numbers, especially in their willingness to challenge the legitimacy of any government that attempts to withdraw from the West Bank and Gaza. By recalling the ancient glory of the Jewish people and its attachment to the land, by looking forward to the reconstruction of the Temple and the coming messianic age, and by a willingness to seek these goals through violence and, if necessary, the expulsion of the Palestinian Arabs, the Jewish fundamentalist movement has become the greatest obstacle to a comprehensive Palestinian-Israeli peace settlement.[14]

Holocaust theologians, in their sorrow and their commitment to survival, and Jewish fundamentalists, in their certainty and violence, contribute in different ways to moving into the present Roskies's understanding of the liturgy of destruction. Yet the liturgy of destruction, which today spawns Holocaust memorials and Jewish settlements, is profoundly transformed in contemporary Jewish life because it takes place within the empowerment of the Jewish people and is intimately linked to it. Within the context of empowerment both the remembrance of the Holocaust and the messianic expectation take on an organized, conscious quality—one might say a strategic sense—that forms the basis of alliances and mutual interests. Clearly there is a difference between the secularist Hillel Zeitlin arriving for deportation dressed in religious garb and the speeches made by American political leaders on behalf of the United States Holocaust Memorial Council. So, too, is there a difference between Orthodox Jews in the death camps praying for the coming of the messiah and Jewish Israeli underground terrorists attempting to blow up the Moslem Dome of the Rock mosque to make way for the messianic age through the reconstruction of the Jewish temple.[15]

The liturgy of destruction, with its elements of remembrance and the messianic, is now in the service of power rather than a precarious survival. Thus it is met with an evident boredom; the need for constant rehearsal seems more and more to pervade the contemporary liturgy of destruction. For many, the liturgy of destruction rings hollow. It does not acknowledge those who have suffered and are suffering today because of that liturgy—the Palestinian people—and reveals a hollowness, almost a deceptive quality, that forces a reevaluation of the liturgy itself. A new inclusiveness in the landscape of the dead and dying is called for if the voices of the Holocaust are to be rescued from an artificial construct that threatens memory much more than the Bitburg affair did.

Thinking the Unthinkable

Though it goes unmentioned and often repressed today, with the founding of the state of Israel, Jews for the first time began to see the suffering of another people, the Palestinian Arabs, in light of the suffering of the Jewish people. Here is the liturgy of destruction in its intuitive and more inclusive sense, which seems closer to reality than the staged and exclusive one heard today. Examples abound: In 1948, an Israeli intelligence officer, Shmarya Guttman, was involved in the occupation of the Palestinian Arab town of Lydda and the subsequent expulsion of its inhabitants. Benny Morris describes it:

All the Israelis who witnessed the events agreed that the exodus, under a hot July sun, was an extended episode of suffering for the refugees, especially from Lydda. Some were stripped by soldiers of their valuables as they left town or at checkpoints along the way. Guttman subsequently described the trek of the Lydda refugees: "A multitude of inhabitants walked one after another. Women walked burdened with packages and sacks on their heads. Mothers dragged children after them. . . . Occasionally, warning shots were heard. . . . Occasionally, you encountered a piercing look from one of the youngsters . . . in the column, and the look said: 'We have not surrendered. We shall return to fight you.'" For Guttman, an archaeologist, the spectacle conjured up "the memory of the exile of Israel" [at the end of the Second Commonwealth, at Roman hands].[16]

Morris continues this description:

One Israeli soldier (probably 3rd Battalion), from Kibbutz Ein Harod, a few weeks after the event recorded vivid impressions of the thirst and hunger of the refugees on the roads, and how "children got lost" and of how a child fell into a well and drowned, ignored, as his fellow refugees fought each other to draw water. Another soldier described the spoor left by the slow-shuffling columns, "to begin with [jettisoning] utensils and furniture and in the end, bodies of men, women and children, scattered along the way." Quite a few refugees died—from exhaustion, dehydration and disease—along the roads eastward, from Lydda and Ramle, before reaching temporary rest near and in Ramallah. Nirm al Khatib put the death toll among the Lydda refugees during the trek eastward at 335; Arab Legion commander John Glubb Pasha more carefully wrote that nobody will ever know how many children died.[17]

In the weeks that followed, a leader of the Mapam party, Meir Ya'ari, lamented: "Many of us are losing their [human] image. . . . How easily they speak of how it is possible and permissible to take women, children and old men and to fill the roads with them because such is the imperative of strategy. And this we say, the members of Hashmer Hatzair, who remember who used this means against our people during the [Second World] war. . . . I am appalled."[18]

Of course, many of the atrocities had little need of direct comparison with ancient or even contemporary Jewish experience in order to have an impact on those whose history was filled with suffering. S. Kaplan wrote of the occupation of the Palestinian village Ad Dawayima, near Hebron, which had surrendered without a fight:

The first [wave] of conquerors killed about 80 to 100 [male] Arabs, women and children. The children they killed by breaking their heads with sticks. There was not a house without dead, wrote Kaplan. Kaplan's informant, who arrived immediately afterwards in the second wave, reported that the Arab men and women who remained were then closed off in the houses "without food and water." Sappers arrived to blow up the houses. "One commander ordered a sapper to put two old women in a certain house . . . and to blow up the house with them. The sapper refused. . . . The commander then ordered his men to put in the old women and the evil deed was done. One soldier boasted that he had raped and then shot her. One woman, with a newborn baby in her arms, was employed to clean the courtyard where the soldiers ate. She worked a day or two. In the end they shot her and her baby.[19]

Another example was a Christian village, Eilaban, that surrendered to Israeli troops and gathered inside the churches while their priests formally surrendered the village. Searching the village, the Israelis discovered in a house the severed heads of two missing Israeli soldiers, which occasioned an order for all villagers to assemble in the village square. The village elders describe the collective punishment imposed upon them:

> Then the commander selected 12 youngsters (shabab) and sent them to another place, then he ordered that the assembled inhabitants be led to Maghar and the priest asked him to leave the women and babies and to take only the men, but he refused, and led the assembled inhabitants— some 800 in number—to Maghar preceded by military vehicles. . . . He himself stayed on with another two soldiers until they killed the 12 youngsters in the streets of the village and then they joined the army going to Maghar. . . . He led them to Farradiya. When they reached Kafr 'Inan they were joined by an armored car that fired upon them . . . killing one of the old men, Sam'an ash Shufani, 60 years old, and injuring three women. . . . At Farradiya [the soldiers] robbed the inhabitants of I£ 500 and the women of their jewelry, and took 42 youngsters and sent them to a detention camp, and the rest the next day were led to Meirun, and afterwards to the Lebanese border. During this whole time they were given food only once. Imagine then how the babies screamed and the cries of the pregnant and weaning mothers.[20]

The flight of villagers from Sa'sa was described in moving detail:

> They abandon the villages of their birth and that of their ancestors and go into exile. . . . Women, children, babies, donkeys—everything moves, in silence and grief, northwards, without looking to right or left. Wife does not find her husband and child does not find his father . . . no one knows the goal of his trek. Many possessions are scattered by the paths; the more the refugees walk, the more tired they grow—and they throw away what they had tried to save on their way into exile. Suddenly,

every object seems to them petty, superfluous, unimportant as against the chasing fear and the urge to save life and limb. I saw a boy aged eight walking northwards pushing along two asses in front of him. His father and brother had died in the battle and his mother was lost. I saw a woman holding a two-week-old baby in her right arm and a baby two years old in her left arm and a four-year-old girl following in her wake, clutching at her dress.[21]

These atrocities and expulsions occasioned some months later a ministerial probe that was discussed in Mapam's executive body. At the start of the meeting Benny Marshak explicitly asked that members refrain from using the phrase "Nazi actions." Later at a cabinet meeting Aharon Cizling told the other cabinet members that "I couldn't sleep all night. . . . This is something that determines the character of the nation. . . . Jews too have committed Nazi acts."[22]

In all of this something is happening that is both ancient and new. The references, in a time of crisis, to an ancient Jewish archetype of destruction, the memory of the exile of Israel with the destruction of the Temple by the Romans in 70 C.E. and to the Holocaust, which already in 1948 functions as an archetype of destruction, are now being made in relation to the suffering of another people at the hands of Jewish people. This is intuitively understood, and even the desire to keep this connection from being spoken belied the obvious, that at least some Jews were seeing in the Palestinian people their own history. And in observing that history, in sad and profound ways, they were recognizing that the history of Jews and Palestinians is somehow, in the expulsions and massacres, bound together.

But it is also clear at the very beginning that the ability to see this bond is intimately related to the ability to admit that Jews are no longer innocent, and this is precisely the most controversial issue. Thus many at the outset wanted to change the intuitive language and instead to address procedural matters and long-range goals, in a sense to bury the intuitive connection. In their minds any comparison from within or later from outside placed the legitimacy of Jewish empowerment in question. And, too, it cast doubt on the entire policy of separating the two communities, which gained strength as the war continued and Israel was, to a large extent, emptied of Palestinians. One cannot help but hear, as these actors saw with their own eyes, the tension between the prophetic—questioning power—and the process of normalization—adjusting for the obvious excess, though continuing pursuit of the general goal. For those who pursued normalization, the time had come for Jews to grow up and to suppress the ancient and contemporary images of destruction that define a landscape better forgotten.

Now over forty years later the connection of Palestinian and Jew can still be found lurking beneath the surface of power politics. After the Palestinian uprising began, Amos Kenan, a columnist for the Israeli daily *Yediot Aharonot*, wrote an essay titled "Four Decades of Blood Vengeance" that takes on the quality of a dialogue with George Habash, head of the Popular Front for the Liberation of Palestine, whom he met in 1948 when the Israeli army conquered Lydda.

Kenan was a soldier who, as a part of the invading and occupying force, kept Palestinian Arabs at a distance. Habash, whose ailing sister lived in Lydda, managed to avoid security and visit her. Habash's sister was thirty years old, married, with six children, and at that point dying. A medical doctor, Habash diagnosed her disease and prescribed the appropriate medicines, but because Lydda was under curfew with no local pharmacies and no access to the outside, his sister died three days later. Because of the curfew it was impossible to bury her properly, and so Habash dug a grave with his own hands and buried his sister in her own backyard. When the curfew was lifted, the survivors of the village, Habash and his sister's six children included, were transferred to temporary prison compounds and later expelled to Amman, Jordan.[23]

Kenan recalls his days of guard duty in Lydda as essentially uneventful and in some senses comical, both because of the lack of military preparedness of many of the military personnel, some of whom had recently arrived from eastern Europe, and the quality, or lack thereof, of the weapons. Since most of the inhabitants of Lydda had fled before the Israel occupation, there were few people to guard. In short, they had a typical military life with much standing around, gossiping, and the inevitable boredom. And it was typical in other, more horrifying ways as well:

> In the afternoon, those of us who couldn't take it any more would steal off to Tel Aviv for a few hours, on one excuse or another. At night, those of us who couldn't restrain ourselves would go into the prison compounds to fuck Arab women. I want very much to assume, and perhaps even can, that those who couldn't restrain themselves did what they thought the Arabs would have done to them had they won the war.
>
> Once, only once, did an Arab woman—perhaps a distant relative of George Habash—dare complain. There was a court martial. The complainant didn't even get to testify. The accused, who was sitting behind the judges, ran the back of his hand across his throat, as a signal to the woman. She understood. The rapist was not acquitted, he simply was not accused, because there was no one who would dare accuse him. Two years later, he was killed while plowing the fields of an Arab village, one no longer on the map because its inhabitants scattered and left it empty.[24]

Kenan then begins to write about blood vengeance, and how difficult it is to square accounts. What he does know is that many have sought and taken revenge, and to his mind all the vengeance has already come:

> Both you and I, George, have already taken vengeance—before and during and after the fact. And both you and I have not taken pity on man or woman, boy or girl, young or old. I know that there is not much difference between pressing a button in a fighter plane and firing point-blank into the head of a hostage. As there is no difference between a great massacre that was not meant to be and one that was meant to be. There is no distinction between justice and justice or between injustice and injustice, as there is no difference at all in what people—weak, transient beings, assured of the justice of their ways and their deeds—are capable of doing to people who are in sum exactly like themselves.
>
> Tears filled my eyes, George, when I read for the first time in these forty years how your sister died. How you dug her a pit with your own hands in the yard of her house in the city of Lydda. I reach out with an unclean hand to your hand, which also is not clean. You and I should die a miserable natural death, a death of sinners who have not come to their punishment, a death from old age, disease, a death weak and unheroic, a death meant for human beings who have lived a life of iniquity.[25]

Two other stories from the Palestinian uprising make this connection of Palestinian and Jewish history in relation to the Holocaust. The first dates from January 1988, one month after the Palestinian uprising had begun, when an Israeli captain was summoned to his superior. The captain was given instructions to carry out arrests in the village of Hawara, outside Nablus. The arrest of innocent young Palestinians is hardly out of the ordinary, but the further instructions provided to the officer—what to do to those Palestinians after their arrest—was disturbing. His conscience would not allow him to carry out these instructions unless he was directly ordered to do so. Having then received the direct order, the captain, with a company of forty soldiers, boarded a civilian bus, arriving at Hawara at eleven o'clock in the evening.

The local *muhktar* was given a list of twelve persons to round up, which he did, and the twelve sat on the sidewalk in the center of the village, offering no resistance. Yossi Sarid describes what followed.

> The soldiers shackled the villagers, and with their hands bound behind their backs they were led to the bus. The bus started to move and after 200–300 meters it stopped beside an orchard. The "locals" were taken off the bus and led into the orchard in groups of three, one after another. Every group was accompanied by an officer. In the darkness of the orchard the soldiers also shackled the Hawara residents' legs and laid them on the ground. The officers urged the soldiers to "get it over with

quickly, so that we can leave and forget about it." Then, flannel was stuffed into the Arabs' mouths to prevent them from screaming and the bus driver revved up the motor so that the noise would drown out the cries. Then the soldiers obediently carried out the orders they had been given: to break their arms and legs by clubbing the Arabs; to avoid clubbing them on their heads; to remove their bonds after breaking their arms and legs, and to leave them at the site; to leave one local with broken arms but without broken legs so he could make it back to the village on his own and get help.[26]

The mission was carried out; the beatings were so fierce that most of the wooden clubs used were broken. Thus was born the title of the article detailing this action, "The Night of the Broken Clubs."

The second story occurred just months after the beatings had begun, when Marcus Levin, a physician, was called up for reserve duty in the Ansar 2 prison camp. When he arrived, Levin met two of his colleagues and asked for information about his duties. The answer: "Mainly you examine prisoners before and after an investigation." Levin responded in amazement, "After the investigation?" which prompted the reply, "Nothing special, sometimes there are fractures. For instance, yesterday they brought a twelve-year-old boy with two broken legs." Dr. Levin then demanded a meeting with the compound commander and told him, "My name is Marcus Levin and not Josef Mengele, and for reasons of conscience I refuse to serve in this place." A doctor who was present at the meeting tried to calm Levin with the following comment: "Marcus, first you feel like Mengele, but after a few days you get used to it." Hence the title of an article written about the incident, "You Will Get Used to Being a Mengele."[27]

The references in these articles to the night of broken glass, "Kristallnacht," and to the Nazi physician Mengele as a way of seeing contemporary Jewish Israeli policy and activity is startling. The resistance on the part of the Jewish community to what one might call the Nazi analogy is understandable and so strong as to virtually silence all such references. Yet during the brutal attempt to suppress the Palestinian uprising, in fact from the very beginning of the Jewish struggle for statehood in Palestine in the 1940s and continuing to the present, the connection between the Jewish experience of suffering in Europe and the Palestinian experience of suffering at the hands of the Jewish people in Palestine and Israel has been, and continues to be, repeatedly made by Jewish Israelis.

What are we to make of these references? First, it is important to see that they are not primarily comparisons between Nazi and Israeli behavior, though some of the behavior may in fact be comparable. Second, these references are not attempts to further political objectives, such as promoting one political party over another or challenging the legitimacy of the state of Israel, though clearly they subvert partisan and bipartisan policies of Israel that lead to these incidents. Rather, the force of the Nazi reference involves and moves beyond comparison and politics and represents an intuitive link between the historic suffering of the Jews and the present suffering of Palestinians. It further represents an implicit recognition that what was done to the Jews is now being done by the Jews to another people. At the same time, the connection of Jewish and Palestinian suffering is prepolitical and preideological; that is, it operates in a terrain filled with images of Jewish suffering that remains untouched by the "realities" of the situation, the need to be "strong," or even the communal penalties for speaking the truth. We might say that the Nazi reference represents a cry of pain *and* a plea to end a madness that was visited upon Jews for millennia and now is visited by Jews upon another people. Thus the vehemence with which such analogies are met when spoken, almost as if a blunt instrument is needed to repress the memories and the aspirations of the Jewish people to be neither victim nor oppressor.

Could it be said that it is impossible today to understand the Jewish liturgy of destruction, the burning of the Temple, the death of the martyr, and the pogrom, the events of exile and Holocaust, unless Jews include as intimate partners those people Jews have expelled, tortured, and murdered as well, those who for most Jews exist without names and histories, the Palestinian people? Could it be said that here in an inclusive liturgy of destruction lies the possibility and the hope of moving beyond the peripheral and the superficial into an engaged struggle—on behalf of the history of the Jewish and the Palestinian people? Might Jews be liberated from policies and attitudes that when understood intuitively are a betrayal of Jewish history, but have been seen as weakness, lack of political maturity, or even self-hate? Could Jews be released from theologies, Holocaust and fundamentalist, that now serve as ideologies that close off critical thought and serve the powerful? To pursue connectedness means a serious reevaluation of parts of Jewish history, but can this painful task be accomplished without the voices and the faces of those whom Jews have initiated into the liturgy of destruction? Can Jews see themselves and their history in a new light without hearing and taking seriously the history and the struggle of the Palestinian people?

Yet even in recent Jewish theological writing there is a noticeable absence of Palestinians, and when they are mentioned it is almost exclusively within a Jewish critique rather than as independent theological voices. In Emil Fackenheim's most recent book, *What Is Judaism? An Interpretation for the Present Age*, his first book after moving to Israel, he does not mention Palestinians even one time. In a massive compilation of essays on critical concepts, movements, and beliefs edited by the late Arthur Cohen and Paul Mendes-Flohr, and titled *Contemporary Jewish Religious Thought*, in 1,076 pages Palestinians are mentioned less than five times. And when Wiesel and Greenberg do mention Palestinians, as they do infrequently, Palestinians exist primarily within the Jewish framework of interpretation. As Greenberg writes, in a tone typical of Jewish writing even when partially sympathetic to Palestinian aspirations, "Ideally, the Palestinians should earn their way—all the way to statehood—by peaceful behavior and policies." Or more to the point: "The Palestinians will have to earn their power by living peacefully and convincing Israel of their beneficence or by acquiescing to a situation in which Israel's strength guarantees that the Arabs cannot use their power to endanger Israel." By banishing Palestinians from the internal landscape of Jewish history, Israel remains essentially innocent. But from a Palestinian perspective who is in need of protection, Israelis or Palestinians? And who, with the experience of the last century on balance, needs assurance?[28]

Wiesel's most extensive discussion of Palestinian issues, in the form of a letter "To a Young Palestinian Arab," also bears scrutiny in this regard. Wiesel begins his letter with an outstretched hand, promising sincerity, which is the only path for those who have suffered. Facing that pain, Wiesel plans to "judge myself as well, since someone else's suffering always puts us to the test." In order to engage in a dialogue, Wiesel counsels the putting aside of politics as a confusing and superficial labyrinth. To be sure, the arguments on both sides are valid; the Palestinians can invoke Palestine's Moslem past as Wiesel can speak of the Jewish past that preceded it. The injustices endured by Arab refugees in 1948 can also be countered by the Jewish suffering in the Holocaust. But the injustice endured by the Arabs is for Wiesel the responsibility of the Arabs themselves: "Your own leaders, with their incendiary speeches, their virulent fanaticism. If only they had accepted the United Nations' resolutions on the partition of Palestine, if only they had not incited the Arab population to mass flight in order to return 'forthwith' as victors; if only they had not attempted to drown the young Jewish nation in blood; if only they had taken into account Jewish suffering also, the Jewish right to also claim its sovereignty on its ancestral land. . . . For thirty years Israel's peace initiatives were ignored; Israel's appeals for mutual recognition were denied; Israel's conciliatory moves were rejected."[29]

As for the Jews who emerged "from the darkest recess of history, from the most hidden marshes of man's and God's imagination," they chose to "opt for man" rather than vengeance. For Wiesel, those who went to Palestine did so to relive an ancient dream together with the Palestinian people, not to displace them. What then divided Wiesel and his Palestinian brother? The use of suffering against others: "Ask your elders and mine; they will tell you that in the immediate postwar years in Europe—in Germany, Hungary, Poland and elsewhere—there were countless collaborators who had every reason to be afraid. But they were not harmed—not by us. And those neighbors of ours who had been present at our agony and had pillaged our homes, sometimes before our eyes, went on living and drinking and sleeping as though nothing had happened. We could have lashed out against them—we did not. We consistently evoked our trials only to remind man of his need to be human—not of his right to punish. On behalf of the dead, we sought consolation, not retribution." The Palestinian Arabs, he implied, had done the opposite. Though Wiesel felt responsible for what happened to Palestinians, he cannot abide by what Palestinians had done with their anger:

> I feel responsible for your sorrow, but not for the way you use it, for in its name you have massacred innocent people, slaughtered children. From Munich to Maalot, from Lod to Entebbe, from highjacking to highjacking, from ambush to ambush, you have spread terror among unarmed civilians and thrown into mourning families already too often visited by death. You will tell me that all these acts have been the work of your extremist comrades, not yours; but they acted on your behalf, with your approval, since you did not raise your voice to reason with them. You will tell me that it is your tragedy which incited them to murder. By murdering, they debased that tragedy, they betrayed it. Suffering is often unjust, but it never justifies murder.[30]

Here is a simple and crucial error in logic that is almost systematic in Jewish analysis when Palestinians, even as supposedly addressed in a letter, are essentially absent. For the Palestinians, the crucial connection in this story is not how Jews reacted in Europe to their former conquerors, but how they acted as they themselves became conquerors in Palestine and Israel. Wiesel's desire to move beyond the confusion of politics is easily stated when the configuration supports Jewish empowerment. But a Palestinian might respond that a face-to-face discussion can only take place in an authentic way if the political situation is changed. Without politics the Palestinian is consigned to Jewish turf. But implicit is Wiesel's condemnation as vengeful the political and some-

times bitter struggle of a displaced people. The Palestinians might reverse Wiesel's framework and speak about a highly organized terrorism
against the Palestinian people.

But how can Jews know how Palestinians might respond? And how
can Jews in Wiesel's sense judge themselves as well—because someone
else's suffering always puts us to the test—if Palestinians are absent from
our history and theology? Or if they are simply interpreted within the
Jewish framework? Who then is to challenge the Jewish framework of
renewal if not one who has suffered under its heel? Credit can at least be
given to Wiesel and to Greenberg for mentioning Palestinians and engag-
ing issues that might one day lead beyond monologue to a genuine
dialogue. How is it possible at this late date for two prominent theologians, David Hartman, a Jewish Israeli, and Michael Wyschogrod, an
American Jew, to publish full-length monographs on the present and
future of Jewish belief and activity without mentioning Palestinians, as if
they did not exist? And would one think it possible that despite Wiesel's
earlier letter to the Palestinians and his dialogue on the uprising (already
discussed), and despite Greenberg's attempts to engage Palestinians in
his work "The Ethics of Jewish Power" their most recent works, published after the uprising had begun and attempting to define a Jewish
liturgy of destruction (Wiesel's *The Six Days of Destruction: Meditations
Toward Hope* and Greenberg's *The Jewish Way: Living the Holidays*), appar-
ently do not even allude to Palestinians? It is fascinating that both books
encourage Christian involvement in commemorating the Holocaust,
even Christian liturgies centered on the Holocaust. They recognize that
those who were the oppressors must incorporate their victims into their
sacred liturgy, but that recognition carries no inkling that Jews face a
similar task with regard to Palestinians.[31]

Still, the problem is not just an absolute absence of Palestinians—for
as we have seen, on the intuitive level Palestinians are ever present—but
rather their banishment from the ideological and theological articulation
of Jewish expression; that is, Zionist ideology and Holocaust theology
represses, even at this late date, the deepest intuitions of the Jewish
people.

On the fringes of the Jewish community some progressive Jews in the
United States are attempting to place the Palestinians in the Jewish
liturgical celebration of Passover, and are thus helping to create a more
inclusive liturgy of destruction. The first attempt in 1984 led to the
development of a Passover Seder that tries to integrate Jewish and
Palestinian voices of suffering, violation, and hope. The Seder focuses on
commonalities between both peoples—the common love for the land,

the common experience of exile, the common oppression—and is dedicated to the dream that both peoples can share the land they love in peace. In alternating rhythms of Jewish and Palestinian speech, the story recalls the mutual destruction of Jew and Palestinian.

HEBRON: 24 August 1929—Police stood by while rioting Arabs killed twenty-three Jews in the upper rooms of the town inn. In all, sixty Jews including children were killed. Again, in 1983, Hebron was the scene of violence, this time Jewish and Arab lives were lost.

DEIR YASSIN: 9 April 1948—The Irgun, the more militant faction of the Jewish resistance, killed over two hundred people in this Arab village and then paraded the survivors in a degrading manner through the streets of Jerusalem.

GUSH ETZION: 12 May 1948—For months Gush Etzion was cut off from Jerusalem. Arab Legion forces surrounded the area and launched an attack. The bloc surrendered. After the surrender many were massacred by Arab villagers from the Hebron area.

KFAR KASSEM: 29 October 1956—This Israeli Arab village near the Jordanian border was placed under curfew; there was no time for anyone to inform workers returning from the fields. Forty-three were lined up and killed.

BEIT NUBA: After the 1967 war—one of a number of towns leveled by bulldozers after the Six-Day War. Its residents were forced to flee.

MAALOT: 15 May 1974—Palestinian guerrillas of the PDFLP seized a school with ninety teenagers inside. Before the Israel Defense Forces stormed the school, the guerrillas machine-gunned the children, killing twenty.

TEL AVIV ROAD: 11 March 1978—Palestinian guerrillas seized two buses filled with passengers on the Tel Aviv–Haifa road. Twenty-five people were killed, including the photographer Gail Gubin.

NAHARIYA: 22 April 1979—Palestinians killed three people on the beach at Nahariya.

NABLUS: 2 June 1980—Bombs were set in the cars of three West Bank mayors. Two suffered serious injuries, as did a policeman defusing one of the bombs.

SABRA AND SHATILA: September 1982—Lebanese right-wing militias massacred Palestinian civilians in two refugee camps in Beirut while the area was under Israeli control: over three hundred bodies were found, hundreds more are still missing.[32]

Palestinian Voices as a Challenge to Jewish History

Still, there is no substitute for concrete Palestinian voices. As it is for any dispossessed people, a reconstruction of history is crucial to self-identity and continuity, and in the last years both scholarly and more popular histories of the Palestinian people have been written. But this history is as crucial to Jews as it is to Palestinians; by understanding Palestinian history one gains a new view of contemporary Jewish history. Or, put another way, the history Jews created and repressed returns as an invitation to change direction.

In 1984 Walid Khalidi published a photographic history of the Palestinians, covering the years 1876–1958, that carried the provocative title *Before Their Diaspora,* one that clearly linked the destruction of Palestine with the history of Jewish dispersion and return. The years covered in this book are sad ones for the Palestinians, for during those almost seven decades the Palestinians were at the receiving end of Zionism, which denied their birthright in their ancestral home, Palestine. Khalidi recalls 1948 as the year of the "Catastrophe," which witnessed the climax of Zionist colonization in the establishment of Israel in the greater part of Palestine, and the displacement of the Palestinian inhabitants from hundreds of towns and villages, whose ruined sites became part of the new Jewish state. In the process, at least ten thousand Palestinians were killed and three times that number wounded; 60 percent of the Palestinian population at the time, some seven hundred thousand persons, were rendered homeless. To Khalidi's mind, the Palestinians may not have been annihilated in 1948, but they were dispossessed of their country.[33]

The decade between 1958 and 1967 was little better. According to Khalidi, Israel refused any gesture of redress, refusing reparations and expropriating Palestinian property. It annexed demilitarized zones in the West Bank, diverted water from the Jordan, and developed a pattern of retaliatory raids on Arab villages grossly disproportionate to the violations used as justification. From a Palestinian perspective, the 1967 war continued with a new ferocity an old policy of displacing Palestinians from their land. Between June and September 1967, Israel expelled across the Jordan River some two hundred fifty thousand inmates of the refugee camps located on the West Bank and the Gaza Strip. Then Israel proceeded to apply to the newly occupied territories the very policy of systematic colonization, pursued by the Zionists in Palestine from the 1880s until 1948, that had created the Palestinian problem in the first place. Thus, again from a Palestinian perspective, the rise of the P.L.O., which answered the historic delegitimization of Palestinians by Zionism with counterdelegitimization, and Israeli terror with Palestinian terror. "The more active the P.L.O. the more steadfast the Palestinians were under occupation, and the more steadfast the Palestinians under occupation the more resolved the Israelis were to extirpate the roots of autonomous Palestinian decision-making, i.e., the civilian and military institutions of the P.L.O. Hence the Israeli devastation of the Jordan Valley (across which the P.L.O. operated from Jordan) in the period from 1968 to 1970. Hence also the Israeli devastation of southern Lebanon and the suburbs of Beirut (the P.L.O's base of operations after 1971), culminating in the siege and bombardment of the Lebanese capital and the massacre at Sabra and Shatila in 1982."[34]

Elia Zureik, a Palestinian sociologist now professor of sociology at Queens University in Ontario, Canada, has drawn up a table outlining a Palestinian understanding of the history of the interaction of Zionism with the Palestine people.

STAGES	PERIOD	SALIENT FEATURES
Dual society (Zionist colonization)	pre-1948	Asymmetrical power relationships mediated by the British presence, exclusivist Zionist institutions; stunting of Arab economic development; Zionist hegemony and eventual Palestinian dispersion
Internal colonialism (pre-1967 Israel)	1948–1967	Marginalization of Palestinian peasants; land confiscation; political manipulation; economic stagnation; residential and occupational segregation; duality of economic and social relations
Dependency of West Bank and Gaza on Jordan and Egypt	1948–1967	Economic and political dependency on Jordan and Egypt, co-optation and political suppression

(*Continued*)

STAGES	PERIOD	SALIENT FEATURES
Accelerated forms of internal colonialism in Israel; colonial dependency of West Bank and Gaza on Israel	1967–present	Further proletarianization of Palestinians in Israel; economic penetration of West Bank and Gaza accompanied by land confiscation and encouragement of Palestinian emigration; political suppression and denial of Palestinian rights
Total control by Israel	Future trend	Depopulation of Palestinians through expulsion and emigration ultimate goal is Zionization of historical Palestine, and, if possible, resettlement of Palestinians in Arab countries[35]

In a series of fascinating books, Edward Said, a Palestinian by birth, now Parr Professor of English and Comparative Literature of Columbia University, attempts to articulate the meaning of Khalidi's and Zureik's analyses of Palestinian history. His books, *The Question of Palestine* and *After the Last Sky*, attempt to offer insights into the position of a suffering community, especially one that has little hearing in the West. For Said to speak of the Palestinians in a rational way is hardly easy, blocked as he is by Israeli and American propaganda. The challenge is to stop speaking about war or genocide—to stop blaming the victims—and to deal with political reality:

> There *is* a Palestinian people, there *is* an Israeli occupation of Palestinian lands, there *are* Palestinians under Israeli military occupation, there *are* Palestinians—650,000 of them—who are Israeli citizens and who consti-tute 15 percent of the population of Israel, there is a large Palestinian population in exile; these are actualities which the United States and most of the world have directly or indirectly acknowledged, which Israel too has acknowledged, if only in the forms of denial, rejection, threats of war, and punishment. The history of the past forty years has shown that Palestinians have grown politically, not shrunk, under the influence of every kind of repression and hardship; the history of the Jews has shown too that time only increases attachment to the historically saturated land of Palestine. Short of complete obliteration, the Palestinians will continue to exist and they will continue to have their own ideas about who repre-sents them, where they want to settle, what they want to do with their national and political future.[36]

To deal with political reality, however, is to discuss Zionism in a historical and concrete way; from the standpoint of its victims, for example, it is a practical system of accumulation and displacement. It is also to see the frustration of the victims as their story is distorted—or more often disappears. Said is startled, for example, when Menachem Begin, former head of the Irgun terror organization, is honored with an honorary doctorate of law at Northwestern University in May 1978, a man "whose army a scant month before had created 300,000 new refugees in South Lebanon," and who consistently referred to "Judea and Samaria" as parts of the Jewish state, thus defying international law. Or he is surprised during the same period at the showing of the mini-series *Holocaust*, at least part of which was "intended as a justification of Zionism," while thousands of civilian casualties were being created by Israeli troops in an operation that a *Washington Post* report compared to the U.S. devastation of Vietnam. For the victims, these represent incredibly contradictory images, yet the contradiction is hardly recognized where Palestinians do not exist. And, of course, these contradictions leave Palestinians wondering whether they do in fact exist: "Do we exist? What proof do we have? The further we get from the Palestine of our past, the more precarious our status, the more disrupted our being, the more intermittent our presence. When did we become 'a people'? When did we stop being one? Or are we in the process of becoming one? What do these big questions have to do with our intimate relationships with each other and with others?"[37]

The Occupation Is Over

The Palestinian uprising beginning in December 1987 and the subsequent declaration of a Palestinian state in November 1988 has said clearly to the Palestinian people, to the Jewish people, and to the world that they do in fact exist as a nation. In fact, the importance of the uprising is such that a division of Palestinian literature may be made according to when it was written—pre- or post-uprising.

Many, both inside and outside Israel, see the uprising as limited to demonstrations and throwing stones. However, within the Palestinian community the most obvious confrontations with Israeli soldiers are an important, though limited, aspect of what Palestinians call the *intifada*. *Intifada*, an Arabic word, means the sudden rising of a person to shake off something that has stuck, in this case shaking off the occupation and all that it has meant politically but also culturally and psychologically. It represents reclaiming self-respect and dignity as individuals and as a community. To assert these newfound strengths Palestinians have concentrated on breaking with the occupation and rebuilding their own societal infrastructure. Thus Palestinians are boycotting Israeli-made products to which there are Palestinian alternatives, like soft drinks, food products, drugs, and clothing. Many mayors, policeofficers, and civil administration workers appointed by Israel have resigned. Palestinian labor in Israel and Palestinian shopkeepers have participated in massive general strikes as well as establishing a schedule of work and opening according to Palestinian directives. Specific committees have been established to provide food and medical supplies for refugee camps under curfew, as well as to assume responsibility for alternative education, health needs, and agriculture. A Unified National Leadership of the uprising has arisen, responsible for making major decisions on a national basis and for writing and distributing leaflets that direct protest activities.

For many, the success of the uprising is due in large measure to the unity achieved through the creative and pragmatic responses of the *intifada* leadership, as well as its emphasis on democratic decision making. At the same time the leadership has made it very clear that the resistance to the forces of occupation is intended to build a Palestinian state next to Israel, not to oppose or undermine the existence of Israel. As Hanan Mikhail-Ashrawi, a Palestinian professor at Bir Zeit University on the West Bank, articulates it:

> As Palestinians under occupation, it is not only our right but our duty to resist occupation and oppression. No self-respecting nation in the world today can wrest respect or recognition from the world community if it does not actively seek to assert its own national integrity and freedom. It must be understood, furthermore, that all allusions to improving the "quality of life" of Palestinians under occupation are inherently unrealistic and in direct contradiction with the aspirations of the Palestinians and the objectives of the intifada. There can be no "quality" of life under occupation beyond the quality of resistance to occupation and rejection of all its manifestations including the unnatural reality of its premises of subjugation and its system of exploitation and inequity. The "quality" argument must be viewed in its correct light as another attempt at "sugar coating" the occupation for both public consumption (hence the contradictory terms "benign occupation") and for local consumption as a means of making an abhorrent situation of oppression palatable to the oppressed. Both rationalizations suffer from political as well as moral blindness and must be exposed as subversive when it comes to dealing with the essence of the problem which is the occupation itself.[38]

Mikhail-Ashrawi articulates some of the strategies and demands of the *intifada*.

Refusal to deal with or give legitimacy to any Israeli-appointed civil authority (police, revenue service, department of motor vehicles, etc.), specifically municipal councils and mayors, which have usurped the rights and responsibilities of an elected national authority.

The rejection of all attempts at creating an "alternative" Palestinian leadership from the Occupied Territories and exposing them as attempts at undermining the unity and legitimate P.L.O. leadership of the Palestinian people everywhere.

The qualitative transformation of the intifada into a full-fledged situation of civil disobedience (more accurately, civil insurrection/rebellion).

The dismantling of Israeli detention camps and centers and the release of all Palestinian prisoners; in addition to the cancellation of the Israeli program of intimidation and terror including the deployment of troops against civilians in populated areas.

The cessation of all Israeli measures aiming at creating new geopolitical and demographic facts in the Occupied Territories such as the confiscation of land, the erection of settlements, the appropriation of resources, the deportation of Palestinians, and the demolition of houses.

Following the unmasking of the occupation, the demand for its immediate end, Israel having been proven totally unfit to remain in charge of a civilian population whose human rights it has constantly violated in direct defiance of the Fourth Geneva Convention.

Instituting free elections under the auspices of a neutral international body whereby the Palestinians in the West Bank and Gaza may elect their own local civil authority.[39]

Though for some Jews the declaration of a Palestinian state was a welcome event, for others it was a dangerous affront. But for the Palestinians it was a bittersweet moment, accepting the two-state solution as less intolerable than the status quo, but giving up the dream of a democratic secular state that would encompass all of Palestine and all the peoples, Jewish and Palestinian, in that state. Muhammad Hallaj, former director of the Council for Higher Education in the West Bank and Gaza and now editor of *Palestine Perspectives*, sees the deficiencies in four areas: because of the partition between Palestinians and Israelis, a part of the country becomes alien to each of the peoples who have the greatest attachment to it; a Palestinian state restricted to one-fifth of the country is unable to accommodate hundreds of thousands of refugees who need a homeland the most; the two-state solution denies the possiblity of Arab-Jewish coexistence and institutionalizes the denial of social pluralism; it continues and institutionalizes the nationalist nature of the conflict, which threatens the future harmony of the two peoples. By contrast, the democratic nonsectarian state that became the official Palestinian policy in the 1960s and signified for the first time the acceptance by Palestinians of a binational state in which Palestinian Arabs and Israeli Jews would share sovereignty and citizenship, with equal rights and obligations, in a common homeland, had advantages that the two-state solution does not. In a vision that from the Jewish perspective in some way harkens back to Judah Magnes, Martin Buber, and Hannah Arendt, Hallaj retains the dream that the two-state solution may be only an interim measure answering the immediate needs of personal security and national pride. For Hallaj, if the Palestinians and Israelis are to move beyond fear and injustice—and not only contain them—they must see beyond the immediate horizon of their nationalist imperatives: "The democratic nonsectarian republic—though proposed by the Palestinians—is a universalist vision of intercommunal relations. But its virtues go beyond its principles. It promises a more spacious home and a richer life for the two peoples who cherish Palestine most. If the two ministates of partition reassure the Palestinians and Israelis, the democratic nonsectarian state liberates them."[40]

While the dream of Palestine remains alive and the practical reality of the need for two states is affirmed, the cost of the intifada continues to escalate. At the end of the first year of the uprising Al Haq (Law in Service of Man), a Palestinian human rights documentary center, published a report appropriately titled *Punishing a Nation: Human Rights Violations During the Palestinian Uprising*. Contained in that report of the first year of the uprising are statistics, including deaths of at least 204 Palestinians in the West Bank alone, and injury of well over thirty thousand people. Included also is a detailed analysis of Israel's concerted response, including the formation of death squads, obstruction of medical treatment, the expanded use of administrative detention and of curfews that prohibit movement of the population for days, even weeks, at a time, the repression of education at all levels, and the supression of any organized activity. But most haunting are the stories themselves recalled by Palestinians. The first is an account of an English teacher, Taha Mousa Nasser, thirty-eight, who was arrested in May 1988 near Hebron. The second, an account of a young woman whose name is withheld, comes from a West Bank refugee camp then under curfew.

> The first session was with Gabi. He was the person who accused me
> of escaping from the Intelligence officer. He cursed me, calling me a bas-
> tard . . . , threatening that he would break my nose. He was humiliating
> me. The session lasted about one quarter of an hour, without beating.
> Then he led me to the cupboard where I was handcuffed with a hood

covering my head. I tried to stand but I couldn't and I couldn't stretch my legs in a normal way. I sat squatting and stayed like that for about five hours until I was led by someone to the interrogation room. The guard had taken the hood off my head but the handcuffs were left on. There I saw Gabi, the interrogator who interviewed me the first time. He said: "We know that you are a member of a teachers' committee, but what we want to know is which political faction you serve and who directs you." I told him that I was a member of the West Bank Teachers' Committee and a member of the Workers' Union in the West Bank and the Gaza Strip, that I wasn't affiliated to any political faction, and that my work was confined to defending the teachers' union rights.

He then started using his hands to beat and box my chest and face and then kicked my genitals, causing me great pain. Immediately after that he ordered the guard to escort me to cell number 11. On 16 June 1988 I was transferred to Atlit Detention Camp. We were transferred in an Egged bus which took about 36 detainees, each pair cuffed together. When we arrived at Atlit and after descending from the bus a soldier led a group of three detainees, of whom I was one, to Section C.

On the morning of 14 July 1988, about 150 detainees, of whom I was one, were transferred to the Beitunia [Ofer] Detention Camp. In the bus our hands were bound in front of us with plastic straps. The soldiers forced us to bend over while seated in the bus until our heads touched our knees. About 100 meters outside of Atlit prison, five soldiers got into the bus and started beating us on our heads and backs with the butts of their rifles. One of the soldiers also beat me on the shoulder with the butt of his rifle and kicked my knees and feet with his heavy boots. I suffered great pain in my shoulders. When we arrived at Beitunia prison near Ramallah, my left shoulder was bleeding. The pain got worse, especially in the top parts of my spine. After my release I was X-rayed at the Maqassed Hospital and it appeared that my spine was badly damaged; I am being treated now.[41]

The following account of a young woman represents an aspect of Palestinian suffering often unreported.

I, the undersigned, am 19 years old. On Monday, November 11, 1988 at 1:30, during a curfew imposed by the Israeli army, while I was sitting with my mother, suddenly—from among the soldiers around the entrance to the house—12 young soldiers entered. When they entered, they began breaking glass objects and dishes with their clubs. When they finished breaking things they saw me and dragged me by my hair to another room and started talking among themselves in Arabic. I understood that they wanted to close the door and that they had sexual intentions. One of them, who was tall, held my right shoulder. I ran towards the back door of the house on the first floor, where we were before. The soldier ran after me fast. Beside the door another soldier was waiting, who pushed me (back) into the house. There were three other soldiers (there) and they dragged me to the room where my mother was yelling, and they were hitting her. They pushed my mother forcefully out of the house and onto the ground.

I was standing because (sic) [and] one of the soldiers, the tall one who had a wheat-colored face, pushed me into a chair and began slapping me and hitting me with his club and with his hands. Beside me were two soldiers and one more beside the door. I got up from the chair and turned towards the door because the soldier who was hitting me said in Arabic, "Good (girl), come and sit beside me or I will shoot you with lead bullets." The three of them pushed me into the chair and started attacking me, hitting me again. I started to scream and they stopped for a while. At this time I heard my mother's yells from outside. At the same time the soldier tried to open my blouse. He was pulling forcefully on my blouse, but I held on to his hand and pushed him (away). I kept trying all the time to get out of the chair and they would threaten to shoot me. While that was going on my mother came into the room and defended me. Then they left the house.[42]

A Palestinian Theology of Liberation

Just as the history of Jewish suffering prompted extended theological reflection in the Jewish community on the themes of survival and the Christian theologies that oppressed Jews, the Palestinian struggle with Israel has also prompted theological reflection by Arab and Palestinian Christians on their own situation and that of their oppressors. Though this theology is specifically for the Christian community affected by the power of Israel, it is also addressed to the Jewish community in Israel and around the world as a critical assessment of those aspects of Jewish theology and activity that oppress the Palestinian people. At the same time, Arab and Palestinian Christians are also addressing their Western Christian brothers and sisters who they find culpable in the oppression of both Jew and Palestinian. Here we find a theology of the oppressed that both implicates the oppressor and envisions a path beyond oppression.

Just days after the Six-Day War ended, for example, a working group of Christian theologians, which included Father George Khodr, metropolitan of Mount Lebanon and professor of Arab civilization at the Lebanese University, the Reverend Samir Kafity, Martine Albert Lahham, and Father Jean Corban, issued a memorandum whose title posed a question, "What Is Required of the Christian Faith Concerning the

Palestine Problem?" To the Christian faithful they hoped to shed light on three matters: the facts of the present situation and what led to them, revelation of the Bible concerning the ideals of Judaism and Zionism, and ideas on a just solution to the Palestinian problem.[43]

For the Christian theologians gathered together, the present state of crisis between Israel and Palestine began with the destruction of the Temple and the consequent expulsion of the bulk of the Jewish community in Palestine. Over the centuries the desire to return to Jerusalem was incorporated into Jewish prayer and ritual. This longing is, to their mind, worthy of respect in the "name of freedom of the spirit." However, the transformation of a religious aspiration into a political claim made the return itself ambiguous. Clearly, the impetus for Zionism was a history of violent anti-Semitism in the Christian kingdoms of Europe, something virtually unknown in the Arabic world since the seventh century, and repentance for Christian "unfaithfulness to the gospel" is essential. The problem is the transference of the sin from West to East; Western Christians are enjoined to search for a solution to anti-Semitism rather than allowing the entire weight to "hang on the innocent population of Palestine."[44]

The early Jewish settlers were accorded the same welcome that other religious refugees were, but the politicization of the settlement with the decline of the Ottoman Empire and the Balfour Declaration of 1917 changed the settlers from a refugee population to a political force. When European anti-Semitism reached its "hysterical climax" in the Nazi persecution, the Jewish communities of eastern and central Europe should have been reintegrated into those societies as others were who had been victims of the Nazis. Because theses states refused to do what was proper and just, they met injustice with injustice: "Because the Christians of Europe and America denied their responsibility for a million Jews who were their brothers, they threw one million Arabs out of their homeland of Palestine. 'What have you done to your brother?' In rejecting one million Jews and in despoiling one million Arabs, the Christians of the West have committed a double crime which cries to heaven for redress." The newly founded state of Israel continued the injustice by refusing to integrate a million refugees whom they had "driven from their homes and lands." This defiance represented for the theologians a racist attitude that Christian conscience could not accept: "As long as the Israelis want to found a state based on this kind of racism, it will continue to be the duty of all Christians to oppose it."[45]

To these theologians, the war just completed had demonstrated once again the violence inherent in a Zionist state that displaced the Palestinian people. In 1967 three hundred thousand new refugees had been created, and a cycle of violence, physical and spiritual, was escalating. Threats of extermination and anti-Semitic demonstrations in some countries and anti-Arab pronouncements in others needed to be condemned "without reserve." Anti-Semitism produced Zionism; Zionism produces new waves of anti-Semitism, which in turn strengthens Zionism. All of this, according to the memorandum, was built on a fundamental confusion, confusion between the well-being of the Jewish people and the interests of the state of Israel. Here these theologians approach what for them is the central political but also theological problem, that is, the confusion between the Jewish people and the state of Israel and between Judaism and Zionism.[46]

From the biblical perspective, there is, according to these theologians, little confusion. The Jews are a people chosen by God, a consecrated people, a nation of priests, whose vocation is to live out in their own history, the history of the whole of humanity. In this way, the Jewish people is prophetic, a witness of God among the nations, chosen to serve the "Salvation of Humanity" rather than to establish itself in any particular national way. Here the comparison is made between the vocation of the Jews and the vocation of the Church; the Church is also called to serve the world rather than enfold itself in a particular race or nation. The creation of an exclusively Jewish state of Israel violated God's plan for the Jews just as the creation of exclusively Christian states, historically and in the present, violates the calling of the Church.[47]

What is the solution for the Palestinian people? First of all, it lies in the Christian uncovering of the true vocation of the Jews, that is, spirit rather than nation building and the integration of Jewish citizens by all nations. The second aspect involves the acceptance of all the inhabitants of Palestine—Christians, Muslims, and Jews–of an ethnic, religious, and social pluralism. This pluralism, which moves beyond the simple tolerance of minorities, is the modern equivalent of universalism. The embrace of their true vocation will move Jews to integrate all Palestinian refugees, to make reparation toward them as certain states have done toward Jews, to accept all the inhabitants of Palestine as citizens with full rights, to promote active participation in the political life of Palestine without any discrimination to use all available resources for the development of all the citizens, and finally to submit to all international decisions regarding Israel and Palestine.[48]

Seven years later, in 1974, Gabriel Habib, one of the founders of the Middle East Council of Churches, refused an invitation to present a paper at the International Symposium on the Holocaust, held at the

Cathedral of Saint John the Divine, and, at the last moment, sent a message instead. The message expresses similar themes but with a greater sense of urgency identifies the Western and Zionist character of the discussion, especially as reflected by the Christians and Jews invited to the conference. According to Habib, the symposium was limited to Jewish and Christian views as they had developed in Europe and North America since World War II and left out Eastern Christians and Muslims as well as Jews of Middle-Eastern background. Though sensitive to Jewish suffering in the West, the symposium posed the problem—Jewish suffering and empowerment—in a way foreign to the East. For Habib, this formulation's lack of balance is a cause of division both among Christians in the West and East and among Jews, whose life in the West and East has differed considerably: "Spiritual Zionism has been emptied by a temporal Zionism, and the traditional Judaism of the East has been subjugated to the technological Jewish ethos of Europe and America. In the conflict within Judaism, we strongly ally ourselves with those Jews who promote a sense of belonging to a common Judeo-Arab community, free from all discrimination. We are thus in accord with the line of Jewish thinkers and militants reaching from Ahad Ha'am to Judah Magnes, Henrietta Szold, and the Ihud movement, without forgetting Simone Weil (*La Pesanteur et la Grace*, chapter on Israel)." In a particularly insightful conclusion, Habib sees the need to develop a critical conscience at the center of Judaism to correct the direction in which Western European and American Jews have led the whole of Judaism—away from solidarity with the oppressed. One way Habib saw to create this critical conscience in Western Christians as well is to open a new dialogue with the East, especially with Muslims. This would help Westerners break out of their "fallacious, anachronistic, and provincial situation and put an end to the fatal epoch of Auschwitz, opening the way, in Palestine, to a new era. Jerusalem will be the symbol of this new era, for all those who claim it as their mother—not through blood, but through faith and hope in a just and human world."[49]

Now, some fifteen years later, the most recent theological development among Palestinian Christians is the call for a Palestinian theology of liberation in Naim Stifan Ateek's book *Justice and Only Justice*, published a year and a half after the uprising began. Here again are theological reflections formulated on the other side of the crucible of Jewish power yet providing Jews insight into the consequences of the power they wield. Ateek, like the Christian theologians and Habib, seeks in his own way a path for Palestinians and Jews beyond opposition and destruction.

Ateek is an Episcopal priest and cannon of Saint George's Cathedral in Jerusalem; he starts his book with an all-too-familiar story. He was born in Beisan, Palestine, twenty miles south of the Sea of Galilee. Ateek's father was born in Nablus and in the 1920s left for Beisan to establish himself as a silver and gold smith. Brought up in an Eastern Orthodox church and later active in the Anglican church, Ateek's father was a pious believer and a successful businessman. When the Jewish soldiers occupied Beisan, Ateek was eleven years old, and both Muslims and Christians fled their homes in fear that what had been done in Deir Yassin might be done to them. Friends pleaded with Ateek's father to go and to take his ten children with him, lest they be murdered. Those who stayed were ordered to leave upon threat of death: the Muslims were sent across the Jordan River; the Christians were taken on buses to Nazareth, as yet unoccupied, where they were unloaded and left. When several months later Jewish soldiers occupied Nazareth, Ateek's father hoped to be able to return to Beisan. As the exile became permanent, there was really no choice for him: at the age of 57 Ateek's father had to begin again. The story of the family's expulsion recalls again the liturgy of destruction:

> My father asked us to carry with us whatever was lightweight yet valuable or important. The military orders were that we should all meet at the center of town in front of the courthouse, not far from my father's shop. My oldest brother and sisters had each carried a few items to the center of town, hoping to leave them there and return to the house for more. Yet when they got to the courthouse, they found that the soldiers had fenced in the area so that whoever reached there was not allowed to leave again. I recall that my father and mother were quite upset because my brother and sisters had not returned. I was asked to run and hurry them back. So I ran to the center of town, only to be caught with them; the same thing happened to both my father and mother when they came themselves. I discovered later—I was not told at the time—why my parents were so terribly anxious: they realized that in one of the baskets left in front of our house to be picked up after was some of the gold we were trying to take with us. In another basket was some fresh bread my mother had been baking that morning when my father came home with the bad news. My brother Michael was worried about a small Philips radio—one of his most precious possessions—that he had bought just before his marriage. When the soldiers occupied Beisan, they ordered people to turn over their radios. It was so difficult for my brother to part with his radio that he hid it in the garden.[50]

Ateek's theology begins with the expulsion and continues with what at first glance seems a sense of conflicting realities that similarly inform his theology—a Palestinian who is at the same time an Arab, a Christian, and an Israeli. After tracing the history of the suffering of the Jews in Europe as a prelude to Zionist colonization and occupation of Palestine, Ateek systematizes the history of Palestinian Israelis in four time periods: 1948–55, a people in shock; 1956–67, a community resigned; 1968–88, a nation awakening; 1988–, the *intifada*. The road traveled between 1948 and today can be seen in two passages from Ateek's book; the first is from 1948, the second 1988:

> Israel's Palestinians were stunned when, within a short period, they had become a minority in their own land. The catastrophe was too great to be believed. Intense bitterness and hatred also developed. On the one hand, profound feelings of recrimination against both the Arab countries and the Zionists were constantly, although privately, expressed. On the other hand, divided families were trying to establish contact with their relatives. Thousands of people attempted to cross the armistice lines in order to be reunited with their families or to return to their homes. Moshe Dayan estimated that between 1949 and the middle of 1954 there was an average of one thousand cases of infiltration per month along the various frontiers, this at the risk of being killed, jailed, or in most cases thrown back across the border.

> Within a forty-year period, Palestinian Arabs in Israel have moved from humiliation and shock to despair and resignation and on to raised consciousness and awakening. From isolation and resignation and on to raised consciousness and awakening. From isolation and fragmentation to entity. From a people robbed of its very identity to one that has regained it. If the establishment of the State of Israel was the antithesis of the Holocaust, then the Intifada of 1988 was the beginning of a process antithetical to the 1948 tragedy of Palestine. Even if the uprising is momentarily quelled, it will remain a turning point in the awakened consciousness of the Palestinians, bringing a new understanding of themselves and a new view of Israel. In fact, Palestinians have already started dating events as pre- or post-uprising. Undoubtedly, a new period in their long struggle for justice and peace has begun.[51]

Ateek sees the problems ahead as many. Over the years Palestinian Christians in Israel, a double minority within the Palestinian Muslim ethos and the Jewish state, have struggled to find their identity and voice. In some ways their leadership has been woefully inadequate, though some improvement in recent years justifies a certain optimism in Ateek's view of the potential for action by the churches. However, the beleaguered Christian minority in Israel, and in the West Bank and Gaza as well, has found little support from Western Christians. On the contrary, theological liberals like Paul van Buren and fundamentalist Christians like Jerry Falwell have, to Ateek's mind, ignored and denigrated Palestinian Christians, in effect warning them that to oppose their own displacement is to sin against the resurrection of Israel, which is God's desire.[52]

The Bible too is problematic, especially as it is often used against Palestinians by Jews, in Israel and outside, as well as by Western Christians and their missionaries. The term *Israel* itself becomes ambiguous when it is applied to contemporary life. What does the verse "Blessed be the Lord God of Israel, for he has visited and redeemed his people" mean for Palestinians today? Which Israel is it referring to and whose redemption? Because of the biblical emphasis on Israel and the contemporary reality of Israeli occupation, Ateek sees the state of Israel as a "seismic tremor of enormous magnitude that has shaken the very foundation" of Christian belief. Thus a major task of Palestinian theology of liberation is to liberate the Bible for Palestinian use, a task that begins with biblical understanding of the land and of justice.[53]

Looking at the Bible from these perspectives, Ateek finds Zionism and the state of Israel wanting. From the biblical perspective the land belongs to God and the people who live on the land, according to their ethical stance. Power is to be used to implement justice; the existence of the poor and displaced signifies abuse of power and therefore a break with God. It is with the poor and the oppressed, the Palestinians, that God sides.[54]

For Christians, the way out of the cycle of violence is nonviolent resistance as exemplified by Jesus and embodied in many ways in the Palestinian *intifada*. Ateek sees nonviolence as both prophetic and peacemaking, combining the elements of justice and mercy and asserting the strength of Eastern Christianity, which is pre-Constantinian in its situation as a powerless minority. The center of this resistance should uphold Ateek's major premise of a solution for Israelis and Palestinians, that Palestine is a country for both the Jews and the Palestinians. Though the ideal would be "one united and democratic state for all Palestinians and Jews," Jewish fears of becoming a minority and their fear of annihilation makes this impossible; thus a two-state solution is the only alternative offering justice and the possibility of peace and stability. For Ateek, this position of the Palestinian leadership and the people themselves represents a paradox; the two-state solution wanted by Jewish settlers in the first place and rejected by the Palestinians is now being offered by the Palestinians and rejected by the Israelis.[55]

To build acceptance of this two-state solution new attitudes must be adopted by both communities. To begin, Palestinians must acknowledge the reality and significance of the Holocaust to the Jewish people:

> The Palestinians need to become really conscious of and sensitive to the horror of the Holocaust, Nazi Germany's attempt to exterminate the Jews. Granted, the Holocaust was not a Middle Eastern phenomenon, and the Palestinians had nothing to do with it; nevertheless, we need to understand the extent of the trauma for the Jews. Our need to be educated in this matter is similar to that of the Eastern Jews, the Sephardim, for whom the Holocaust was also not part of their frame of reference. Admittedly, we as Palestinians have refused to accept, much less internalize, the horrible tragedy of the Holocaust. We have resisted even acknowledging it, believing that we have been subjected to our own holocaust at the hands of the Jews. Many Palestinians have doubted that the Holocaust even occurred; they could not believe that those who suffered so much could turn around and inflict so much suffering on the Palestinians. We have also refused to admit or acknowledge its uniqueness, pointing to the attempt to destroy the Assyrian and Armenian Christians in this century.
>
> Be that as it may, a new attitude is expected of us vis-à-vis the Holocaust. We must understand the importance and significance of the Holocaust to the Jews, while insisting that the Jews understand the importance and significance of the tragedy of Palestine for the Palestinians.[56]

For their part, Jews have to admit that they have wronged the Palestinian people:

> The new attitude of the Israeli Jews toward the Palestinians should be simply this: We are sorry that we came to you with arrogance and a feeling of superiority. We came with good and not so good reasons. But we are now here in the land. Forgive us for the wrong and the injustice that we have caused you. We took part of your country. We ignored you. We pretended that you did not exist, or even worse, that you did not matter. We stereotyped you, convincing others that you are all terrorists. We have refused to recognize that you have any rights, while we insisted that you should recognize and legitimate our right to your land. We have insisted, and convinced the United States and others to insist, that you recognize our claim to your land. And amazingly, many governments in the world have agreed with us. We have refused to negotiate with your representatives, rejecting them as terrorists. Here, too, we have extracted a pledge from the United States government that it will not negotiate with your representatives. We have done this and much more. We have

wronged you. Now, we recognize that the healthiest solution to any
conflict is the use of negotiation and compromise, as opposed to power,
repression, and control. We are willing to negotiate with your representatives, the P.L.O. and we choose to live in peace with you. We want to stay
a part of the Middle East. We want to live among you, Muslims and
Christians. Your own country of Palestine today used to be our country
two thousand years ago. We still have many cherished historic memories
that keep pulling us to it. It is our "holy land," too, our "promised land."
There is room for both of us here.[57]

Ateek's analysis brings forward into the present many of the central
themes of Arab and Palestinian Christians, and those of Palestinians with
Muslim backgrounds analyzed earlier, as they have witnessed the slow
but sure process of destruction. The images are difficult for Jews: that of
occupying the land, uprooting a people, creating ghettos, expelling,
raping, torturing, murdering. We see a theological struggle to separate
that which part of the Jewish community insists is inseparable—Judaism
and Zionism—and a call for the reemergence of the prophetic Jewish
tradition, in their eyes essentially nonstatist. The return of the Jews to
Palestine, legitimated by Jewish and Western Christian theology, is unfair and unjust—in short, a disaster for the Palestinian people. Rather
than aberrational, the brutality of the occupation army is in continuity
with Zionist policy from the beginning, a reality Palestinians know intimately in their history and their bodies. From the beginning of the
twentieth century, theirs has been a liturgy of destruction as well, ignored by much of the world. There is also a call for confession of past and
present injustice as if this, rather than the disappearance of Israel, might
allow a path of reconciliation to emerge. To be sure, the state of Israel in
and of itself is a symbol of oppression for Palestinians, but the hope is
that the people of Israel and Palestine, Jew, Christian, and Muslim, will
overcome what the state represents and live together in a unity characterized by mutual respect, diversity, and pluralism.

What does this emerging Christian theology have to say to Jewish
theology? To begin with, it reminds Jews of a time, less than fifty years
ago, when the possibility of theological legitimation of a state was a
debatable proposition in the Jewish community. It also seeks to clarify a
crucial issue that has been lost to that legitimation; that is, the state of
Israel was formed outside the arena of contemporary Jewish suffering, in
Palestine rather than in Europe. Why should the Palestinian people
suffer for the recognized sins of Europe? Furthermore, while recognizing
the tragedy of the European catastrophe for the Jews, Arab and Palestin-

ian Christian theologians separate the settling of Jewish refugees from the establishment of an exclusive Jewish state. Rather than logically expressing an evolving history within the Middle East, the movement of refugees into a state repeats a pattern of Western colonialism in which "inferior" indigenous peoples are displaced. In doing this, the refugees pervert the idealistic rhetoric of saving a remnant people and oppress another people. One might say that Arab and Palestinian Christian theology has much to say to the shifting perspective of a Jewish theology that now for the first time in two thousand years is called to legitimate rather than to confront state theology. If, in Holocaust theology, Jews continue their tradition of confronting the world with the suffering imposed on the Jewish people, the Jewish tradition of dissent, especially after the uprising, forces Jews to confront one another. With Arab and Palestinian Christian theology, for the first time, others confront the world and the Jewish people with the suffering caused by Jewish power. Thus, beyond the specifics, Christian theology emanating from the Middle East is a challenge and a warning: Jews are becoming everything they protested against.

Just as the Holocaust has reached liturgical expression, the Palestinian tragedy has achieved a like expression. David Roskies's version of a Jewish response to destruction—the recalling of the ancient archetypes, the reunification of diverse classes and religious and nonreligious sensibilities in the European ghettos, the movement from a literature of consolation to a literature that prompts action, even uprising—is occurring today among those who live on the other side of Jewish power. In fact, for Palestinians, the Jewish liturgy of destruction has come to legitimate that which it originally resisted: statelessness, deportation, murder. Thus Palestinians insist that the Jewish liturgy of destruction be complemented by a similar Palestinian liturgy.

That liturgy now inclusive of Palestinian and Jew might be exemplified in the statement of Mubarak Awad, a Palestinian Christian advocate of nonviolent resistance, upon his deportation from Israel in June 1988.

> I am a Palestinian in an enemy court.
>
> I am a Christian in a court of Jewish justice.
>
> I am from occupied Jerusalem in an Israeli High Court.
>
> I accepted to come to court knowing all the odds. I gave you legitimacy and recognized you as a State and recognized your High Court of Justice because I am searching for true peace. Only peaceful means can achieve peace. If peace is the sign of victory, victory has to be for both Palestinians

and Israelis. Both must be winners; there can be no losers. This would be the great measure of justice.

Moral and judicial responsibility is not a historical or religious debate. It is the reality that I face today with the rest of the Palestinian people. You have the power, the law and the gun pointing in my face. I am armed with hope, truth and nonviolence pointing toward your conscience. If the uprising will not open your eyes and soul to tell you we need freedom I don't know what will.

I am here to fight my deportation order. Uprooting me from my family, land, friends and culture is a disgrace. As a government Israel is doing all it can to rid Palestinians from their land. It is deliberate, through unjust laws that we can't change, with tricks and unfair practices. You are depriving me of my basic human and religious rights.

As a Palestinian I never hated you. I don't hate you now. And I will never hate you.

But as a Jerusalemite I am telling you—I will be back.[58]

The liturgy of destruction heard from the Palestinian side confirms the initial and ongoing Jewish intuition that Palestinians are as intimate to Jewish history as Jews are to Christian history. The victors in Israel, like the victors in Europe, create a history that is univocal in its outlook and violent in its expression. After the celebration of victory its hollowness becomes evident, the oppression of others more obvious. The search begins for a way back to the community vocation that affirms rather than destroys. The original desire to be neither victim nor oppressor returns, yet paradoxically the critical thought necessary to break through the ideologies and theologies that legitimate power rest with the defeated and marginalized. Thus, the renewal of Christianity in the West rests to a large extent in Jewish hands, that is, with those who lived on the other side of Christian power. It is the Jewish people who provide insight into the betrayal of Christian witness. What is startling for Jews, as indeed it was at first for Christians, is that today Palestinians call the Jewish community to account. For they have lived on the other side of Jewish power and see through the ideological and theological justifications of their oppression. For Christians after the Holocaust Johann Baptist Metz, the German Catholic theologian, wrote, "We Christians can never go back behind Auschwitz: to go beyond Auschwitz if we see clearly, is impossible for us by ourselves. It is possible only together with the victims of Auschwitz." For Jews today it might be said, "We Jews can never go back behind empowerment: to go beyond empowerment, if we see clearly, is impossible for us by ourselves. It is possible only together with the victims of our empowerment, the Palestinian people." Thus the inclusive liturgy of destruction sees the history of Palestinian and Jew as now intimately woven together, the bond of suffering as the way forward for both peoples. From this vantage point, Mubarak Awad's pledge that he will one day return to Jerusalem should be seen as a hope for the Palestinian people and for the Jewish people as well.

CHAPTER 5

Holocaust, Israel, and Christian Renewal

The inclusion of Palestinian voices in contemporary Jewish life as a critical challenge to Jewish power is impossible without the prodding of Western and, most specifically, American Christians. In fact, the neglect of Palestinian voices in Jewish life is intimately tied to the refusal of American Christians to hear those voices and, if heard, to speak the truth to their Jewish ecumenical partners. We might say that the Jewish-Christian ecumenical dialogue since the 1960s has been tied to Holocaust theology, with its emphasis on suffering and empowerment. Christians have willingly and sometimes unwillingly accepted that theology almost as a new gospel. The acceptance of Holocaust theology from the Christian side means repentance of past sins against the Jewish people and acceptance of Israel as central to Jewish identity. However, the importance of Holocaust theology to Christian theology has often made Christians silent partners to Israeli policy and formed a barrier to an honest critique of the Middle East situation. It is no exaggeration to suggest that Christian renewal in the West is intimately tied to the affirmation of their Jewish brothers and sisters. Yet at this point in Jewish history, the ability of Christians to speak honestly to Jews is a key to the future renewal of the Jewish people. Of course, the relationship of Jews and Christians is as complex as their history together is long—and the relationship of Western Christians with the Arab world is similarly complex. Paradoxically, the relationship between Jews, American Christians, and Palestinians, a triangular relationship between former and present enemies, may provide an avenue for the three communities to move beyond a parochialism that threatens them all.

Jews and the Crisis of Christian Liberalism

Edmund Wilson, a well-known American essayist and cultural critic with a particular interest in Jews, Hebrew, and the Hebrew scriptures, traveled to Israel in 1955. His book *Black, Red, Blond and Olive* includes a long section on his journey to the newly established state. He was hardly blind to the methods used in the birth of Israel and comments disapprovingly that in Israel "the terrorist habit has been established" and with it an "element of moral fanaticism." Though his writing contains an ambivalence both about the state of Israel and Jews themselves, when it comes to the Palestinian Arabs he is unequivocal in his condemnation:

> So the position of the Arabs in Israel—especially as one sees them in the country—is rather like that fierce but still picturesque, pathetically retarded people, cut off from the main community but presenting a recurrent problem. In a large Arab town like Acre, the squalor of the swarming streets inspires in an Israeli the same distaste that it does in the visiting Westerner. For the Jew, who takes family relations so seriously and who, in Israel, has labored so carefully with the orphans from Poland and Germany, and the children of the illiterate Yemenites, the spectacle of flocks of urchins, dirty, untaught, diseased, bawling and shrieking and begging in the narrow and dirty streets, inspires even moral horror. If the restrictions imposed on marriage by the ancient rabbinical law are considered by many too rigid, the facility of divorce for the Arabs, which, together with their nomadic habits, encourages the father of a family simply to abandon his offspring and move on to take a woman in another place, must be felt to be an evil far worse. It is not that a certain contempt for the Arabs is not natural for anyone trained in the West, nor is it that any ruthlessness of Israel is not matched by the rather stupid obstinacy of the Arab refugees in Jordan, who have refused offers of U.N.R.W.A. to accommodate them in other localities and continue to insist on returning to their villages and farms in Israel. I am occupied here solely with bringing out the operation in Israel of a certain Jewish tendency toward exclusiveness—I shall deal later on with the converse of this, the life-giving elements of the Jewish tradition—as a limiting and sometimes destructive influence.[1]

This view of Palestinian Arabs was echoed by one of the most influential Christian theologians of the post–World War II period, Reinhold Niebuhr. In an article written in 1946 titled "A New View of Palestine," Niebuhr, like Wilson, emphasizes the role of Jews and later Israel in helping to modernize a backward, illiterate culture:

There is, I know, not sufficient consideration in America either of Arab rights or of the embarrassment of Britain in dealing with the Arab world. I find it baffling, on the other hand, that the average person here speaks of Arab "opinion" without suggesting that such opinion is limited to a small circle of feudal overlords, that there is no middle-class in this world and that the miserable masses are in such abject poverty that an opinion is an impossible luxury for them. One difficulty with the Arab problem is that the technical and dynamic civilization which the Jews might have helped to introduce and which should have the support of American capital, and which would include river-development, soil-conservation and use of native power, would not be acceptable to the Arab chieftains though beneficial to the Arab masses. It would have therefore to be imposed provisionally, but would have a chance of ultimate acceptance by the masses.[2]

One year later in a signed letter to the *New York Times*, Niebuhr and six others wrote of their support for partitioning Palestine. For Niebuhr, whoever analyzed the Middle East had to admit that there was only one vanguard of progress and modernization in the Middle East, Jewish Palestine. A second factor for progress was Christian Lebanon, which, from Niebuhr's point of view, was artificially subdued by the Pan-Arabists and Pan-Islamists of the Arab League against the will and sentiments of Lebanon's Christian majority. Niebuhr saw Jewish Palestine and Christian Lebanon as islands of Western civilization confronted by the hopeless picture of an Arab-Moslem Middle East.[3]

Niebuhr's interest in the Jewish people was a long-standing one and in a sense paradigmatic for the emerging Christian renewal. As a young pastor in Detroit in the early 1920s, he was frustrated by the few converts from Judaism to Christianity, blaming it on "the unchristlike attitude of Christians" and "Jewish bigotry." By 1926 he abandoned missionizing Jews altogether, seeing the Christian-Jewish encounter as mutually beneficial, with liberal Jews speaking of Jesus in positive terms and Judaism acting as a counterweight to the otherworldliness to which Christians were prone. With his move to New York in 1928, Niebuhr was drawn to Zionist thought, especially the binationalism of Judah Magnes. By the early thirties Niebuhr understood that Hitler was bent on at least the cultural annihilation of the Jews, and from that time on he was a strong and public advocate of the Zionist cause.[4]

In a two-part essay titled "Jews After the War," published in February 1942, Niebuhr outlines his position regarding Jews, anti-Semitism, and Zionism, which, at the same time, goes to the heart of his emerging critique of Western liberal assumptions and philosophy. In effect, for

Niebuhr, the Jews represent the dialectic of universalism and particularism it would be necessary to resurrect in the postwar, postliberal world. Thus he argues to ensure the democratic rights of individual Jews in the West and at the same time argues that Jews as a people have a right to a collective existence in Palestine. The assimilability of the Jews and their right to be assimilated are not in question; this is the conviction that should prompt the program of the democratic world, which consists in maintaining and extending the standards of tolerance and cultural pluralism. But the other aspect of the Jewish problem is not met by this strategy: that for Niebuhr is the simple right of the Jews to survive as a people. Though there are both Jews and Gentiles who deny that the Jews have a will to survive as a people, the evidence of contemporary history refutes them. Modern liberalism has difficulty seeing this aspect of human existence because its individualist and universalist presuppositions and illusions prevent it from seeing what Niebuhr feels to be some rather obvious facts in the collective life of humanity. In Niebuhr's view the type of liberalism that fights for democratic rights but not the collective existence of the Jewish people is informed by a false and unrealistic universalism, as well as by a failure to deal with the West's decided lack of interest in absorbing the vast numbers of Jewish refugees.[5]

Niebuhr recognizes that the dual strategy of democratic rights and collective existence in Palestine is difficult for Jewish liberals to accept as well: "Non-Zionist Jews have erred in being apologetic or even hostile to these aspirations on the ground that their open expression might imperil rights painfully won in the democratic world. Non-Jewish liberals have erred equally in regarding Zionism as nothing but the vestigial remnant of an ancient religious dream, the unfortunate aberration of a hardpressed people." At the same time, he understands that a Jewish Palestine will be possible only with the support of the two great liberal democracies, the United States and Great Britain, who after the defeat of Hitler can make the "necessary political arrangements." This includes guaranteeing that Palestine is set aside for Jews, that restrictions on Jewish immigration are dropped, and that the Palestinian Arabs are compensated. Niebuhr also understands that a Jewish Palestine involves an injustice to the Palestinian Arabs and that it is absurd to expect people to regard the diminution of their sovereignty over their land as "just,": "What is demanded in this instance is a policy which offers a just solution of an intricate problem faced by a whole civilization. The solution must, and can, be made acceptable to the Arabs if it is incorporated into a total settlement of the issues of the Mediterranean and Near Eastern world; and it need not be unjust to the Arabs in the long run if the same

'imperial' policy which establishes the Jewish homeland also consoli-
dates and unifies the Arab world. One may hope that this will not be
done by making the Jewish homeland a part of an essentially Arab
federation."[6]

Both Wilson and Niebuhr were participating in a Western tradition of
viewing Arabs and Muslims as threatening and backward, in need of
Western assistance. They were also carrying on a history of Christian
Zionism, begun with the Protestant Reformation, that though always
ambivalent toward Judaism and the Jews, sought and often sponsored a
Jewish return to the land. These two traditions took on a certain urgency
with the knowledge of the Jewish Holocaust and the Jewish refugee
problem when World War II came to an end.

But beyond the tradition and the urgency lay a reevaluation of the
teachings of the Western Christian tradition vis-à-vis the Jews, teachings
that had clearly laid the groundwork for the Nazi death camps. This
reevaluation, begun by theologians like Reinhold Niebuhr, went on
quietly during the 1950s and early 1960s as an issue peripheral to the
Christian community. But with the Second Vatican Council and the
publication of Rosemary Radford Ruether's ground breaking study *Faith
and Fratricide: The Theological Roots of Anti-Semitism*, the issue assumed
central importance. Gregory Baum, who had participated in this discussion since the early fifties, set the stage for this new level of discussion in
introducing Ruether's book. For Baum, it was not until the Holocaust
destroyed six million Jews that some Christian theologians became willing to face the question of Christian complicity in a radical way. At this
point few theologians have been willing to listen to the message of the
death camps. "While it would be historically untruthful to blame the
Christian Church for Hitler's anti-Semitism and the monstrous crimes
committed by him and his followers, what is true, alas, is that the Church
has produced an abiding contempt among Christians for Jews and all
things Jewish, a contempt that aided Hitler's purposes. The Church
made the Jewish people a symbol of unredeemed humanity; it painted a
picture of Jews as a blind, stubborn, carnal and perverse people, an
image that was fundamental in Hitler's choice of the Jews as the scape-
goat. What the encounter of Auschwitz demands of Christian theologians, therefore, is that they submit Christian teaching to a radical
ideological critique." As Baum correctly points out, the radical and most
troubling conclusion of Ruether's work is that Christian anti-Jewishness
did not grow as an aberration. Rather, it was and continues to be the left
hand of Christology, linked to the Church's proclamation of Jesus as the
Christ.[7]

As the Six-Day War galvanized the Jewish community, it also crystallized the search for a Christianity devoid of anti-Jewishness and issued into an ecumenism based on the significance of these events. For example, it was at this time that discussion of the Holocaust and Israel became central themes in Christian writing and that repentance for causing Jewish suffering and affirmation of the centrality of Israel to the Jewish people became keys to reevaluation of Christian theology itself.

Israel and Christian Renewal

Alice and Roy Eckardt's book *Encounter with Israel: A Challenge to Conscience,* published in 1970, bears scrutiny as an example of this revived interest in Judaism and Israel after the 1967 war. It is clear from the beginning that though they declare themselves pro-Israel, the Eckardts are aware of some of the complexities of the Arab-Israeli conflict. Though the tendency is to see Israel as either holy or demonic, the Eckardts think it necessary to fight both enmity toward and uncritical adulation of Israel. For the Eckardts, Israel has the same right to exist as any country, but to see Israel as God or messiah is mistaken. To be pro-Israel, to celebrate the reality of Israel, is not to abandon even Israel's enemies. From a theological view, though religious faith has a place in the inspiration of the reborn Israeli state, the Eckardts do not believe that Israel's right to exist as a sovereign nation can be validated through the theological presupposition that once upon a time God gave the land to the people of ancient Israel, without qualification and for all human history. "Those who, either as Christians or as Jews, identify 'religious Zionism' in terms of theological absolutism, and that seek to promote that point of view, will find that we disagree with them. We are not Christian Zionists."[8]

Still, despite this limitation, the burden of acceptance rests with those Arabs intent on "politicide," and the Eckardts equate their effort with the work of Adolf Hitler. "Adolf Hitler never exaggerated and never kept silent concerning his intentions. Neither do the present heirs of his gospel. The very words they use comprise a fearsome repetition of history. Countless Arabs have proclaimed countless times that Israel is 'a cancerous growth' within 'their' body. The growth must be cut away before it brings death to the whole Arab world. And these are not just words. Year upon year, Arab deeds have been suited to the threats. Threat and deed have vied in their viciousness. Had the Israelis ever fallen prey to the myth that Arabs did not mean what they said, the entire country of Israel would have long since become a hugh death camp. There would be no Jewish refugee camps." Thus Israel's military victory in 1967 was, to the Eckardts, "an averted pogrom, a pogrom that would have been exceeded in its vastness only by the Nazi inferno." The Palestinian Arab demand that Israel be destroyed is a euphemism for annihilation of the Jews.[9]

For the Eckardts, on a theological level Israel represents a rebirth of Jewish faith, a response to an unbroken trust so that the ancient spiritual covenant can be reborn and realized in the life of a free Jewish people. To those Christians who argue that divine judgment was responsible for the historic dispersion of Jewry, they should also see divine support in the rebirth of Israel. Religious and secular Jews can find in this rebirth following the Holocaust the realization of Ezekiel's vision of the dry bones being gathered together for new life in the land of Israel. As the Eckardts conclude, "Perhaps only the Jew feels the full power of these words. Yet can we not identify with him?"[10]

The problem is that most Christians, at least according to the Eckardts, remain anti-Jewish, ignorant of the long history of Christian anti-Jewishness and ready to exchange the old weapon of Jesus Christ against the "unbelieving Jews" with a new weapon of a "militant aggressive" Israel that "threatens world peace" and harms "innocent Arabs." Though the weapon has changed, the vilification is the same. As for the response of church bodies to the 1967 war, the Eckardts quote Franklin Littell's sense of shame, which is also their own:

> When I saw with an awful sense of human mortality and fallibility the way in which the Protestant spokesmen of the Establishment responded to the need of Israel in June, I saw the nakedness of my father—the theological nakedness as well as the political ineptitude. The incident was not merely personal—autobiographical: I don't see how we can discuss the Christian-Jewish dialogue and the State of Israel without grasping the nettle. We must draw the knife and begin with this time which was so difficult for some of us "younger theologians," men who had hoped that—in the age of the [German] church struggle, in the age of the salvaging of Europe, in the age of the reestablishment of Israel—our fathers in the faith might have learned a new language and a new sense of responsibility towards the Jewish people and Israel.
>
> The spokesmen of the Establishment are not, of course, vulgar anti-Semites . . . they are too enlightened and humanitarian for that. They are not openly anti-Israel; they are just sympathetic to the governments which pledge Israel's destruction. They are not against Judaism; they just enunciate an emancipated New Covenant which has escaped from the irritating particularism of the Old. They are not openly vindictive toward Jewish history; they just express timeless truths and general humanitarian propositions which avoid the essential Jewishness of Christianity.[11]

For the Eckardts, this represents a fundamental betrayal of Jesus himself, who has been coerced into many roles during the life of the Church but in his own life knew only one, as a Jew of Palestine. Therefore, whether one likes it or not, Christian destiny is tied to a man who if he were living today would be an Israeli Jew. Still, the shame of Western Christians extends beyond the betrayal of the Jews to the betrayal of the Arabs on this very point: Western Christians have done almost nothing to educate Christian Arabs as to the rightful claims of the Jews in Israel.[12]

Despite the lack of progress on many fronts, the Eckardts also find encouraging signs, especially because some Christians are coming to know *with* Jews—that is, in the self-understanding of what it means to be Jewish—rather than simply speaking about them from a Christian understanding. They voice support for theologians and church leaders who recognize the reunification of Jerusalem as crucial to Jewish self-understanding and the reality that for Jews Israel has become the equivalent to a sacrament in Christian faith. "By the very nature of our own faith, we who are Christians are linked to the Jewish people and thereby to the people of Israel. The Christian is involved in the State of Israel, because he is, by faith, within the Jewish family. He is 'part of that people.' He is affected in his very existence, not merely as a human being (as a man, he will simply be humanitarian) but as a Christian. It is by virtue of his Christian existence that for him, Israel can never be just one more country. Christianity is devoid of spatial ties to the extent that it is on its own. But through its indissoluble bond with the Jewish people and the Jewish faith, the Christian faith is yoked spiritually to Eretz Yisrael." This means that "the tears of the Israelites are our tears; the laughter of the Israelites is our laughter. When Israel is attacked, we are attacked. When latter-day churchmen make their pathological and immoral charges against the people of Israel, we are more than ashamed. We receive their accusations as a personal insult, as though our own mother were being defiled. And then we grieve over their heresy-in-action." Ultimately the rebirth of Israel is an undeserved gift to Christians, who are privileged to be allowed to live and worship there freely and whose role is to support Jewish life and defend it against defamation and destruction.[13]

Paul van Buren has also taken on the challenge of reevaluating Christianity in light of the Jewish people. In the first two volumes of a projected four-volume series, *A Theology of the Jewish Christian Reality*, van Buren writes of the necessity for Christians to understand their historic and contemporary links with the Jewish people. To begin with, Christians carry on their liturgical and theological conversation with a predominantly Jewish vocabulary, for example, the law and the prophets, creation and covenant, judgment and resurrection. And this vocabulary reflects the Church's worship of the God of Israel. For Christians, there is no choice in the matter, for "not we but God's dealings with Israel made our talk possible in the first place. It marks the way as made for us, not by us, something for us to receive."[14]

The rejection of the Jews by the Church, beginning in the second century and continuing to the present, makes the assertion of Christian dependence on the Jews seem contradictory. But the real contradiction, according to van Buren, is presented by the contemporary history of the Jews, in their suffering and their return to the land. The Holocaust and the birth of Israel have brought to the attention of Christians, in a poignant way, the fact that Jews are alive and continuing with the covenant, a covenant Christians once thought to be abrogated:

> We do not have to decide whether the events of 1933 to 1945 in Europe or those begun in 1948 in the Land promised to their fathers are of greater or lesser importance than other reorienting events of their past. We need only observe that they appear to be exercising a comparable reorienting effect upon the church, leading us to read the book which we carry with new eyes. When the people whose history the church has held to be revelatory are again figuring so centrally in events of our days, we have, on the face of it, at least an occasion to ask whether we do not see today something of the ways of God with His people and of the Way in which His people walk. Consequently, we have grounds to consider afresh the Way the church is to walk. The alternative, if we would be honest, is to stop speaking of God as the Lord of history and agree that He stopped being that centuries ago.

For van Buren, Christians, or from his perspective Gentiles, have been called into the Way of Israel's God and thus the suffering and rebirth of God's Chosen is the place of transformation for the Gentile as well.[15]

Van Buren sees the birth of the state of Israel as part of the continuing testimony of God's fidelity to the Jewish people, and the Six-Day War of 1967 assumes a major place here. Since 1967 the Jewish state has been on the "map of God's creation," and according to van Buren, "we are witnesses today to the opening of a new era in the continuing life of God's people." Zionism represents the fulfillment of the Diaspora longing for a return to Eretz Yisrael; for Israel was a people that needed its land, and the land in return needed Israel. The land "desolate and untended" needed its people to care for it. For van Buren, those who reject that return—the United Nations, which condemns Zionism as racism; the Middle East Council of Churches, which accepts Judaism but not Zionism; blacks in the United States, who accept a burgeoning anti-Jewishness—do not hear or understand the fidelity of God in the contemporary world. "Zionism is the modern expression of Israel's age-old longing to unify its response to its calling by the unique God: to be itself in the place to which God called it to serve him." The resistance to Zionism should give way to gratitude and thanksgiving, for God's fidelity to the people once chosen means that God is faithful to others as well. Instead of resisting Israel, people of the First and Third Worlds should see the state of Israel as a model to be emulated.[16]

Van Buren understands that the witness of the Jewish people in Israel today is, to be sure, far from perfect. However, the problems come primarily from external hindrances, first among them the fact that Israel has not known peace with its neighbors:

> It has had to maintain itself since birth in constant military preparedness for yet another attack by its neighbors, who from the beginning have sought the disappearance of the Jewish state. The partition of the land, for which many of the neighboring Arab states would now settle, was rejected by them when it was offered by the United Nations General Assembly (with Jewish agreement) in 1947. Instead, the Arab countries all attacked the new Jewish state, and Israel's borders ever since have been armistice lines. Israel's border with Egypt is the first to be established by a peace treaty, the stability of which, after thirty-four years of hostilities, is more a matter of hope than certainty. With the uncertain exception of Egypt, Israel's neighbors have forced Israel to be constantly prepared to fight, hardly an ideal condition for a people called to bear witness to the Creator and Redeemer of all.[17]

The work of the Eckardts and van Buren is representative of an important segment of Christians who are struggling with their own complicity in the suffering of the Jewish people. They represent the possibilities and limitations of the ecumenical movement as it has developed over the past decades. Jews, those who have been seen as "other," have questioned Christian triumphalism and legitimacy, and that questioning has led to a significant reevaluation of what it means to be a Christian. Yet Christian understanding of authentic Judaism and Jewish commitment, though somewhat nuanced, is essentially within the framework of Holocaust theology. Though they are flawed like other peoples, there is an essential innocence about the Jewish people, and though they refuse the label Christian Zionist, for these Christians Israel remains a portent of redemption. Those Christians who are critical of Israel run the risk of being accused of being anti-Jewish; dissenting Jews are in a similar position, being seen almost as deviants. With all its beauty and struggle, the work of the Eckardts and van Buren limits Christian and Jewish dissent and thus makes it more difficult to hear Palestinian voices in their own right.

The Palestinian Uprising and Christian Theology

Robert McAfee Brown is another Christian theologian whose work has been affected by Holocaust theology. This is most evident in his study *Elie Wiesel: Messenger to All Humanity*, in which Brown attempts to immerse himself in the Holocaust world of death and destruction. Clearly Brown sees Wiesel as a challenge to Jews and Christians, indeed the entire world, as a storyteller and a witness who raises questions most would like to avoid. For Brown, Wiesel confronts the world and especially Christians with moral dilemmas posed in the form of questions: How could a decent people with the highest form of Western culture engage in the murder of six million Jews? How could the world remain silent as the Jews were slaughtered? How can the world remain indifferent today, when similar horrors loom on the horizon? How can we believe in human goodness or God after the Holocaust and in the face of the difficult challenges that face us today? For Brown, listening to Wiesel provides insight into these questions, but more, forces a confrontation with some of the most difficult questions of twentieth-century life. Though it is impossible for Brown and others who were not in the death camps to enter Wiesel's world, it is possible to allow Wiesel to enter our world. This is a shattering experience, but Brown believes it is only through taking the risk of listening to the survivor that the ability to celebrate life may be reclaimed.[18]

With Brown's respect for Wiesel in mind, and his continuous gestures of solidarity with the Jewish people and with Israel over the years, it is interesting to see his latest commentary on the uprising, titled "Christians in the West Must Confront the Middle East." As a person known for his prophetic writings about many areas of the world, Brown's reluctance to criticize Israel has been obvious both to those who await his words and to himself. In the first place Brown has been reluctant to speak because of Jewish suffering and Christian complicity in that suffering, the understanding of which has "cast a heavy shadow over my view of the world, my understanding of God, my estimate of human nature and my theology of the church." In a world devoid of affirmations of Jews and Judaism, Israel has been a solace of affirmation for Jews and therefore worthy of support. For Brown, the limitation of this approach is that it fails to take with equal seriousness the rights of Palestinians, their displacement from the land, and the oppressive conditions under which they have been forced to live ever since. The second reason for Brown's reluctance to speak is that the Holocaust was only the latest of almost two thousand years of Christian anti-Jewishness; a challenge to the existence of the state of Israel almost certainly will be interpreted as a continuation of that history, thus earning the label anti-Semitic. For Brown, the shortcomings of this approach lie in the failure of all involved to distinguish clearly enough between the religious faith, Judaism, and the modern political entity, Israel. A final reason for silence is a Christian desire not to aid in any way "*enemies of Israel* who *are* anti-Semitic, terrorist, chauvinistic, unreasoning, or all of the above." Brown sees that the shortcoming here is the failure to distinguish between fanatical criticism and creative criticism; a terrain for public discourse must have options beyond supporting either Palestinian displacement or Israeli annihilation. In sum, Brown finds himself caught between two concerns, both legitimate and difficult to resolve: the commitment to Israel because of past Christian anti-Jewishness, and the commitment to the liberation of all oppressed people arising from Christian faith, a commitment that must include Jews in the past and Palestinians in the present.[19]

What allows Brown to break his silence is that Jews, for the first time and in great numbers, have broken their silence. And though criticism by non-Jews may be difficult to accept, providing a "kind of moral blank check" to Israel is helpful neither to Palestinians nor to Israelis; speaking the truth should be seen as an act of loyalty rather than disloyalty. Still, Brown warns against demagogic criticism like comparing Israelis to Nazis, as such a comparison denies the reality of the situation. The problem for Brown is similar to the one Greenberg surfaces, that is, the double standard of Israel as seeming special and thus being criticized for behaving like other nations. Instead of a double standard Brown suggests a dialectical tension between Israel as special and Israel as normal, thus though its fears of annihilation are understandable in relation to its memory, in its operation as a state in warfare or dealing with refugees, for example, it is to be judged like any other nation. With this in mind Brown makes a plea to Israel: "You, more than all the other peoples of the earth, know what it is like to be refugees, sojourners, displaced persons, people whose lands have been overrun time and again by invaders. Your psalms and liturgies invoke that sense of homelessness as something to be overcome. The Torah calls on you to welcome the sojourner, to feed the hungry, to care for the sick and dying. Could you not exercise that kind of concern for the Palestinians 'within your gates' today?"[20]

Brown concludes his essay with a discussion of a possible liberation theology for the Middle East, the elements of which include theological reflection growing out of the immediate situation; a true liberation achieved for all, rather than for some at the expense of others; a preferential option for the poor that leads to the empowerment of the weak, the Palestinians, as well as the now strong Israelis; recognition of the inherent risk in the liberation struggle, that the once-oppressed Jews will continue to oppress and that the oppressed Palestinians, once liberated, may oppress the once more powerful Israelis. The more specific list of ingredients to be part of the solution from Brown's perspective include: a homeland for both Jews and Palestinians; safeguarding the rights of all minorities; respect for one another's borders; bilateral deescalation of the military forces; a willingness to have all parties judged by the same moral and political standards; an acknowledgment that everyone will have to settle for less than initially hoped for.[21]

Another Christian theologian involved in a reappraisal of the Christian stance is Rosemary Radford Ruether, who deepened her own perspective with her trip to Israel and Palestine in 1987. Since the publication of her book *Faith and Fratricide* in 1974, Ruether has become well known and respected for her critique of Christian triumphalism as a way of solidarity with the Jewish people. To her, the anti-Judaic myth that grew up in the early Christological formulations regarding Jesus lives on in the present, thus deflecting the critique of Christendom and nourishing the roots of anti-Jewishness. A vital key for understanding aspects of Western history is therefore lost, and Christian theologians continue writing Christologies that are implicitly, if not explicitly, anti-Jewish. This selective ignorance is then passed on in the churches in a way that continues to reinforce the stereotype of the carnal, legalistic, and obsolete Jew. "This very suppression of Jewish history and experience from Christian consciousness is tacitly genocidal," Ruether writes. "What it says, in effect, is that the Jews have no further right to exist after Jesus. We repress the memory of their continued existence and our dealings with them so that it appears that 'after Christ' Jews disappear, and only Christians remain as the heirs of Jewish history and the people with a future." Yet if Christian theologians would only listen to the experience of the Jewish people within Christendom, and in their continued life today, then Christian anti-Judaism would have to end:

> Today, European Jewry is gone, swept away by the Holocaust. To be sure, some Jews continue to live in Europe. But European, especially German, Jewry as a cultural phenomenon, which made such brilliant contributions to modern culture and scholarship, has been destroyed. In

North America, the promise and the ambivalences of the emancipation are still intact. In Russia, the condition of ghetto Jewry mingles with the totalitarianism of the modern revolutionary state. It is in Israel that the myth of Christian anti-Judaism comes to an end. Here, the dispersion is overcome, and the Jewish people regathered into the ancient homeland, contrary to that Christian theory that denied this possibility. The Zionist messianic vision of the Return confronts the Christian doctrine of eternal misery and dispersion of the Jewish people to the end of history. Yet, the hope for a people "at ease in Zion" still eludes the Jewish state, as it struggles with the effects of Western imperialism which, now, set one victimized people against another.[22]

While detailing the distortions of Christology with regard to the Jews (and later with regard to women as well), Ruether is also active in the discussion of Christian responses to the state of Israel. In her article "Anti-Semitism and the State of Israel: Some Principles for Christians," written just a month after the October 1973 war, Ruether begins by affirming the connectedness of the Holocaust and Israel and by decrying Christians and Arabs who use Jewish empowerment as a rallying point for an underlying anti-Jewishness. The difficulty for Christians lies in their own continuing theological tradition that sees the Jews after Christ as existing on the periphery, a detached and wandering people. By contrast, for Ruether, Zionism arose as a liberation movement vis-à-vis the heritage of Christian oppression. To recognize Israel is to reevaluate Christology. "In the light of the Holocaust . . . Christians today must unequivocally reject any viewpoint that smacks of the tradition of eternal exile and reprobation. They must recognize Israel itself as an event that rebukes this idolatrous misuse of biblical messianic hope. They must affirm the equal legitimacy of Judaism as a people of God and a vehicle of salvation. This affirmation of continued Jewish existence must affirm Israel as a vehicle for Jewish survival." The Arabs, on the other hand, turn justified grievances into the language of holy war, republish the infamous and fallacious so-called protocols of the elders of Zion, and deny the right of Israel to exist.[23]

At the same time Christians cannot let past history silence them with regard to present abuses, nor can they assert from a Christian viewpoint the obsolete theological right of Israel to exist as a political state. For Ruether, the only persons who can speak legitimately of Israel as the "Zion of God" are Jews who use this vision to move beyond survivalism to an inclusive solidarity with all peoples. Such a person recovers the prophetic stance of internal self-criticism and realizes that Israel is in danger of becoming an oppressor. The difference between survival and overkill is important; the recognition by the Arab states and Palestinians of Israel's right to exist is crucial; Israel must understand that the acquisition of territories in the 1967 and 1973 wars puts it in the unenviable and self-defeating position of ruling over Arab peoples it is not prepared to enfranchise. Ruether believes that for Israel to retain these territories on a permanent basis is to "commit Israel to a course of expulsion, covert destruction or political suppression of these people that can only feed internal revolt and demoralization of Israeli citizens." By contrast, acceptance by its neighbors may lead to Israel's feeling itself to be part of the Middle East rather than a transplanted European colony, and a nation that can express itself creatively rather than simply through military might. A solution comes into view that may mean, among other things, the return of some territories, communal self-government in local areas, the revival of interest in a binational state or an independent Palestinian state, with the possibility of implementing a policy of equality for remaining Arab minorities in Israel.[24]

By 1989, Ruether, with her husband, Herman Ruether, was detailing the intransigence and violence of the Israeli government vis-à-vis the Palestinian people. In their book *The Wrath of Jonah: The Crisis of Religious Nationalism in the Israeli-Palestinian Conflict* and in her subsequent writings, Ruether takes on the difficult task for the Christian of speaking truth to Jewish power without being or being considered anti-Jewish. For Ruether, the starting point, the critical analysis of Jewish suffering in European history and the response of the Jews to that history, must now be complemented by a critical analysis of how one response to that suffering, Zionism, has in the past and present affected the Palestinian people. Second is how Jewish and Christian theology has helped to legitimate Zionism in the past and the present, as well as the need to develop Jewish and Christian theologies that oppose the injustices inherent in Zionist ideology and practice. At the same time, Ruether finds it difficult or impossible for Christians to analyze the historical or theological patterns unless and until they come into contact and solidarity with the Palestinian people. Thus comes the crucial question that Brown broached earlier: whether Christians can be in solidarity with both Jews and Palestinians.[25]

The answer for Ruether, as for Brown, is yes, but only when the myths of Israelis as innocent and Palestinians as terrorists are exposed. By analyzing Zionist and Palestinian history, Ruether concludes that the chief impediment to peace has not been historically and is not today the Palestinian people but an expansionist and violent state of Israel. This impediment to peace lies in the concept of Israel as an exclusive Jewish state and also in Israel's position as an occupying power. Underlying both these realities is the refusal to recognize, alongside Jewish nationalism, a parallel Palestinian nationalism and right to self-determination. Though Ruether believes that a Jewish homeland should be understood as a powerful part of contemporary Jewish identity, this understanding does not on the face of it give Jews a political right to found a state, much less to displace the Palestinian people in the process. Thus for Ruether three myths need to be overcome: that Jews have an *a priori* right to the whole of Palestine, that the Arab Palestinians do not have a parallel claim on the land as a national community, and that Israel must be oriented toward European people and culture and not be part of the Middle East. It is these three Zionist myths that have walled "Israel into a segregated, hostile, and violent relationship to the rest of the communities of people that live around it."[26]

Although Ruether acknowledges that Jews have a fear of annihilation that comes from the Holocaust and now has been transferred to the Arabs, Palestinians cannot be expected to address this almost pathological fear that Jews have of them, "since it makes little sense to their own experience as refugees and as an oppressed community with no state, little land, no army worth mentioning and so little political clout that only by suffering endless assaults does it keep itself before the attention of the world at all." For Ruether, the struggle to demythologize the innocence of Israel is less an academic question than a struggle for the survival of the Palestinian people. In her most recent essay, "The Occupation Must End," Ruether details the brutal response of Israel to the Palestinian uprising in terms of injuries and deaths, now approaching eighty thousand, and the assault on Palestinian culture and education as a way of punishing and humiliating a people.[27]

Ruether finds it difficult to communicate these facts to Christians in the West, because the flip side of anti-Jewishness has become a philo-Semitism. This is true especially with regard to liberal Christians, who in their sensitivity to and guilt for anti-Jewishness have compensated by idealizing Jews and elevating them to superior wisdom and morality. "When faced with the possibility that an organized group of Jews have done some pretty bad things to another group of people, many sensitive, anti-anti-Semites are thrown into agonized emotional conflict. We fear that we might be slipping back into negative stereotypes of Jews and quickly censor the thought that 'maybe those Jews are bad people after all.' This suggests to me that we Christians, with a history of negative stereotypes of Jews, have a hard time dealing with Jews as complex beings like ourselves." Christian thinking about Jews therefore swings between two unrealistic polarities—Jews as superior to Christians, paragons of wisdom and moral insight, and Jews as inferior to Christians, untrustworthy and lacking in true capacity for moral and spiritual life. As Ruether envisions it, the task is to see Jews as different, with their own particular history and culture, and similar, with the same human attributes and propensities as others. Christians are just going to have to face the complexity of human nature in Jews as they learn to face it in themselves: the reality of the Jews in Israel has been of a dominant conquering power displacing another people and seeking to make them disappear.[28]

The challenge for Christians is to see Jews as they are, but the conflict in Israel and Palestine also challenges the Jewish people to move beyond a particularity that emphasizes uniqueness in order to justify exclusivity, which in turn seeks to confer a special holiness and thus rights to the land that supersede the claims of others. Ruether suggests instead that Jews choose the universalist tradition in Judaism, which affirms Jewish particularity in solidarity with the particularity of other peoples. This ethic of mutual solidarity does not mean an anonymous universalism that contains (as it did in the past) a hidden agenda of ending Jewish distinctiveness, an agenda Jews rightly resist. "Rather, one must locate it in the concrete relations between different people who are actually called, either by choice or by historical circumstances, to live side by side with each other. The quest of Israeli Jews and Palestinian Arabs for a just and peaceful coexistence is an instance of the difficulty and challenge of that ethical commandment." Ultimately, to choose a different path, more than innocence and exclusivism needs to be given up. The understanding of Israel as redemptive is also thrown into question, for religious messianism in Holocaust theology and fundamentalist groups, rather than a healing and unifying force, has become a force of violence within the Jewish community as well as outward toward Palestinians. As Ruether comments:

> The *sabra*, redeemed from Diaspora weakness, with a gun in one hand and a plow in the other, has become a military-political-industrial ruling elite. Many Jews no longer work the land with their own hands or do any kind of manual labor. For many, such labor is now seen as "Arab work," unbefitting a Jew. Some Israelis have become an urban managerial elite, ruling over lower classes and races who do the manual labor. The dream of redemption through labor has evaporated in the reality of a colonialist, capitalist organization of the economy. The class and race hierarchy of labor, relegation of Palestinians to third-class citizens or stateless subjects of military rule, also destroys the messianic myth of Israel as model social democracy, a "light to the nations," in terms of democratic and socialist ideals.[29]

Thus for Ruether Zionism becomes a false messianism.

> False messianism rests on a false construction of the relationship between unredeemed human reality and human hopes. False messianism evokes a dream of redeemed life, whether that be expressed in romantic, liberal, socialist, or religious norms. It uses this dream to cover up contrary realities. Symbol is separated from ethical substance and then used to conceal the contradiction between symbol and ethical substance. False messianism demands deception. Those who glorify their activities as redemptive must lie about contradictory realities. The deception, in turn, must be covered up, and those who would expose it vilified. The large amount of deception, coverup of deception, and vilification of those who seek the truth has been typical of Israeli state propaganda. This pattern of deception is not unlike that found in other modern forms of failed messianism, such as state communism, fascism, and even the American self-perception of its foreign policy as "making the world safe for democracy."[30]

The response of the Jewish community to Brown's and Ruether's analyses is instructive. Brown's original essay on the crisis, which contains many of the points in his essay analyzed earlier, drew high marks from many Jews and was featured in *Interreligious Currents,* a publication of the Department of Interreligious Affairs of the Union of American Hebrew Congregations. Brown's basic requirement that a Christian critique of Israel "spring from our love of Israel, from our desire that Israel be all that it is destined to be, both for its sake and our own," was greeted warmly by the editor, Annette Daum, who saw this as an appropriate ground rule for responsible discussion about Israel between Christians and Jews. According to Daum, too often Christian statements lack historical context, holding Israel "responsible for Palestinian frustrations which have been fueled by forty years of *Arab* rejection and refusal to absorb Palestinian refugees as well as by twenty years of Israeli occupation." Still, Jews cannot expect socially conscious Christians to be silent with respect to the Palestinian refugees. From Daum's perspective, what Jews have a right to expect from Christian leaders is accurate background information, historical perspective, and avoidance of "selective condemnation when considering Middle East issues." Selective condemnation encourages the worst elements among the Palestinians and increases Israel's fears, thus encouraging a cycle of violence. Daum concludes that Christians and Jews need to "create a moral climate that would challenge Arabs and Israelis to break this cycle of violence; to end four decades of unrelenting, unholy warfare."[31]

The Wrath of Jonah fared quite differently. In a review of the Ruethers' book titled "The Philo-Semitic Face of Anti-Semitism" and published in

Tikkun, David Biale, director of the Center for Jewish Studies at the Graduate Theological Union in Berkeley, mounted the offensive. Citing the book as part of the problem rather than the solution, Biale sees the Ruethers' "polemic" as an "anti-Zionist diatribe cloaked in the sweet light of Christian universalism; as such it stands as a singular warning of how a Christian critique of Israel can slide unwittingly into the swamp of anti-Semitism." Because, according to Biale, the Ruethers do not believe that the Jews have a right to a state, he believes they fail the "minimum litmus test" of any progressive solution to the Palestinian-Israeli conflict by viewing the conflict in asymmetrical terms: right against wrong rather than a clash of two equally legitimate rights. At the same time, to propose the choice of Jewish universalism as the essence of Judaism is for Biale a continuation of Rosemary Ruether's critique of Christian universalism, though now applied to its victims. "The purpose of *Faith and Fratricide* was to divest Christianity of its own form of chauvinism, namely, anti-Semitism, so that it might become its true universalist self. The purpose of *The Wrath of Jonah* is to do the same thing for Judaism, the parent religion of Christianity. Christian universalism comes from the 'true' Judaism, but the Jews have strayed from their calling by espousing tribal nationalism. The correct role for Jews is to fight for these universal, pluralistic values in the countries of the Diaspora, the true Jewish homelands."[32]

Anti-Semitism with a philo-Semitic face is now clear to Biale. Having in her previous book disposed of the belief that the Jewish exile is a punishment for rejecting Jesus, Ruether now embraces the Jewish existence in the Diaspora as a positive vocation. "She, after all, is willing to fight for Jewish rights in the Diaspora. But the Jews—that stiff-necked people—are (once again) ungrateful and prefer to defend themselves with their own arms in their own state. Having betrayed their calling to remain dispersed among the nations, Jews surely deserve the wrath of the righteous Christians." Biale concludes his review with a plea for normality: "Progressive Jews are engaged today in a fateful struggle over the future of Israel and, indeed, the future of the Jewish people. We desperately need all the allies we can get. But the last thing we need is modern versions of the medieval sermons that Jews were forced to listen to in Christian churches, or well-meaning attempts to liberate the Jewish community. We wish to be neither oppressors nor victims, neither heroes nor puppets in someone else's theology. We wish, in short, to be a normal people."[33]

The writings of these Christians who have struggled to break out of a tradition that sought to displace and vilify the Jewish people can only be, in the first place, applauded. The limitations of each of the writers must also be seen and respected within the historical context as well; a new relation to the Jewish people cannot be forged overnight if it is to have substance and depth. Moreover, there is a complexity to these writers often overlooked in the polemics filled with urgency and danger.

There is little question that historically Christian commentary on the Jewish people has been a process of internal analysis and adamant posturing carried on without reference to Jewish theology. The Jewish people have presented questions to Christian believers—those relating to God's fidelity and the messianic fulfillment in Jesus are just two examples—and this questioning has often led to a desire to bury the questions by burying those who carry, or more to the point, embody the questions. With the Holocaust and the founding of Israel, the questions have persisted and shifted. Jews became the test for Christian authenticity in a way that led to a deeper search for fidelity rather than a desire to annihilate the other. We see this especially in Alice and Roy Eckardt and Paul van Buren. The reappropriation of the Gentile way as coming from and remaining within the original covenant, differentiated and intimately related to the Jews as the chosen, is complex and often strained. Ultimately the *raison d'être* for the search may bear more fruit than some of the arrival points suggested. For there is in both the Eckardts' and van Buren's framework of analysis a certain burden of authenticity for Christians and Jews difficult to carry over time. Though they maintain a perspective on the diversity and humanness of Jews as a concrete people, the burden of chosenness as well as the celebration of Jewish renewal can be confining for the Jewish people, even at times oppressive. Because Jewish renewal in the state of Israel is seen as part of the continuing convenantal relationship, there is, despite protestations to the contrary, an innocence maintained and at least a hidden redemption implied. Criticism by Christians, then, can only come within this framework as identifying flawed human acts to which Jews, like anyone else, are prone. A specific and substantive political analysis is mitigated by the preordained rightness of the general project; there is no possibility that the framework might be flawed, because that would threaten the Christian understanding of God's fidelity to the Jewish people and ultimately God's fidelity to Christians as well.

The framework of innocence and redemption, which places the Jews at the center of the religious drama played out in Israel, also places the Palestinians on the periphery permanently. Their role is relegated to acquiescence in or hindrance to the unfolding drama. An active Palestinian voice, one that struggles with the issues, seeks clarity and definition, or stands in a genuine opposition with its own integrity, is missing from most Christian commentators. It is wrong to accuse the Eckardts or van Buren of wishing ill to the Palestinians or lacking, at least on a superficial level, knowledge of their suffering. Rather, Palestinians exist only in relation to the Israelis and therefore become invisible. In a sense a reversal of the original Christian drama takes place in which Jesus is the center and the Jewish people exist in relation to their acceptance or rejection of him; the continuation of Jewish life after Christ is seen solely and negatively within the drama of Christian salvation. The rebirth of Israel provides a similar salvific story with Palestinians in the supporting, most often negative, role. The consequences of such a role are obvious.

By discarding the importance of the political in favor of the overtly religious or, more to the point, seeing the political acts of Jewish empowerment as carrying the force of a religious mandate, the Eckardts and van Buren disarm political dissent and even religious dissent by both Christians and Jews. If, for instance, the Palestinians are seen as major actors with all the rights ascribed to Israelis and presenting a legitimate prior and immediate claim to the land, then the framework of innocence and redemption has to change. From the Palestinian point of view the claims to innocence and redemption are ludicrous, but for the Eckardts and van Buren Palestinians have simply missed the point. The European tragedy of Jewish displacement befalls the Palestinians in their own land as a form of divine justice, cutting short arguments involving domestic and cultural life. The framework of the Eckardts and van Buren's analysis fails to even fully address the fact that secular Jews and Diaspora Jews make up the vast majority of the Jewish people.

Brown's response to the Palestinian uprising struggles within the framework of Holocaust theology. The ecumenical deal accepted by post–Vatican II Christians—repentance for past sins against the Jewish people and acceptance of Israel as central to Jewish identity—remains intact, though shaken. For Brown, as for many other progressive Christians, the difficulty seems more and more to revolve around the accepted ideal and the increasingly harsh reality of Israel. But here too we find the reality of Israel as a challenge to Jewish self-definition and Christian self-definition as well. Though Brown has spent a lifetime coming to grips with Christian complicity in injustice and evil, it is still another step, perhaps as painful, to realize that Jews are creating an all too similar history in Israel and Palestine today. Could it be that Brown, like other progressive Christians, sees the Jews as the harbinger of the first more innocent Christians and that the end of Jewish innocence in a sense challenges the possibility of recovering that innocence for Christians?

Could it be that a Judaism beyond innocence and redemption also challenges Christianity at a fundamental level to move beyond even the possibility of recovering innocence and redemption?

This, it seems, is the challenge of Rosemary Ruether's political analysis of Israeli and Palestinian history and her religious analysis of false messianism. If the left hand of Christology is anti-Jewish and the left hand of Zionism anti-Palestinian, then reform of Christology and Zionism is absolutely necessary and yet not enough. The problem, when recognized politically and religiously, is less managerial and aberrational than foundational. For Ruether, the displacement of European history into the Middle East is a disaster that can only be remedied by admitting that the entire Zionist enterprise is flawed. The insistence by Jews and Christians on the messianic character of Israel simply covers up the fundamental problems of exclusivity and expansionism, thus blunting the ability to critique Israeli reality and distorting for Christians and Jews the actual, concrete history and present.

Yet for those Jews who move beyond innocence and redemption, Ruether represents a new partner in dialogue and a bridge to the Palestinian people. Her understanding of false messianism applies across the board, and she offers an honesty shorn of religious and political mystification. If the Eckardts, van Buren, and Brown extend a much-appreciated hand to the Jewish people, Ruether calls us to an intriguing, and to some a dangerous, path. In a world beyond innocence and redemption, what is the religious calling? Can Jews after a history of dislocation and death recognize their own evolving complicity and thus undergo a conversion in their stance toward their former and present "enemies"? Can there be mutual conversions of Jew, Christian, and Palestinian toward one another?

CHAPTER 6

Beyond Innocence and Redemption

Just days after the beginning of the Palestinian uprising Thomas Friedman, a reporter for the *New York Times*, wrote a provocative article with the telling title "How Long Can Israel Deny Its Civil War?" His thesis, backed by statistics from the West Bank Data Project, was that the new outbreak of hostilities was simply an escalation of a decade of violence. "There is a new trend in Palestinian resistance," Friedman quotes Meron Benvenisti, director of the West Bank Data Project. "Palestinian violence is largely out in broad daylight by individuals and groups who spontaneously express their feelings, undeterred by the consequences of their actions. The fact that there are more killings shows the rising frustration level of the occupiers and the occupied. Before, the Palestinians were afraid of the Israeli soldiers, but they are not any-more." As Friedman concludes his article, "Indeed, maybe the real last-ing effect of the past two weeks of violence will be to force Israelis and Palestinians to realize that they have been talking about their conflict in obsolete language. Yes, it is still territorially based—but the territories in dispute are not the West Bank and Gaza strip, but all of Palestine." A year and a half later in June 1989, with over five hundred Palestinians dead and fifty thousand injured, the Israeli army chief of staff, Dan Shomron, was reported by the *Times* as saying that only harsher measures can halt the uprising. "People ask why we don't end the *intifada*. Whoever de-mands the wiping out of the *intifada* has to remember that there are only three ways to achieve it: transfer, starvation or physical extermination—that is, genocide." [1]

This, then, marks the distance traveled from the trial of Adolph Eichmann to Jerusalem. When Friedman writes of civil war and Shomron speaks of genocide, they are voicing a reality that remains unspoken: that the occupation is over and now the options are narrowed to justice, expulsion, or annihilation. Described as a war of attrition, the best that can be claimed is that the uprising is "under control." These are the words of Defense Minister Yitzhak Rabin, who in December 1989 promised to continue the "confrontations, the hitting, the arresting, the introduction of the plastic bullet, the rubber bullet and the curfews on a large scale."[2]

With the narrowed choices before the Jewish community, what does Jewish theology have to say at this most critical time? As we have seen, Irving Greenberg has written at length, yet his analysis seems impotent before the need to make a fundamental choice rather than a corrective maneuver. The framework of Holocaust theology itself mitigates serious discussion and decision on the fundamental challenge before the Jewish people: to move beyond innocence and redemption and to realize the cost of Jewish empowerment. And what do other theologians who work in the shadow of Holocaust theologians, the progressive Jewish theologians like Arthur Waskow, have to contribute? Waskow's essential response to the uprising and the Israeli measures to repress it is that if one loves Israel one should work to correct its policies; if one has given up on Israel, work for Jewish renewal in the United States. From other theologians, there is silence, or tired repetition of old arguments.[3]

Confronting State Power

The challenge to the Jewish community now is a critical retrieval of the tradition of dissent and the incorporation of Palestinian voices in the Jewish experience. What has been offered by theologians and commentators thus far lacks the empathy and ability to achieve this. The litmus test posed by David Biale, a symmetry of suffering and rights between Jews and Palestinians over the last forty years, is a false symmetry. The Palestinians have been done a great historical wrong by the Jewish people. The only way forward, it seems, is a solidarity with the Palestinian people that is at the same time confessional and political. Could we say that the task of Jewish theology is to lay the groundwork for solidarity with the Palestinian people and that any theology that does not pose that as the central question is a theology that legitimates torture and murder? To carry out this task means first of all that Jewish self-perception needs to be radically altered and the framework of discussion drastically reoriented. And if the tradition of dissent is to be politically efficacious before Shomron's options are invoked, that is, if Jews are serious about dissent and not simply demonstrating that Jews have in fact protested, then a new Jewish self-understanding needs to be created. Unfortunately, it is doubtful that mainstream theologians will be of help in this matter, for like Holocaust theologians they, at least in their theological writings, pretend Palestinians hardly exist. The works of Eugene Borowitz, Michael Wyschogrod, and David Hartman exemplify this neglect and this failing.[4]

The initial dilemma Jews face may be stated in the following way. For the first time in two thousand years Jews have a state of their own. Jewish dissenters inside and outside Israel have to confront a state power controlled by Jews with a theology that tells Jews that to confront Jewish state power is to delegitimate it and thus confrontation is an act that leads to suicide. Of course, this dilemma is complicated by the fact that 75 percent of the Jews in the world live outside Israel and thus confront that state's power outside its political framework. And finally, there is no way of confronting Israeli power without breaking through the myths of innocence and redemption that are used by Jews to legitimate the state. From these perspectives, with the testimony available, there is little choice but to commit the excommunicable sin—undermine the legitimacy of Israel. If this, however, is the option, many Jews would agree with Roberta Strauss Feuerlicht when she writes, "Zionists executed the psychological coup of the century by taking Palestine from the Arabs and then pretending Jews were Arab victims. Yet this wrong cannot be righted by another. Israel exists and must continue to exist; the alternative would mean another holocaust."[5]

But this is precisely the dead end of Jewish dissent, the place where the rough edges are unfolded and the litmus test invoked. There is no state in the world that can or does, in an ultimate sense, base its existence on moral right, despite rhetoric to the contrary. The recognition of a state, its basis, lies in its ability to govern a specific territory with enough consent, volunteered or coerced, to allow that governance. Israel, like the United States or the Soviet Union, India or Guatemala, exists as a state for better and for worse because it has the requisite power and consent to govern. To lose that ability to govern is to change political leadership; threats from the outside can be met with moral and political suasion, but ultimately the military guarantees survival. Thus Israel exists because it exists, that is, because it is able to assert enough power and gain enough consent to survive. This of course is true for a Palestinian state as well; it can be claimed as a right, it can be declared to exist, but it will come into being only when it is able to govern a territory with enough power and consent to make it viable.

So the argument is not about the existence of Israel but, rather, about the question of a Jewish state. At this point in history there is little doubt that to participate fully in Israeli society one has to be of Jewish descent, though beyond birth to Jewish parents there seems little demanded. What helps Jews rise in Israeli society is what helps people to rise in many societies: social and cultural background, class, and education. What then is the context of the term Jewish in the title Jewish state? This is the crux of the matter and why many Jews sense that normalization is hardly enough. And we are now aware that many of Israel's "normal" policies over the years—organized displacement and continuous expansion, for example—are rejected, at least by the tradition of dissent, as unacceptable to Jewish history and struggle over the millennia. To frame this discussion in a prophetic-normalization dichotomy is to miss the significance and depth of the questions placed before Jews by Jewish history and the inclusive liturgy of destruction.[6]

The term self-determination, that Jews deserve the ability to decide their own fate in their own country like all other peoples, and that the denial of that right is perforce a sign of anti-Jewishness is, like the term Holocaust, ambiguous and lacking in context. For most groups and individuals, historically and in the present, the ability to determine their own future is part of sometimes successful, other times unsuccessful struggles within communal and nation-state systems. Aside from the larger question of the meaning of self-determination, self-determination as regards Jews is also complex. Some measure of self-governance is found in Diaspora Orthodox Jewish communities, as it has been found throughout the last two thousand years, and the offer of participation in a pluralist arena of self-determination seems to achieve (not without its difficulties, of course) what most Jews appear to want: participation in the public realm with others of like and unlike mind. It would be hard to argue, for example, that the Jewish community does not participate in the American political process. On the contrary, everything points to the opposite conclusion; that is, it participates and influences the process well beyond its small numbers in the American population.[7]

Pluralism is thus crucial to the discussion of self-determination. Dissenting groups, both Jewish and non-Jewish, in the United States are no further from state power than dissenting groups in Israel. There is clearly a pluralism in Israel, found in different political parties, associations, and interest groups, that is similar to that in other countries, except that in this case the major and minor participants are Jewish. Yet, over 18 percent of the Israeli population within the 1967 borders, and over 40 percent if the occupied territories are included, are, as Palestinians, removed from the normal acts of self-determination. This Palestinian population suggests a possibility of pluralism beyond that within the Jewish community. The uprising points to a large population, pluralist in its own ways, yearning to participate in the process of self-determination—yet forced to act outside the legal processes of Israeli society.

Today Jews throughout the world participate in pluralist activities of self-determination, including in Israel. Yet the historical question remains of the need, in nineteenth- and early twentieth-century Europe and during and after the Holocaust, for a self-governing Jewish community. In retrospect, a minority of Jews felt strongly about this need, strong enough to leave their homes or, if refugees, to choose a more difficult life in Palestine than was available in other countries. The quest for identity and for some of the attachment of that identity with the ancient Jewish homeland is hard to deny; one would not want to argue with it. The problem lies less in the desire than the actuality, for self-determination has a price for which another people pays dearly.

From the literature, however, self-determination had a twofold and sometimes contradictory *raison d'être:* the desire to be free to define oneself, and the renewal of Jewish spirit and culture. This first purpose involved political independence, the government and the army; the second cultural and spiritual regeneration, the land and the university. Self-determination was seen as a means for the unencumbered development of Jewish life, though priority, political or cultural, was crucial to how one saw that development and what one was willing to do to achieve it.[8]

Ultimately the quest for self-determination was and remains a historical one. What is the mission and witness of the Jewish people? What does it mean to be Jewish? Is Jewishness achieved best within an almost totally Jewish framework or in an environment with others accepted in the personal and public arena as equals? Substantive questions, like these of course, are always found and worked through in a historical context. Judah Magnes, for example, found it important for Jewish renewal in the first half of the twentieth century to have an enlarged Jewish community in Palestine. But he also placed limitations on the importance of Jewish return by refusing to displace another people in pursuit of that goal, as he also limited the definition of Jewish self-determination by arguing for autonomy and integration with the Palestinian Arabs.

The question then and now, as Magnes, Buber, and Arendt saw it, is not whether Jews should live in Palestine but how the community in Palestine is to be organized. A binational state with Jewish autonomy, integrated into a larger pluralistic structure was one possibility. Another possibility was an exclusive Jewish state, which would create the consequent need for territory filled with Jews and free of Arabs. It is this latter choice that underlies the continuing expulsion of Palestinian Arabs. Settlements are created; the West Bank and Gaza are left economically underdeveloped; and the territories are *de facto* annexed, leading to the expulsion of the population to Jordan and Lebanon. These actions are components of a logical policy deriving from the choice of communal organization. The Palestinians are therefore right: the choice to pursue a small or enlarged Jewish state demands either subservience of the Arab population or, better yet, their disappearance into neighboring countries. However, Palestinians were not alone in this understanding: dissenting Jewish Zionists felt that this policy would defeat the intent of Jewish renewal and instead create a cycle of violence and destruction in which Jews would be either master or victim, or both at the same time.[9]

Self-determination in an exclusively Jewish state, even when 18 or 40 percent of the people are non-Jewish, creates a further question relating to Jewish history: Are Jews essentially a ghetto people? The irony of the demand for self-determination today, especially for those who live in democratic pluralistic states, is that Israel can be seen in a ghetto framework, seen as an isolated, ingathered community unable to move freely in the area that surrounds it, in constant fear of annihilation, and dependent on others for moral, political, economic, and military support. In this way Israel can be seen as approaching a ghettolike reality in continuity with the ghettos of eastern Europe, albeit an empowered ghetto. The Zionist dream that all Jews will come to live in Israel by choice or through emigration forced by anti-Jewishness at a future time has undergone a painful reversal. As Feuerlicht comments: "Israelis should not be preparing to receive American Jews; American Jews should be preparing to receive Israelis."[10]

The ghetto quality of Jewish Israeli life is, with its concomitant choices, encouraged at least partly in Holocaust theology. Between the lines and sometimes directly within innocence and redemption is the foreboding image of a future holocaust. Wiesel's travel to Israel during the 1967 war was not undertaken in anticipation of sharing a victory toast but with a sense of defeat and annihilation. Anyone who reads Holocaust theology and who has spoken with Jewish Israelis realizes that one subtext of life in Israel is the prospect of annihilation or, because of Israel's power, a fight to the finish. The Masada complex, Jews choosing suicide rather than be conquered by the Romans, has been analyzed *ad nauseam*, yet the truth of that complex can only be seen as relational, in the context of innocence and redemption. Only then does the last stand of the Jewish people make sense. There is a feeling in Holocaust theology and in Israel, beneath Wiesel's tears and the *sabras'* toughness, that Israel is a dream that cannot last. This time, however, because of the power of Israel, others will perish as well. One might call innocence, redemption, and the last stand a dangerous and unholy trinity that threatens the Jewish people more gravely than the Christian Trinity ever had the power to do. Thus self-determination has traveled to the last stand of the Jewish people: Holocaust is past *and* future.[11]

Though the trinity that ends in the "last stand" is present in Holocaust theology, the operative trinity today is innocence and redemption coupled with expansion. This is the unspoken reality that Holocaust theology refuses to deal with. Arthur Hertzberg points this out in his letter to Wiesel: refusing to say no explicitly to expansion is to support it, because this has been and is the policy of the Israeli government. Even the Jewish voices in response to the uprising, which say no to occupation, hardly touch on this point of continuity in Israel's history. It is as if the policy of settlement and occupation that began in the 1890s is an aberration, a correctable mistake rather than a logical and consistent policy relating to the promotion of a Jewish state. The underlying ideology of state power, Likud and Labor, remains untouched, as do the first legs of the trinity, innocence and redemption. In short, to advocate the end of the occupation without discussing how the occupation is integral to the triumph of state power in Israel is to miss the significance and the possibility the uprising presents: to reappraise the entire venture. In the end the distance between Elie Wiesel and Michael Lerner, while important in the contemporary political arena, may not be as great as it at first glance seems.

Thus the task presented is to forge a new relationship to the state of Israel, rather than oppose it or dissociate oneself from it. The reality is that Jews are connected together, though in ways different than the command of state loyalty in the name of religion. That part of the literature of dissent that argues the sense of peoplehood as false, stressing primary loyalty to the state a Jew lives in—for example, the classical Reform dissent of Elmer Berger—is ultimately superficial as a way of opposing Zionism. Fackenheim is closer to the truth when he argues the commanding voice of Auschwitz as a voice speaking to the Jewish people, though his emphasis on survival almost as an end unto itself empties that voice of meaning as it is used to oppress another people.

Is there a path for the Jewish people that leads beyond American liberalism and Israeli expansionism, that is connected with the Jewish people but not so self-involved that it becomes a form of idolatry? One path might be what Orthodox Judaism once was, which is now found only among the "extreme" sects of Hasidic Judaism: a self-contained Jewish community that carries on its business wherever it is, fulfilling the law and awaiting the Messiah. The neoorthodox position of Arthur Waskow tries to combine orthodoxy and contemporary life, that is, innovative prayer and ritual with ancient tenets and beliefs, as well as a heightened political commitment from a perspective rooted in Judaism. It has found a willing audience among a minority of Jews searching for their roots. Yet its appearance of addressing the Jewish issues of our time along with American political issues is more a matter of feeling than substance. Holocaust theology quite rightly surfaces Holocaust and Israel as the central questions of our time, and neoorthodox reform movements skirt these issues with alacrity.[12]

One of the major problems that both Holocaust and neoorthodox theology share in different ways is a self-defeating self-involvement—a preoccupation, as it were, with being authentically Jewish. The United Jewish Appeal dinners and the weekend *hauvorot* of progressive Jews gathering to celebrate the Sabbath, all fine in their own right, can become engines of self-affirmation that emphasize return to land or return to self. Both represent a view of history that is oriented around Jewish experience and outlook. Both Holocaust theology and neoorthodox reform, though different in many respects, come to the same destination, Jewish affirmation.

Although Jewish affirmation is important, it is not enough. The Jewish people in Israel and America have overwhelmingly and consistently rejected religious language, the language of ritual and prayer, as the vehicle of Jewish affirmation and have for at least two decades accepted Israel in its place. However, once the presumed innocence and redemption is challenged, that affirmation has to change, and the Jewish people are left with difficult questions. Is there Jewish life beyond neoorthodox Judaism and the state of Israel? Is it possible to move beyond ancient archetypes of Yavneh, where rabbis gathered after the destruction of the Second Temple and began rabbinic Judaism, and Masada, where almost a thousand Jews committed suicide rather than be conquered by the Romans? Again Holocaust theology is instructive here. In his essay "To Be a Jew," Elie Wiesel writes: "Thus there would seem to be more than one way for the Jew to assume his condition. There is a time to question oneself and a time to act; there is a time to tell stories and a time to pray; there is a time to build and a time to rebuild. Whatever he chooses to do, the Jew becomes a spokesman for all Jews, dead and yet to be born, for all beings who live through him and inside him. His mission was never to make the world Jewish but, rather, to make it more human." And in his essay "Cloud of Smoke, Pillar of Fire," Irving Greenberg writes: "After the Holocaust no statement, theological or otherwise, should be made that would be not credible in the presence of the burning children," and, "The victims ask us above all not to allow the creation of another matrix of values that might sustain another attempt at genocide."[13]

The way forward is not to abandon the dialectic that Holocaust theology poses, or to skirt it, but to reassert and broaden it, to see Holocaust and empowerment as ways of connecting Jews to the world rather than isolating them from it. It is to see ourselves as Jews in history rather than simply creating a Jewish history. The question of survival and the assertion of Jewishness, as articulated by Wiesel and Greenberg, take second place to the quality of Jewish witness. In a sense this is to restate the obvious; as Jews we are in history with others, and Jewish particularlity should be a sign of affirmation to ourselves and to others as well. The singled-out condition about which Fackenheim writes needs to be transformed as a calling into history for the sake of others, as a sign of fidelity and solidarity. Attempts to move beyond vulnerability to the self-assured strut of a people who know who they are and will defend that affirmation against everyone and everything to the end only create a people who hasten that end. If Jewish history teaches Jews that survival is fragile and must be guarded, it also tells us that survival without witness is ultimately meaningless.[14]

Today more than anything Jews need clarity of thought—freedom to think through relationships with the Holocaust and with Israel unencumbered by the threat of excommunication. The tradition of dissent provides one such avenue, as exemplified by Judah Magnes and Noam Chomsky. The liturgy of destruction provides another in the voice of the Palestinian people. Paradoxically the bridge between the tradition of dissent and the liturgy of destruction may be Christians, who now participate in both.

The Hidden Tradition

In April 1944 Arendt published an essay titled "The Jews as Pariah: A Hidden Tradition." Arendt defined the new tradition as that part of the Jewish community that is fully integrated into neither the general identifiable Jewish community, nor non-Jewish society. This tension of involvement and distance allows for critical thought to develop and mature. A boundary position comes into being where critical inquiry is possible and necessary. According to Arendt, the hidden tradition began almost two hundred years ago with the Enlightenment and Jewish eman- cipation in western Europe, which allowed greater participation of Jews in society even as they remained outsiders in the social and political realms. The outcast status gave rise to two particular types of Jews in society: the "conscious pariahs" who transcended the bounds of nation- ality to "weave the strands of their Jewish genius into the general texture of European life," and the "parvenus" who tried to achieve status by raising themselves above their fellow Jews into the respectable world of the Christians. Arendt, along with others, chose to place herself as a conscious pariah and thus endure a dual difficulty that all conscious pariahs share, becoming marginal in relation to European society and to the Jewish community as well. As Ron Feldman analyzes their situation, conscious pariahs were "neither parochially Jewish, like their Eastern European cousins, nor were they part of the wealthy Jewish upper class of bankers and merchants that controlled Jewish-Gentile relations." The conscious pariah constituted a hidden tradition because there were few links among those who affirmed their pariah status—for example, Hein- rich Heine, Sholom Aleichem, Franz Kafka, and Walter Benjamin—or between them and the rest of the Jewish community. Standing exclu- sively neither inside nor outside their Jewish or European heritage, conscious pariahs used both as platforms from which to gain insight into the other.[15]

This understanding of the hidden tradition allowed Arendt an ex- traordinary independence and clarity of thought, in short, a freedom to think about the crucial issues facing the Jewish people in Palestine in the 1940s and later in the Eichmann trial in the early sixties, that is, the issues of Holocaust and empowerment.

As we have seen, Arendt's understanding of Palestine revolved around the support for a Jewish homeland and a political framework in which Jews and Arabs could interact from positions of equality. In the kibbutzim, Arendt saw "a new form of ownership, a new type of farmer, a new way of family life and child education, and new approaches to the troublesome conflicts between city and country, between rural and in- dustrial labor." Thus from Arendt's perspective Palestine could become a model of how to overcome the problems that led to totalitarianism in Germany, the problems of a mass society and deterioration of the nation- state. According to Arendt's biographer, Elizabeth Young-Bruehl, the possibility of Jewish-Arab cooperation foreshadowed an answer to the problem underlying racism, the possibility of a new concept of humanity; she saw the problem of the underlying imperialism as one of "organizing a constantly shrinking world which we are bound to share with peoples whose histories and traditions are outside the western world." In Palestine, Arendt hoped to see the elements of her political theory realized: new social forms, local political councils, a federation, and international cooperation. In a paradox that was not lost on her, she hoped that the victims of totalitarianism could offer a vision of institutions and government beyond totalitarianism. Her hopes for the Jewish community in Palestine were in conformity with her understanding of the forms that the postwar world would develop, empires and federations, and her conviction that the Jewish people would survive only if they chose the model of federation.[16]

In covering the Eichmann trial in Jerusalem, Arendt became famous and even more controversial. As on the question of Palestine, her clarity and independence of thought rankled many. Yet it is precisely in this ability to refuse conformity that Arendt's analysis of Eichmann takes on significance. Originally published as a five-part series in the *New Yorker*, her analysis was published later as a book titled *Eichmann in Jerusalem.* The controversy involved these main points: Arendt's portrait of Eichmann as banal rather than overtly sinister, her analysis of the European Jewish Councils and their role in the Nazi program of mass death, and her questions concerning the nature of the trial and the political reasons for it. Arendt's analysis of Eichmann led her to two startling and controversial judgments: that Eichmann, having a bureaucratic mentality, carried out the laws of his state without differentiating between right and wrong, and that the corruption of the Nazis affected other countries and societies, including that of the Jewish victims themselves. Her challenges were thus posed as the need for a law of humanity to create new legal and moral categories for those involved in state-instigated crimes or, in Arendt's own words "administrative massacres." A shift in moral perspective was also necessary to address the new factor of corruption of the victims as well as the oppressor that made judgment more difficult. In short, Arendt explored the reality of Eichmann within and beyond the confines of the Jewish community and saw the discussion of his persona and work in political and systemic terms rather than simply in the images of the liturgy of destruction. Or to put it another way, the attempt to destroy the Jews offered a paradigm of future destruction beyond the Jewish community.[17]

Arendt's conclusions about the normality of Eichmann, about the difficulties of judgment that "extermination per se was more important than anti-Semitism or racism," remains her most controversial conclusion. The reasons she supported his hanging were controversial also:

Let us assume, for the sake of argument, that it was nothing more than misfortune that made you a willing instrument in the organization of mass murder: there still remains the fact that you have carried out, and therefore actively supported, a policy of mass murder. For politics is not like the nursery: in politics obedience and support are the same. And just as you supported and carried out a policy of not wanting to share the earth with the Jewish people and the people of a number of other nations—as though you and your superiors had any right to determine who should and who should not inhabit the world—we find that no one, that is, no member of the human race, can be expected to want to share the earth with you. This is the reason, and the only reason, you must hang.[18]

The reaction to Arendt's articles is in retrospect easy to understand but was at the time somewhat unexpected. In a fascinating exchange of letters between Gershom Scholem and Arendt, the issues behind the issues become clear. Scholem, a German Jew by birth and a leading scholar on Jewish mysticism, left Germany for Palestine in the 1920s. Scholem was part of an important German Jewish circle of intellectuals, writers, and artists in the 1920s that included Walter Benjamin. Scholem begins his letter to Arendt by noting the difficulties and complexities inherent in writing about the catastrophe of European Jewry. Yet it seems to him that at each decisive juncture of her analysis the weakness of the Jewish people is emphasized, her work thus losing a sense of objectivity and "acquiring overtones of malice." In fact, so much of this malice is present that Scholem is left with a sensation of bitterness and shame toward and for Arendt. To his question of why he should have such a feeling, Scholem answers:

In the Jewish tradition there is a concept, hard to define and yet concrete enough, which we know as *Ahabath Israel,* "Love of the Jewish people. . . ." In you, dear Hannah, as in so many intellectuals who came from the German left, I find little trace of this. A discussion such as is attempted in your book would seem to me to require—you will forgive my mode of expression—the most old-fashioned, the most circumspect, the most exacting treatment possible—precisely because of the feelings aroused by this matter, this matter of the destruction of one-third of our people—and I regard you wholly as daughter of our people, and in no other way. Thus I have little sympathy with that tone—well expressed by the English word "flippancy"—which you employ so often in the course of your book.

Arendt's response to Scholem is striking. To the trouble Scholem had with regard to Arendt's love of the Jewish people, she writes:

I found it puzzling that you should write "I regard you wholly as a daughter of our people, and in no other way." The truth is I have never pretended to be anything else or to be in any way other than I am, and I have never even felt tempted in that direction. It would have been like saying that I was a man, not a woman—that is to say, kind of insane. I know, of course, that there is a "Jewish problem" even on this level, but it has never been my problem—not even in my childhood. I have always regarded my Jewishness as one of the indisputable factual data of my life, and I have never had the wish to change or disclaim facts of this kind. There is such a thing as a basic gratitude for everything that is as it is; for what has been *given* and was not, could not be, *made;* for the things that are *physei* and not *nomq*. To be sure, such an attitude is pre-political, but in exceptional circumstances—such as the circumstances of Jewish politics—it is bound to have also political consequences though, as it were, in a negative way. This attitude makes certain types of behavior impossible—indeed precisely those which you chose to read into my consideration.[19]

Arendt predicted much earlier in relation to the question of Palestine what she experienced directly in controversy surrounding her interpretation of Eichmann. The issue would revolve around Jewish unity rather than thought, demonstrable commitment to a people rather than rootedness in a people as a platform for free inquiry.

It would be frivolous to deny the intimate connection between this mood on the part of Jews everywhere and the recent European catastrophe, with the subsequent fantastic injustice and callousness toward the surviving remnant that were thereby so ruthlessly transformed into displaced persons. The result has been an amazing and rapid change in what we call national character. After two thousand years of "Galut mentality," the Jewish people have suddenly ceased to believe in survival as an ultimate good in itself and have gone over in a few years to the opposite extreme. Now Jews believe in fighting at any price and feel that "going down" is a sensible method of politics.

Unanimity of opinion is a very ominous phenomenon, and one characteristic of our modern mass age. It destroys social and personal life, which is based on the fact that we are different by nature and by conviction. To hold different opinions and to be aware that other people think differently on the same issue shields us from that god-like certainty which stops all discussion and reduces social relationships to those of an ant heap. A unanimous public opinion tends to eliminate bodily those who differ, for mass unanimity does not stop at certain well-defined objects, but spreads like an infection into every related issue.[20]

And thus the crux of the matter that Arendt exemplifies: Arendt's critical thought is challenged primarily through questions that threaten to close off the dialogue. For her, the reality of Jewishness is a given, a way of entering a broader history and making a contribution to it that at the same time is a contribution to her own people. To Arendt, Zionism, anti-Jewishness, even the mass murder of Jews in Europe involves political questions, influenced by culture and religion and imbedded in a concrete historical context capable of being analyzed and transformed. Indeed, this is the task of the postwar world in which the Jewish people have a role: to recreate a civilization worthy of the name. It is in this context of the recreation of a livable world that Jewish contributions are needed and Jewish life safeguarded.

The reasons for Arendt's ability to see these questions, to analyze them, and to continue on through legitimate and malicious criticism are instructive. Important is her connection with and independence from two cultures, European and Jewish. To be sure, the marginalized status is a difficult one, but it is one that allows her to draw on the riches of European and Jewish culture while remaining free from the confines of both. In a sense she draws upon and participates in a dialogue between cultures that has often been bloody but that she continues to believe, even after the Holocaust, could help lay the foundations for a world beyond death and destruction. Her intuitions as well as her intellectual vision encompass the need for dialogue partners.

If Hannah Arendt was part of the secular hidden tradition of Jewish life, basing her critical thought from both European and Jewish culture, Martin Buber might be seen as an example of the religious aspect of the hidden tradition. Like Arendt, Buber was a refugee from Nazi Germany and supported a Jewish homeland. While Arendt was in the early sixties becoming one of the best known and controversial secular Jewish philosophers, Buber was similarly known and controversial as a preeminent biblical and religious scholar.

Though there are many aspects of Buber's theology that warrant discussion, as does his Zionism, which was close to that of Magnes and Arendt, what is important here is Buber's ability to develop a theology that supports Jewish renewal in a way that reopens the Jewish dialogue with the world, often without use of overt theological language. In fact, for Buber, this was the cornerstone of theology: genuine conversation lay at the heart of the religious quest.

As someone who lived through the darkness of Europe and who struggled for an autonomous and integrative solution in Arab and Jewish

Palestine, Buber was hardly shielded from the demands of the hour. He recognized the faith questions raised by recent history and outlined them in his book *Eclipse of God*, published in 1952.

> Such is the nature of this hour. But what of the next? It is a modern superstition that the character of an age acts as fate for the next. One lets it prescribe what is possible to do and hence what is permitted. One surely cannot swim against the stream, one says. But perhaps one can swim with a new stream whose source is still hidden? In another image, the I-Thou relation has gone into the catacombs—who can say with how much greater power it will step forth! Who can say when the I-It relation will be directed anew to its assisting place and activity!
>
> The most important events in the history of that embodied possibility called man are the occasionally occurring beginnings of new epochs, determined by forces previously invisible or unregarded. Each age is, of course, a continuation of the preceding one, but a continuation can be confirmation and it can be a refutation.
>
> Something is taking place in the depths that as yet needs no name. To-morrow even it may happen that it will be beckoned to from the heights, across the heads of the earthly archons. The eclipse of the light of God is no extinction; even to-morrow that which has stepped in between may give way.[21]

But again, like Arendt, though from a religious perspective, Buber articulates theological questions posed by World War II and the Holocaust both to the Jewish community and to the world. For Buber, the questions are common ones, and though particularity in language and tradition is important, it is in contributing to the whole of humanity that the mission of each people is to be fulfilled. True, Buber's understanding of particularity and universality are pronounced from the beginning of his work. What is amazing and instructive is that despite the century and his experience in it, Buber maintains that understanding over time. Neither the Holocaust nor the state of Israel overwhelms his theological ability to see clearly.

Like Arendt, Buber maintained a dialectical tension between Jewish and European culture, though Buber's dialectic involves greater immersion in the Jewish community. However, even within the Jewish community Buber maintained another subtle yet sometimes overt distance. His critical Zionism within Israel, lived over three decades, is one example, but theological and liturgical matters also play their role. Because of his sense of the living word refusing codification and systematization, Buber had great difficulty with his Orthodox brethren; his argument with the rationalization of Jewish life in western Europe and his proposal for immediacy and depth of religious experience occasioned angry exchanges with the great chronicler of Jewish mysticism Gershom Scholem, and with other Jews divorced from religion altogether. The ironic quality of his position within the Jewish community is found here: the most famous religious Jew in the world hardly set foot inside a synagogue.[22]

Buber's isolation within the Jewish community allowed him to remain in contact even with those who had forced him into exile and attempted to annihilate his people. Thus when in September 1953, within a decade after the liberation of the death camps, Buber was invited to Germany to accept the Peace Prize of the German Book Trade at Frankfurt am Main, he agreed. His accepting of the prize, indeed, his agreeing to publicly acknowledge being in Germany, was as controversial as, and in some ways anticipated, the reception to be accorded Arendt's *Eichmann in Jerusalem*.

Buber delivered his acceptance speech, "Genuine Conversation and the Possibilities of Peace," to an audience of tens of thousands listening through loudspeakers. Buber began his talk with a discussion of the Holocaust:

> About a decade ago a considerable number of German men—there must have been several thousands of them—under the indirect command of the German government and under the direct command of its representatives, killed millions of my people and my fellow-believers in a systematically prepared and executed procedure, the organized cruelty of which cannot be compared with any earlier historical event. I, who am one of those who remained alive, have only in a formal sense a common humanity to those who took part in this action in any capacity. They have so radically removed themselves from the human sphere, so transposed themselves into a sphere of monstrous inhumanity inaccessible to my power of conception, that not even hatred, much less an overcoming of hatred, could have arisen in me. And who am I that I should here presume to "forgive"?

Buber continued:

> When I think of the German people of the days of Auschwitz and Treblinka, I see, first of all, the great many who knew that the monstrous event was taking place and did not oppose it. But my heart, which tells me of the weakness of men, refuses to condemn my neighbor because he was not able to bring himself to become a martyr. Next there emerges before me the mass of those who remained ignorant of what was withheld from the German public, but also did not undertake to discover what reality lay behind the rumors which were circulating. When I think of these men, I am seized by the thought of the anxiety—likewise well-known to me—of

the human creature before a truth which he fears that he cannot stand. But finally there appears before me, from reliable reports, some who have become as familiar to me by sight, action, and voice as if they were friends—those who refused to carry out or to continue to carry out the orders and suffered death or put themselves to death, or those who learned what was taking place and opposed it and were put to death, or those who learned what was taking place and because they could do nothing to stop it killed themselves. I see these men very near before me in that special intimacy which binds us at times to the dead and to them alone; and now reverence and love for these German men fills my heart.[23]

Having made the distinctions among those who were complicit, those who were ignorant and silent, and those who opposed mass death, and identifying personally with the difficulties inherent in each response, Buber then shifts to the contemporary struggle, preparation for the "final battle of *homo humanus* against *homo antihumanus.*" For Buber, this struggle cuts across national and religious lines to become a solidarity—Germans and Jews alike—in the battle for a true humanity. This act of solidarity is the task of the survivor, who "must obey precisely there where the never-to-be effaced memory of what has happened stands in opposition to it." The task of the survivor and all those throughout the world who stand on the side of the human is to rekindle the conversation of peace, genuine conversation whose foundation despite all is trust.[24]

Seen through the persons of Arendt and Buber, the hidden tradition as expressed in the first half of the twentieth century comes into view. In it, there is a willingness to stay in tension, to maintain a critical distance while being fully involved in communal, national, and international affairs. And there is further a grounding in tradition, humanist and religious, that does not seek to subvert one with the other or place them together in a false unity. An instructive example of this critical interaction is how both Arendt and Buber, Jews who gathered at the Eichmann trial, as did the entire world, differed about the sentence. As we have seen, Arendt favored the death penalty; Buber opposed it. "I do not accept the state's right to take the life of any man," Buber wrote, ". . . as long as it depends on us, we should not kill, neither as individuals nor as a society." In a statement given to *Newsweek*, Buber said: "The death sentence has not diminished the crime—on the contrary, all this exasperates the souls of men . . . killing awakens killing." Buber's proposal for Eichmann's punishment was as controversial as Arendt's reports from the Eichmann trial in Jerusalem. As a symbol of the Holocaust, Eichmann should be given a life sentence working on a kibbutz farming the soil of Israel. This would force Eichmann to confront the fact that he and the Nazis had failed, for the Jewish people live on.[25]

Perhaps this tension of secular and religious in the hidden tradition is best exemplified by the German critic and philosopher Walter Benjamin, a friend of both Arendt and Buber, who committed suicide during World War II to avoid being arrested by the French police. In his "Treatise on History," written in the spring of 1940 shortly before his death, Benjamin sees the forces of material history shaped and challenged by a theological voice that is hidden and too often employed by the powerful to legitimate injustice. Though "wizened" and kept out of sight, theological insight speaks for the dead and the dying in a world of power; its weak "messianic" power is subversive of those who use politics and theology to murder. Here Benjamin sees the continual need to prevent politics and theology from becoming a "tool of the ruling class." Thus the task of every generation is to "wrest tradition away from a conformism that is about to overpower it." The role of the historian is to keep politics and theology honest by speaking for the dead. The hidden quality of Benjamin's theological insights can be found in the following passage from his treatise:

> A Klee painting named *Angelus Novus* shows an angel looking as though he is about to move away from something he is fixedly contemplating. His eyes are staring, his mouth is open, his wings are spread. This is how one pictures the angel of history. His face is turned toward the past. Where we perceive a chain of events, he sees one single catastrophe which keeps piling wreckage upon wreckage and hurls it in front of his feet. The angel would like to stay, awaken the dead, and make whole what has been smashed. But a storm is blowing from Paradise; it has caught in his wings with such violence that the angel can no longer close them. This storm irresistibly propels him into the future to which his back is turned, while the pile of debris before him grows skyward. This storm is what we call progress.[26]

Benjamin concludes his essay.

> The soothsayers who found out from time what it had in store certainly did not experience time as either homogeneous or empty. Anyone who keeps this in mind will perhaps get an idea of how past times were experienced in remembrance—namely, in just the same way. We know that the Jews were prohibited from investigating the future. The Torah and the prayers instruct them in remembrance, however. This stripped the future of its magic, to which all those succumb who turn to the soothsayers for enlightenment. This does not imply, however, that for the Jews the future turned into homogeneous, empty time. For every second of time was the strait gate through which the Messiah might enter.[27]

Benjamin's insight: our experience forbids us to conceive history in fundamentally theological terms, however little one thought to try to write it in atheological terms.

What Benjamin adds to the secular-religious dialogue of Arendt and Buber is the subversive quality of not only being on the boundary of Jewish and European culture, and not only being in a critical dialogue with the humanist or religious traditions, but also being within a critical tension of secular and religious within oneself and by extension within the larger community. The challenge for Arendt and Buber is the war-torn secular and religious traditions and the recreation of values that might guide the Jewish community and the world. However, for Benjamin, the goal is always to keep both traditions honest by subverting their tendency to conform to power.[28]

It is here that the challenge of Arendt, Buber, and Benjamin comes into focus. To desert, in a time of crisis, the boundary position between cultures, within a tradition, or even between traditions within oneself, is to jeopardize the possibility of genuine conversation and thus abandon the subversive aspect of the boundary itself. The person and the community, instead of critically interacting with history, are in danger of being overwhelmed by it. To be sure, the Holocaust, Eichmann, and Jerusalem look very different from the vantage point of the hidden tradition than from Holocaust theology, but one sees a challenge to the broken dialectic, the self-absorption, the sense of isolation we have analyzed earlier.

The triumph of Holocaust theology in the late 1960s and early 1970s, coinciding with Buber's and Arendt's deaths in 1965 and 1975, respectively, spelled the end of the hidden tradition of European Jewry. This tradition, which had given so much to the world, had in fact ceased to exist as a fertile ground of Jewish critical thought with the Nazi rise to power in the 1930s and certainly with the discovery of the death camps in 1945. First and foremost, German Jewry and other great centers of Jewish life literally ceased to exist with the Holocaust, and the major Jewish population of the world shifted to the United States and Israel. The territory, culture, and questions raised by this shift were clearly different from those in Europe, and the events themselves, Holocaust and Israel, the concentration on the singularity of Jewish suffering and the actual empowerment of Jews in Israel, began to narrow the opinions and perceived options of the Jewish people. Those who spoke within the hidden tradition were those whose primary formation occurred before and in the first few years after the war. Simply stated, Arendt, Buber, and Benjamin are historically impossible to ideologically replicate.

The narrowing of the secular and religious options is instructive and today can now be seen more clearly with the hidden tradition in mind. Today one is either secular or religious, a humanist or a practicing Jew. In the secular community one is either a leftist or a businessperson completely cut off from the religious Jewish community. To be Jewish in this sense is to remember the Holocaust and to support Israel, politically and financially. To be religious is to attend synagogue, to remember the Holocaust and support Israel. A progressive Jew with religious tendencies—that is, a critical thinker—feels, and in some ways is, unwelcome in the organized Jewish community. An overtly religious critical thinker is likewise in limbo. Those who carry forward the tradition of dissent of Magnes and Chomsky and the hidden tradition of Arendt and Buber have no place to call home.

However, the revival of the hidden tradition so important to the future of the Jewish community does not begin *ex novo*, and it cannot avoid the themes articulated by Holocaust theology. For in the final analysis it is Jewish suffering and Jewish empowerment and the articulation of both by Holocaust theology that brings the European phase of the hidden tradition to an end. Holocaust theologians understand correctly that if after Holocaust and empowerment any future boundary position is possible, it has to emerge within the formative events of our time. That is, they succeed in creating a framework for Jewish commitment and articulation after the European catastrophe and with the rebirth of the Jewish nation, but paradoxically a framework over which they have little control. The Holocaust is of course finished and waiting to be interpreted; Israel emerges as an actual state power, something that Wiesel and Fackenheim hardly understand and that Greenberg strains to cope with. In this they represent a significant portion of the Jewish people, torn, as Feuerlicht comments, between Jewish ethics and Israeli power. Stated another way, they are Jews torn between the remembrance of suffering and the reality of an independent and powerful state that they do not control but must always legitimate—thus the strained arguments, the twisted logic, the shrill voices. In short, as many voices of the tradition of dissent have pointed out, the Jewish people are entangled in a contradiction of incredible proportions to which there seems no egress. To continue in this way is to continue to manufacture half-truths and lies, to justify thoughts and ideas that would not be justifiable in any other arena.

Paradoxically, Holocaust theology contains aspects of the hidden tradition itself. The early writings of Irving Greenberg are important here. His understanding that after the Holocaust the testing of authenticity occurs in the presence of the burning children; his discussion of moment faiths, "moments when Redeemer and vision of redemption are present, interspersed with times when the flames and smoke of the burning children blot out faith—though it flickers again"; his announced end of the easy dichotomy of atheism and theism, both of them now within each person—all point to a renewed understanding of the hidden tradition. As Greenberg recognizes, his understanding of "moment faiths" derives in part from Buber's "moment Gods," in which God is known momentarily and God's presence and our awareness are fused in life, though these moments are interspersed with the routine and the more mundane. Greenberg appropriately understands that historical events have forced a new appropriation of Buber, in effect, adjusting for the demonic in culture and society. In short, Holocaust theologians have had it in mind to overcome a certain innocence about the reality and potentiality of life that was present even in many of the survivors. As Greenberg points out at the conclusion of his 1974 essay, and which he prophetically comments is the task of his future work, the Holocaust demands above all a redistribution of power. "No one should ever have to depend again on anyone else's good will or respect for their basic security and right to exist. The Jews of Europe needed that good will and these good offices desperately and the democracies and the church and the communists and their fellow Jews failed them. . . . To argue dependence on law, on human goodness, or universal equality is to join the ranks of those who would like to repeat the Holocaust." Though this statement seems incredibly broad and universal in its application, taking the Jewish experience as paradigmatic for the world, one can see already in 1974 (and still more so later) the thrust of the analysis: Jews have been betrayed even by their own. No one will ever betray us again.[29]

Yet it is the absolute refusal of betrayal, the absolute fear of vulnerability—what in short can become the absolute fear of the world—that has betrayed the original dialectical tensions of Holocaust theology and overwhelmed the aspects of the hidden tradition buried within it. The betrayal takes place in the insistence that empowerment and the organization of that empowerment, especially in the state of Israel, cannot be questioned, that empowerment has reached the status of a sacred symbol that must be legitimated at every turn. The question of vulnerability and renewed openness to the world is subsumed by the principle of empowerment. The prophetic is consumed by the sign of a maturity that now lies in correcting abuses of a power that cannot be controlled and that in its essence is beyond questioning.

A Coalition of Messianic Trust

Perhaps, paradoxically, it is in dialogue with our former enemies, Western Christians, and our present "enemies," Palestinians, that the possibility of Jewish renewal of the hidden tradition can take place. Such a dialogue addresses the two formative events of our time—Holocaust and Israel—and provides an avenue for healing and repentance so crucial to the emergence of critical thought. Only after healing and repentance can the commanding voice of Auschwitz be realized in its particularity with its universal implications and the liturgy of destruction expanded so that we can be honest with ourselves. It is in this framework that our relation to Holocaust and Israel may move beyond innocence and redemption, which have become for Jews and Palestinians burdensome and oppressive.

If Martin Buber led the way in the 1950s with a willingness to reach out to the German people, it is Johann Baptist Metz, a German Catholic theologian, and Gustavo Gutierrez, a Latin American liberation theologian, who provide glimpses of the difficult path from the Christian side, as well as the possibility of life for Jews beyond the Holocaust.

Metz's essay "Christians and Jews After Auschwitz" is worth contemplating in this regard. He begins with a question to his fellow Christians: "Will we actually allow Auschwitz to be the end point, the disruption which it really was, the catastrophe of our history, out of which we can find a way only through a radical change of direction achieved via new standards of action? Or will we see it only as a monstrous accident within this history but not affecting history's course?" Metz answers his own question by asserting that the future of Christianity is dependent on an affirmative answer to the first question: a radical change of direction is demanded. However, this cannot be accomplished through abstract reflection on dogma or even on the complicity of the Church; it cannot be accomplished by personal Christian reflection or even institutional action alone. The change can occur only by embracing the suffering and the heirs of that suffering.[30]

According to Metz, Christians are from now on "assigned to the victims of Auschwitz—assigned, in fact, in an alliance belonging to the very heart of saving history." Thus Metz considers insulting and incomplete any attempts at Christian theology and language about meaning when they are initiated outside the Holocaust or try in some way to transcend it. Meaning, especially divine meaning, can be invoked only to the extent that such meaning was not abandoned in Auschwitz itself.

This is why Metz responds to the question whether it is possible for a Christian to pray after Auschwitz in the affirmative: "We can pray after Auschwitz because people prayed *in* Auschwitz."[31]

Metz's understanding of history is dynamic, as a calling forth of memory and as a movement into the future. The alliance Metz projects within saving history, that is, within the particularity of being Jewish and Christian but also somehow affecting both together at the deepest level, is a call to the common task of resistance, that might include new suffering. This saving historical alliance would, in the first instance, mean the radical end of every persecution of Jews by Christians, surely an understandable goal of dialogue. But again, Metz moves beyond dialogue. If any persecution were to take place in the future, it could only be a persecution together, of Jews and Christians—*as it was in the beginning*. The reason for this common persecution in the beginning—the refusal to recognize the Roman emperor as God that called into question the foundations of Rome's political religion and thus branded Christians and Jews as atheists—is a call to political activity in the contemporary world. Still more, however, is the vision of embrace that arises from this analysis. Metz cautiously suggests that Jews and Christians could arrive one day at a "coalition of messianic trust in opposition to the apotheosis of banality and hatred present in our world." Thus the memory of suffering is a call beyond dialogue to an embrace that lies at the very root of the struggle to be faithful in a world of injustice and oppression.[32]

Metz calls Christians to carry the victims of their history with them into the future. Put more strongly, there is no future for Christianity unless the victims of Christian history are heard in the present. But can the victims of Christian history embrace their oppressors? Can the victims of Christian history, in this case the Jews, specifically in the contemporary manifestation of the Holocaust, enter this coalition of messianic trust by choice, open to the transformations that lie before them, including the possibility of persecution? Is the call of Auschwitz the same for Jews as it is for Christians? And if we know that only a minority of Christians has embarked on the road that Metz so hauntingly outlines, can we expect more than a minority of Jews to see such a road as possible after Auschwitz? And what does it mean if a minority of Jews and Christians affirms this coalition of messianic trust—not in the theological abstraction but in political action that may lead to suffering?

Though, for Gustavo Gutierrez, the answers are far from clear, the questions raised by the Holocaust are present in his own people. Queried whether, because of the suffering he witnesses, Gutierrez doubts the existence of God, he responds, "Existence no; God's presence everyday." Here Latin American theologians are quite close to Holocaust theologians. That is why Elie Wiesel can feel a camaraderie with Gutierrez, expressed in a greeting on the occasion of Gutierrez's sixtieth birthday.

> I feel very close to Gustavo Gutierrez, even though we have not met one another. We share a common passion for Job—whose situation intrigues and saddens us at the same time—and a need to believe that God has not abandoned creation. Some theologians would describe our approach as "liberative." And indeed, why not? I feel at home with the term "liberation." Because we are created in the image of God, we human beings ought to be free just as God is free. And, like God, we should want to be vehicles of freedom for others. Or, to put it another way, those persons are truly human who recognize themselves in the freedom of others, and who measure the extent of their own freedom by its relationship to that of their fellow human beings. It was in order that we might be free that God chose to create us. Persons who live in fear, in oppression, in hunger, in misery, are not free. What remains free, however, is their thirst for freedom, their desire to free themselves—the part of them that God, as only God can do, loves to enlighten in the fulfillment of hope.
>
> Yes, I feel very close to Gustavo Gutierrez. Along with him, I believe that God is not an abstraction but a living presence. To the prisoner, God represents memory, to the starving, a smile; and to the wandering exile, a companion on the way.
>
> The mystical tradition teaches us that even God is in exile. In the process of freeing the oppressed from their oppression, and the humiliated from their shame, we are likewise freeing God.[33]

Gustavo Gutierrez's recent meditation on the Book of Job is also important in this emerging solidarity of Christians and Jews. If for Metz the ability to pray continues for Christians after Auschwitz because some Jews continued to pray in Auschwitz, and if this connection allows a coalition of messianic trust in the future as once existed in the past, Gutierrez's thought allows Jews to see the possibility of God amid suffering as a call to commitment within the present.

Gutierrez's book *On Job* revolves around the question of how one can speak about God amid suffering, especially the suffering of the innocent. "How are we to talk about a God who is revealed as love in a situation characterized by poverty and oppression? How are we to proclaim the God of life to men and women who die prematurely and unjustly? How are we to acknowledge that God makes us a free gift of love and justice when we have before us the suffering of the innocent?"[34]

Gutierrez begins by differentiating between the questions that modernity poses, that is, how it is possible to believe in God in a world of technology, science, and affluence—questions posed to the Western

Christian world—and the question that innocent suffering poses to those on the margins of society, that is, how it is possible to believe in God when your experience is one of abuse and injustice, as it too often is in the Third World. For Gutierrez, the distinction of these two situations is illustrated in the difference between Blaise Pascal, the great European philosopher, and Job:

> In Pascal's case, the wager has to do with the existence or nonexistence of God. The question Pascal asks is: "Which will you choose?" In Job the choice is between a religion based on the rights and obligations of human beings as moral agents, and a disinterested belief based on the gratuitousness of God's love. Pascal employs a crystal-clear, almost mathematical logic in responding to the questionings of the modern mind and the first manifestations of unbelief. In Job the challenges arising from the suffering of the innocent are met in a tortuous trial in which progress is made through a series of violent jolts. Pascal warns that a choice must be made between unbelief and God, and points out that not to choose is to choose: "You must wager. There is no choice; you are already committed." In Job the choice is between a religion that sets conditions for the action of God and applies a calculus to it, and a faith that acknowledges the free initiative at work in God's love; to make no choice is to live in despair or cynicism.[35]

For Gutierrez, Pascal issues his wager to bourgeois nonbelievers; the wager in Job is issued in the world of the nonpersons. Pascal's wager is the first step to meet the challenge of modernity; the wager in Job starts on the garbage heap.[36]

According to Gutierrez, Job undergoes two transformations of viewpoint as he begins to reject the doctrine of retribution for the suffering of the innocent. The first occurs when he realizes that the suffering of the innocent is broader than his own individual suffering and that the real issue is the suffering and injustice that mark the lives of the poor: "Those who believe in God must therefore try to lighten the burden of the poor by helping them and practicing solidarity with them." The speeches of God to Job occasion the second shift, in which Job begins to understand that justice is found within a horizon of freedom formed by the gratuitousness of God's love. Thus the Book of Job for Gutierrez poses two types of language about God, the language of prophecy, which opposes at every turn the suffering of the innocent, and the language of contemplation, which within the commitment to justice allows a vision beyond the present and the actual. "In the Book of Job, to be a believer means sharing human suffering, especially that of the most destitute, enduring a spiritual struggle, and finally accepting the fact that God cannot be pigeonholed in human categories." In contemporary times this is what Luis Espinal, a priest murdered in Bolivia, was doing when he wrote: "Train us, Lord, to fling ourselves upon the impossible, for behind the impossible is your grace and your presence; we cannot fall into emptiness. The future is an enigma, our road is covered with mist, but we want to go on giving ourselves, because you continue hoping amid the night and weeping tears through a thousand human eyes." For Gutierrez, this is what Job did: "He flung himself into an enigmatic future. And in this effort he met the Lord."[37]

Thus the questions of Job are contemporary questions for the poor and suffering of Latin America. They are for Gutierrez similar questions to the ones faced in the Jewish Holocaust. Yet while the questions flowing from the Holocaust remain, the suffering has ended. For Latin Americans, however, the suffering increases daily. Gutierrez sees the Holocaust as an "inescapable challenge to the Christian conscience and an inexcusable reproach to the silence of many Christians" during the Nazi period, but for Latin Americans the question is not precisely "How are we to do theology after Auschwitz?"

> The reason is that in Latin America we are still experiencing every day the violation of human rights, murder, and the torture that we find so blameworthy in the Jewish Holocaust of World War II. Our task here is to find the words with which to talk about God in the midst of the starvation of millions, the humiliation of races regarded as inferior, discrimination against women, especially women who are poor, systematic social injustice, a persistent high rate of infant mortality, those who simply "disappear" or are deprived of their freedom, the sufferings of peoples who are struggling for their right to live, the exiles and the refugees, terrorism of every kind, and the corpse-filled common graves of Ayacucho. What we must deal with is not the past but, unfortunately, a cruel present and a dark tunnel with no apparent end.[38]

Therefore in Peru, as in all of Latin America, the question shifts: "How are we to do theology while Ayacucho lasts? How are we to speak of the God of life when cruel murder on a massive scale goes on in 'the corner of the dead'? How are we to preach the love of God amid such profound contempt for human life? How are we to proclaim the resurrection of the Lord where death reigns, and especially the death of children, women, the poor, indigenous, and the 'unimportant' members of our society?"[39]

If Metz and Gutierrez articulate the Jewish and Christian experience of suffering, as well as raise questions about God's presence amid that suffering, Carter Heyward, an Episcopal priest, continues the relation and moves it forward. In her first book, *The Redemption of God: A Theology of Mutual Relation,* Heyward attempts to rethink Christology through the ethical demands of justice and the suffering of the innocent. The Holocaust figures prominently in her analysis, and two chapters of her book deal with the questions of theodicy raised by Elie Wiesel. For Heyward, the questions posed remain; they suggest patterns of relation that bind us as human beings together and in so doing suggest a different way of addressing one another and God. The Holocaust and other human suffering, especially the suffering of women, call Christians to reevaluate their understanding of God and Christology itself. Jesus becomes neither Lord nor divine but rather brother and sister: "Jesus is to be remembered, not revered. Remembering Jesus does not warrant Jesusolatry or Christolatry, idolatry of a male God. Remembering Jesus does not warrant the worshipping of Jesus, but rather compels us to be open to the God of Jesus, the one whom Jesus called 'Abba': Daddy. Moreover, to remember Jesus does not mean that we 'imitate' Jesus, but rather that, like him, we seek to act with God in our own time, under the political, social, psychological, physical, and institutional conditions of our own place." Heyward's reimaging of God and Jesus are to some extent indebted to and remarkably close to the early Wiesel and Irving Greenberg as well.[40]

Heyward's passion for justice takes her deeper into feminist analysis and to many of the troubled areas of the Third World. In August 1984 she, along with other teachers and students of the Episcopal Divinity School in Cambridge, journeyed to Nicaragua to investigate the impact of American foreign policy on the Nicaraguan revolution and the call of Christian faith in response to these policies. For us, the important aspect of Heyward's sojourn among the Nicaraguan people is the discovery of what she terms *revolutionary forgiveness.* This forgiveness of those who have harmed the people, the former guards of Somoza, the contras, and those who arm the contras, the government of the United States, at first startled Heyward and her companions. Yet upon reflection its logic became clear. Revolutionary forgiveness had nothing to do with forgetting injustice but, rather, understanding and overcoming it. To begin with, an important distinction between persons and oppressive systems has to be made, and revolutionary forgiveness has as its corequisite that systems and structures of injustice be changed. Heyward writes:

> Those who forgive must be wise as serpents, and the act of forgiving must be as strategically potent as it is spiritually potent. Which is why, at this time, the Sandinistas cannot forgive the contras. People cannot simply "forgive"—invite back into their lives on a mutual basis—those who continue to do harm to them and their people. We do not believe that any of us can forgive those who continue to violate us. Otherwise "for-

giveness" is an empty word. Forgiveness is possible only when the violence stops. Only then can those who have been violated even consider the possibility of actually loving those who once brutalized and battered them. Only then can the former victims empower the victimizers by helping them to realize their own power to live as liberated liberators, people able to see in themselves and others a corporate capacity to shape the future.[41]

This is how Heyward interpreted Tomas Borge's forgiveness of his torturer: "His act of forgiveness was an invitation—in spite of what had happened—in which Borge was signaling his desire that this man come into right-relation with him and with the Nicaraguan revolutionary movement. To try to forget acts of violence which have been done to us is foolish, probably impossible. To base forgiveness on remembering what happened is to move toward the future in the belief that we will be stronger together than we would be apart. Borge may have determined also that after persons are forgiven they are at least as likely to join those who forgave them as to repeat their violent behavior. Forgiveness can also be a pragmatic political act."[42]

Thus, for Heyward, revolutionary forgiveness hardly sentimentalizes injustice or allows it to continue. Instead, it carries with it a knowledge of power that seeks to transform injustice, to remember as a way of creating a future beyond injustice, to confess in order to acknowledge wrong relations, to repent as a commitment to stop the injustice, and to provide solidarity with the victims of injustice.[43]

Heyward's understanding of revolutionary forgiveness as acts of reconciliation within the context of achieving justice brings us to consider again Rosemary Radford Ruether's description of false messianism as the use of a dream of a redeemed life to cover over lies and deception. False messianism is in opposition to revolutionary forgiveness and undermines the very possibility of breaking the cycle of injustice. We might say that false messianism deliberately makes revolutionary forgiveness impossible as it seeks to label those who see through it as traitors who endanger the existence of the community. Ruether contrasts false messianism with prophetic hope, which seeks a "self-critical and transformative relationship to the divine call and future hope." Prophetic hope judges historical reality by its distance from the ideal rather than covering up this distance with deception. Thus prophetic hope calls the critic to reform reality, beginning with oneself, to bring self and society closer to the divine ideal. "It is by keeping human hopes and ideals as critical measuring rods to judge historical reality, rather than using them as ideological self-sacralization, that one keeps redemptive hopes from being turned into false messianism." The signs of prophetic hope are similar to the process of revolutionary forgiveness. "When one person is not another's evil, one peoples' redemption is not another peoples' damnation. Graced moments are moments of repentance that create reconciliation and overcome enmity."[44]

The importance of the analysis of Christian thought now comes into focus. Metz's search for a coalition of messianic trust, Gutierrez's realization that the massacres of the innocent continue in the corner of the dead, Heyward's revolutionary forgiveness, and Ruether's prophetic hope are all rooted to some extent in the Jewish Holocaust; each attempts to rethink Christian commitment in that light. That is, they have taken the challenge of Jewish history as a confrontation with their own and as a challenge to create a Christianity of justice and compassion. What is ironic is that the process of dialogue has shifted to become a newly thought-out Christian theology challenging Jewish theology and history. Could it be that the issues of trust and forgiveness, suffering in the present and prophetic hope, represent critical thought that cannot (at this point) be generated within the Jewish community? Could it be that the new dialogue partner for the revival of the Jewish hidden tradition will be less modern secular thought than the critical Christianity being fashioned by such theologians as we have analyzed? In touch with the Jewish experience and searching for a Christianity beyond false piety and triumphalism, Metz, Gutierrez, Heyward, and Ruether may be where Arendt and Buber and the deepest inclinations of Wiesel and Greenberg find a connective challenge. But this can only happen if Christians offer and Jews receive critical solidarity, that is, a solidarity that moves beyond frightened silence or paternalistic embrace. Critical solidarity at this point in Jewish history means confronting Jewish theology and policies that legitimate oppression. Here, Ruether is the only one of these theologians to take this most important step. To take the Holocaust seriously without condemning the brutality of the Israeli occupation is no longer enough.[45]

A critical solidarity brought forth through our former enemies may presage a conversion favoring our present "enemies," the Palestinian people. If Metz is correct that Christians in the West can only move forward with the victims of Christianity, the Jewish people, it is also true that the Jewish people can only move forward with the victims of Jewish empowerment, the Palestinian people. In fact, the challenge of the Palestinians in their struggle for freedom and dignity is one that necessitates the revival of critical thought. The issues they raise in their rebellion against oppression are exactly those that are in need of reclamation:

separation of religion and power, the use of Jewish history as a path of generosity rather than oppression, the renewal of Jewish life as a contribution to creative and pluralistic cultures rather than a univocal and thus stultifying imposition of one culture on another. As important is the recognition of Jewish history in the faces of the other: Palestinian suffering, diaspora, ghettoization, deportation, and murder. Emmanuel Levinas, the French Jewish philosopher, wrote that ethics arises out of the face of the other. One might expand this to say that critical thought about the systems of oppression and the theologies that legitimate them arise when we begin to be with and understand those who suffer from that oppression. Paradoxically, the critical thought and ethical possibility ensuing from such an encounter are also a bridge back to the deepest ethical impulses of the very community now betraying those values in oppression. If Jews represent the road back to the values of the Western Christian tradition, Palestinians represent a similar road back to the values of the Jewish tradition. Of course, intent in and of itself is hardly the issue; the Jewish struggle vis-à-vis Christians and the Palestinian struggle vis-à-vis the Jews is the challenge.

Yet beyond challenging others in their very being, Palestinians have also presented concrete avenues to begin the Jewish process of recovering ethics and values. The declaration of a Palestinian state on the West Bank and Gaza, recognition of the state of Israel, in effect nullifying the P.L.O. charter provision calling for the elimination of Israel—all are difficult steps that are practical, concrete invitations to Israel to settle historical grievances and begin anew. And if these seem too sweeping to begin with, other concrete proposals from within the occupied territories have surfaced as a basis for the start of negotiations. At a press conference in January 1988, a broad spectrum of West Bank and Gaza Palestinian leaders and representatives of nationalist institutions demanded that Israel.

> Abide by the 4th Geneva Convention pertaining to the protection of civilians, and declare the Emergency Regulations of the British Mandate null and void.
>
> Comply with Security Council Resolutions 605 and 607 [relating to recent deportations]. . . .
>
> Release all prisoners arrested during the recent uprisings. . . . Rescind all proceedings against them. . . .
>
> Cancel the policy of expulsion and allow all deported Palestinians . . . to return to their homes. . . . Release all administrative detainees. . . . Accept applications for family reunions. . . .
>
> Lift the siege of all Palestinian refugee camps and withdraw the Israeli army from all population centers.

Conduct a formal inquiry into the behavior of soldiers and settlers, and take punitive measures against all those convicted. . . .

Cease all settlement activity and land confiscation and release lands already confiscated. . . . End the harassment of the Arab population by settlers in the West Bank and Gaza and in the Old City of Jerusalem.

Cancel all restrictions on political freedoms including restrictions on freedom of assembly and association. Hold free municipal elections under the supervision of a neutral authority.

Remove restrictions on participation of Palestinians from the territories in the Palestine National Council . . . to ensure a direct input into the decision-making processes of the Palestinian nation by the Palestinians under occupation.[46]

The steps suggested have now been complemented with a foundational approach that enjoins critical thought on both the Jewish and Palestinian sides. Naim Ateek's work analyzed in chapter 4, especially his challenge to Jews to admit that they have wronged the Palestinian people and to Palestinians to understand in a deeper way the European trauma through which Jews have recently passed, provide the foundational approach that, though not probing every issue of concern to either side, allows the themes enunciated earlier—trust, the continuation of suffering in the present, revolutionary forgiveness, and prophetic hope—to develop. Ateek's approach allows a process of insight and activity that moves beyond an ethic of retribution toward a future of mutual involvement, recognition, and ultimately integration. Thus he allows Jews to feel the birth of a Jewish state was necessary if they also admit that from the Palestinian perspective it was also wrong. Palestinians can continue to assert that in the process of building a Jewish state Palestinians were wronged, even as they try to understand the reasons some Jews had for such an undertaking. Ateek thus forces both sides to discard the ideological blinders that mask a false messianism: Jews are no longer innocent; Palestinians will not reclaim all of Palestine. In fact, ultimately the dreams of Jewish innocence or Palestinian restoration will give way to a desire to live in a creative environment of mutual trust that, after a long and bloody history, brings out the best in both peoples.[47]

The Revival of Critical Thought

The revival of the hidden tradition of Jewish life, that is, the resumption of a boundary position vis-à-vis political and religious power, is joined by those Western Christians and those Palestinians of

Christian and Muslim background who seek a path beyond injustice and suffering. Thus, a new political and theological framework for the Jewish people is suggested as Western Christians and Palestinians similarly search out a framework requisite to the history within which they are living. It could be that the boundary position once located between the Jewish community and European civilization is now to be found at the intersection of the Jewish, Western Christian, and Palestinian communities. If we take as the task of theology the creation of a framework to nurture the questions a people needs to ask about the history it is creating, it is here in the intermingling of difficult and bloody histories that a future may be born.

First and foremost, this new configuration suggests that deabsolutization of Israel is crucial to Jewish politics and theology. Jews are essentially a diaspora people who choose to live among the peoples of the world. In essence, understanding this relativizes the geographic location of any particular Jewish community while appreciating the specific qualities of each; we begin for example to speak about the Jewish community in America and the Jewish community in Israel and Palestine. The communal organization of each community and its relation to its neighbors is less defining and more flexible, responding to the needs of the hour rather than defending an imposed order that no longer serves those needs. It may be that at this point a state organization of the Jewish community of Israel is important, but that hardly means forever. Realizing this frees Jewish theology from legitimating a state that is simply an organizational tool that furthers or hinders the essential hope of the community. In the case of the Jewish community, legitimating the state of Israel means also becoming court theologians in the United States in order to ensure its economic and military aid to Israel. As Christians found out long ago, and Jews are beginning to find out today, theologies that legitimate states tend to legitimate injustice. As I. F. Stone, a secular Jewish journalist, once remarked, "all governments are liars," and though it is startling to many Jews, Israel as a state is hardly exempt.[48]

Deabsolutizing the state of Israel means at the same time de-absolutizing the Holocaust. The effect is to rescue the Holocaust both from trivilization and a dramatization that ultimately sees the Holocaust as part of the Jewish future rather than its past. Placing the Holocaust in its historical framework also liberates Israel from the throes of redemption, a function it cannot fulfill. The Holocaust then regains its historical call to end the suffering of the Jewish people and all peoples, including and especially the Palestinian people. Thus the particular experience of suffering speaks to a world of suffering rather than simply to Jews. The call becomes one of solidarity and connectedness rather than to an affirmation characterized with anger and the experience of isolation. The dialectics of suffering and empowerment, innocence and redemption, specialness and normalization surfaced in chapter 1 are confronted and transformed by this solidarity. As Jewish theology is freed from state building in Israel and state supporting in the United States, its vocation as an agent of critical reflection becomes possible again.

In this framework Israel becomes, at one level, a state like any other, capable of good and bad but unworthy of ultimate loyalty. Thus the framework of statehood is relativized even as the bonds between Jewish communities may grow stronger. What once evoked a theological commitment immune from criticism is now returned to its rightful place in the political arena, deserving of respect when functioning as an agent of justice, subject to criticism from the perspective of Jewish history and theology. A major element of this critical relationship to the state is helping the state bring the Jewish people into closer proximity to the Palestinian people. If the state succeeds in this task, then it paradoxically acts less like a state and more like an agent of Jewish ethics.

Jews have too often been confused on this point; to do what is necessary in Israel and Palestine means challenging a rhetoric that says that the state of Israel is completely different from other states. Solidarity with the Palestinian people means preparing for a transformation of the Jewish state into something else, perhaps a confederation or even a unified state with autonomous and integrated communities, much like the structures the early dissenters in Zion spoke of. All states are "liars"; all states seek perpetuation of their structure as a matter of course. However, the revival of critical thought may push the state of Israel to do what states are loath to do—act beyond their perceived and often enshrined interests.

The politics of Israel, even its military operations, assumes a different place in light of Jewish critical thought. Again, the challenge is whether these elements of Israel broaden the intersection of Jew and Palestinian, Jew and Arab, or narrow it. The myth of Israel's weakness is debunked by a concrete and critical evaluation of its power, and future conflicts are relegated to the business of statecraft, rather than the fear of another holocaust. The responsibility for preventing a military defeat is first and foremost a political venture to minimize the possibility of conflict. But where the interests of a state are served by exacerbating conflict then military victory or defeat can be looked at with a critical eye. At any rate, it is crucial to demythologize what every state at some point in its history experiences, military defeat. Israel's power in the Middle East is superior at this point, but in the last two wars, the Yom Kippur War in 1973 and the invasion of Lebanon in 1982, Israel, though not defeated, could hardly claim victory.[49]

It must be stated unequivocally that a military defeat of Israel would be from the Jewish Israeli side horrible, but in no way comparable to the Holocaust. Defeat would represent a political and military failure of a state organization with consequences for the Jewish community living in that state. It would represent a failure of an empowered community to come to grips with its environment. But it would not threaten the continuation of the Jewish people, as so often prophesied by Holocaust theologians. To consider military defeat is merely to prevent the kind of thinking that makes such defeat almost inevitable. The time for Israel to seek peace—which can only come with justice—is now, while the state has superior power. To see its success in war as redemptive or its failure in war as another holocaust is to take from the state of Israel responsibility for its primary role: to be a vehicle at this point in history in minimizing and then overcoming the division of Jew and Palestinian.

To shift perspectives on Holocaust and Israel is to refashion the current trends of Jewish identity, at least as defined by Jewish institutional leadership and Jewish theology. Rather than avoiding the perils of statecraft or responsibility, as Greenberg suggests, the framework for Jewish identity must question the process of normalizing that which was and ought today to be considered abnormal. Because Jews as a people are no longer innocent, and because Jews are in danger of becoming everything we loathed about our oppressors, Jews must use this experience to choose a new direction. The shift in Jewish identity occurs not by bypassing the formative events of Jewish history, the Holocaust and the state of Israel, but by reevaluating them in the light of Jewish experience with suffering and power. The task is not so much realizing the imperfections of exerting power but reorienting that power before it is too late. The stories of the broken clubs and Mengele are less exaggerations or aberrations than warnings that the entire history of Jewish suffering and struggle is in danger of being perverted, becoming in a strange twist that against which it protests. This warning also expresses intuitive connections with the Palestinian people. When today we speak of the formative events of Holocaust and Israel, Jews need to add the experience of the Palestinian people as a formative event for the Jewish people as well. To do so brings Jews beyond innocence and redemption to a posture of humility and confession. Could it be that underneath the expressions of

Jewish pride and power lies the desire to be free of the limitations they impose? Could it be that Jews know they are wrong and are looking for a way beyond the oppression of others?

At the intersection of Jewish, Western Christian, and Palestinian thought and activity lies the revival of the hidden tradition of Jewish life. It is here that the most intimate and urgent questions are raised. And it is from this particular configuration that the future contribution of the Jewish people to the world will be made. That there is no theological movement of any consequence in Jewish life that promotes the revival of the hidden tradition, hence no Jewish theology that promotes critical thought, is a lamentable fact to be faced. The point where Jewish thought meets other traditions thus is often spoken of in secular terminology. The opportunity created by this meeting of traditions may give birth to a theology but is not a theology itself. Hence those who use overt theological language may mistake the revival of the hidden tradition for mere humanism, as if this itself were a critique, while mistaking its theological language for theological integrity. This is as typical of theological orthodoxy as it is of states: mistaking rhetoric for substance. Like the state of Israel, however, contemporary Jewish theology faces a test that portends its own transformation: that is, solidarity with the Palestinian people. This is where the realm of critical thought may join forces with overt religious language and move beyond the division of secular and religious. And here too lies the possibility of moving beyond innocence and redemption, beyond a false normalization, to the deepest impulses of the Jewish people.

Afterword:
The Task Before Us

On 19 June 1967, less than a week after the conclusion of the 1967 war, Bernard Avishai, a Canadian Jew, left for Israel to explore an ambition that his father, who had emigrated from Bialystok to Canada many years earlier, had failed to explore: life in Israel. On June 28, Avishai and a friend of the family, who had fought as a paratrooper in the Old City just days earlier, went to Jerusalem for the first time.

> All morning we walked around the ridges overlooking the Old City; not yet disturbed were markers made of piles of stones and helmets, on places where his friends had been killed. In the baking noon sun, we drove our straining Citroen *deux chevaux* up to the old Mandelbaum Gate, the checkpoint that had divided the Israeli city from the Jordanian since the 1948 war. We'd expected to be stopped there, and had practiced how to con the guard into letting us go on to the Old City. But we found no checkpoint and no guard. Anxiously we flipped on the radio—to hear that the city had been declared united and annexed to Israel just twenty minutes before. The announcer played "Jerusalem of Gold," and tears rolled down my companion's cheeks.[1]

For Avishai, Israel implied something he lacked in Canada, something authentic, continuing, dramatic, even redemptive. In 1972 he and his wife left for Israel to begin a new life, only to return to Canada three years later disappointed with the reality of Israel and realizing that his Jewish roots were not in Israel but in North America.

After his return to Canada he wrote a book, *The Tragedy of Zionism: Revolution and Democracy in the Land of Israel*, that details the contradictions inherent in and the fundamental choices before a Jewish state, that is, Zionism or democracy. In effect, Avishai sees the continuation of

Zionist ideology as the end of the critical thought needed to move beyond Zionism into a pluralistic nation-state framework that provides all its citizens, Jewish and Palestinian, a formal constitution and bill of rights. At the conclusion of his book, Avishai writes of the contradictions of Jewish existence both in Israel and in North America and the difficulty of renewing the spirit and ethical quality of Jewish life. His final lines are haunting:

> In a way, an American Jew may have nothing more to look forward to than being a critic whose subject is the Torah; if spiritual life in the modern world must be vicarious, then better to struggle along with the children of Israel at Sinai than to dance even with the pioneers at Degania. To be sure, deciding to be Jewish because this is interesting is itself an American conceit: Abraham intended to sacrifice Isaac to something more terrible than the pursuit of happiness. But Jewish life will either become more interesting in this country or it will disappear. American Jews will have to retrieve or get at something more skeptical in the Jewish spirit. And some will have to write elegies to the Zionists' tradition, just as the Zionists once wrote elegies to Orthodoxy. This was mine.[2]

We have now in effect come full circle if we add to the elegies of Orthodoxy and Zionism the additional elegy to Holocaust theology that the foregoing analysis represents. The formative events of Jewish life in the twentieth century have spawned and buried so many Jewish movements and ideologies that it is difficult to maintain our balance. Is it the fate of Jews to be divided by movements and tendencies we hardly understand or control? And is not the fascinating panoply of possibilities haunted by the engines of power that chart Jewish destiny without our consent, oppress another people, and in so doing oppress us as well? Yehoshafat Harkabi, professor of international relations and Middle East studies at Hebrew University in Jerusalem, believes that this is Israel's fateful hour and that what is at stake is the survival of Israel and the status of Judaism. Our analysis confirms and moves beyond this statement: what is at stake is everything Jews have stood for, struggled for, and suffered for.[3]

The task before us is to confront that which threatens the foundations of Jewishness, drawing strength from the tradition of dissent and raising up the liturgy of destruction to include both those who persecuted us and those whom Jews persecute today. This is the avenue to critical thought and activity that moves beyond innocence and redemption to recover the ethical tradition at the heart of Judaism. The elegies, as it were, are now complete and ideologies of power relativized. What we are left with are Jewish communities in the United States and England, for example, and a Jewish community in Israel and Palestine organized as a state with a military arm. If it is true that there was little to celebrate and much to lament at the fortieth anniversary of this community's organization as a state in 1988, the fiftieth anniversary represents a forbidding challenge. For by 1998 the fundamental choice will have already been made: to continue the expansion and militarism and its disastrous results for Palestinians and Jews, or to change radically and embark on a new road. The task before us thus is neither soothing nor encouraging. Only a confrontation with state power and the legitimating force of that power—Zionism and Holocaust theology—hold forth the prospect of a faithfulness that is Jewish in context and efficacious in reality.

Notes

Chapter 1. The Birth of Holocaust Theology

1. For analytical studies of the Holocaust, see Raul Hilberg, *The Destruction of the European Jews*, 3 vols., rev. ed. (New York: Holmes & Meier, 1985), and Lucy S. Dawidowicz, *The War Against the Jews, 1933–1945* (New York: Holt, Rinehart & Winston, 1975). For descriptions of what the liberators of the camps found, see Abraham L. Sachar, *The Redemption of the Unwanted: From the Liberation of the Death Camps to the Founding of Israel* (New York: St. Martin's, 1983), 1–22.
2. The 1950s saw many writers question the foundations of Western civilization. Two examples are Lewis Mumford, *The Transformations of Man* (Gloucester, MA: Peter Smith, 1956), and Albert Camus, *The Rebel: An Essay on Man in Revolt* (New York: Vintage, 1956).
3. For moving accounts of the life and destruction of the Jewish community in Vilna, known as the "Jerusalem of Lithuania," see Chaim Grade, *My Mother's Sabbath Days: A Memoir*, trans. Channa Kleinerman and Inna Hecker Grade (New York: Knopf, 1986), and Lucy S. Dawidowicz, *From That Place and Time, 1938–1947: A Memoir* (New York: Norton, 1989).
4. A useful description of the movements birthed in the nineteenth century can be found in Jacob Neusner, *Death and Birth of Judaism: The Impact of Christianity, Secularism and Holocaust on Jewish Faith* (New York: Basic Books, 1987), 75–186.
5. Wiesel's first major discussion of the Holocaust took the form of an autobiography and was originally published in France in 1958. It was translated and published in the United States with the title *Night* (New York: Avon, 1969). Wiesel's range of writing is extensive, and his novels are important to more fully understand the nuances of his thought. For one such attempt at analysis, see Robert McAfee Brown, *Elie Wiesel: Messenger to All Humanity* (Notre Dame, IN: Univ. of Notre Dame Press, 1983). Also see Alvin A. Rosenfeld and Irving Greenberg, eds., *Confronting the Holocaust: The Impact of Elie Wiesel* (Bloomington: Indiana Univ. Press, 1978). Suffice it to say that my analysis of Wiesel in this chapter and throughout the book is to highlight the major themes of his thought vis-à-vis the Holocaust and Israel as it has helped to articulate the experience and historical situation of the Jewish people.
6. Elie Wiesel, "A Jew Defends Eichmann," in *Against Silence: The Voice and Vision of Elie Wiesel*, vol. 2, ed. Irving Abrahamson (New York: Holocaust Library, 1985), 171–72.
7. Elie Wiesel, "The Day of Judgment," in *Against Silence*, 176.
8. Elie Wiesel, "Because of You," in *Against Silence*, 179.
9. Ibid., 180.

10. Elie Wiesel, "The Death Sentence," in *Against Silence*, 184–85. Wiesel continued: "The accounting with Germany must continue for generations, with the Eichmann trial serving as a constant reminder. Whenever a German hears the name Eichmann, he should feel guilty, not innocent—Eichmann is no longer alive, but his accomplices are." See Elie Wiesel, "No Punishment Befitting The Crime," in *Against Silence*, 186.

11. Elie Wiesel, "Israel Twenty Years Later," in *Against Silence*, 191, 190.

12. Ibid.

13. Elie Wiesel, "At the Western Wall," *Hadassah Magazine*, July 1967, 4.

14. Ibid., 7.

15. Ibid., 6. Wiesel was aware that the victory would bring criticism of Israel as well: "The world already envies our victory. Already we can hear the strident voices: Israel is taking a hard line; Israel should show special patience, forgiveness and magnanimity toward her enemies. There will be pressures, attempts to squeeze out this or that compromise. Even our 'friends' are not likely to forgive us for a victory so impolitely swift, so complete, so magnificent. It is understandable. We have suddenly stripped them of the chance to pity us or even help us" (p. 8).

16. Elie Wiesel, "A Moral Victory," in *Against Silence*, 187. For an almost identical understanding of the 1967 war and its place in Jewish history, see Abraham Joshua Heschel, *Israel: An Echo of Eternity* (New York: Farrar, Straus and Giroux, 1969).

17. Emil Fackenheim, "Jewish Values in the Post-Holocaust Future," *Judaism* 16 (Summer 1967): 270.

18. Ibid., 271.

19. Ibid., 272–73. Fackenheim continues: "How can we possibly obey these imperatives? To do so requires the endurance of intolerable contradictions. Such endurance cannot but bespeak an as yet unutterable faith. If we are capable of this endurance, then the faith implicit in it may well be of historic consequence. At least twice before—at the time of the destruction of the First and of the Second Temples—Jewish endurance in the midst of catastrophe helped transform the world. We cannnot know the future, if only because the present is without precedent. But this ignorance on our part can have no effect on our present action. The uncertainty of what will be may not shake our certainty of what we must do" (p. 273).

20. Emil Fackenheim, *God's Presence in History: Jewish Affirmations and Philosophical Reflections* (New York: New York Univ. Press, 1976), 84.

21. For Fackenheim, Israel is to be revered as a response to the Holocaust; "However—in equal reverence for all the innocent millions, the children included, who had neither the ability, nor the opportunity, nor the desire, to be willing martyrs—it must be *rid totally of every appearance of being an explanation*." This is a crucial distinction in Holocaust theology. See Emil L. Fackenheim, "The Holocaust and the State of Israel: Their Relation," in *The Jewish Return into History: Reflections in the Age of Auschwitz and a New Jerusalem* (New York: Schocken Books, 1978), 281. As to opposition to the reality of Jewish empowerment, see Emil L. Fackenheim, "Post Holocaust Anti-Jewishness, Jewish Identity, and the Centrality of Israel: An Essay in the Philosophy of History," in *World Jewry and the State of Israel*, ed. Moshe Davis (New York: Arno Press, 1977), 11–31. After criticizing opposition to Israeli policies from the First World and Second World as anti-Jewish, Fackenheim reflects on the Palestinian Arabs: "That Palestinian Arabs should have become hostile to the 'invaders' is understandable, and perhaps natural or even inevitable. But one wonders whether, had these invaders not been Jews, their hostility—to say nothing of the Arab world—would have remained implacable. Indeed except in the context of Muslim and post-Muslim Arab anti-Jewish attitudes, Arab policies toward Israel would appear to be unintelligible." (p. 16).

22. On the question of God, see Wiesel's *Night*. Also see Fackenheim, *God's Presence*, and idem., *To Mend the World: Foundations of Future Jewish Thought* (New York: Schocken Books, 1982). For an even more confrontational approach with the Jewish God of history, see Richard L. Rubenstein *After Auschwitz: Radical Theology and Contemporary*

Judaism (New York: Bobbs-Merrill, 1966). For a more recent discussion by Rubenstein, see Richard L. Rubenstein and John K. Roth, *Approaches to Auschwitz: The Holocaust and Its Legacy* (Atlanta: John Knox Press, 1987), 290–338. A different aspect of Rubenstein's contribution to the Holocaust discussion is found in the following chapter.

23. Irving Greenberg, "Cloud of Smoke, Pillar of Fire: Judaism, Christianity and Modernity After the Holocaust," in *Auschwitz: Beginning of a New Era?* ed. Eva Fleischner (New York: Ktav, 1977), 9–19.
24. Ibid., 28, 29.
25. Ibid., 27. According to Greenberg, this act of redemption ensures the survival of the Jewish people. See Irving Greenberg, "The Interaction of Israel and the Diaspora after the Holocaust," in *World Jewry and the State of Israel*, ed. Moshe Davis (New York: Ayer, 1977), 259–82.
26. Ibid., 32.
27. Ibid., 22.
28. Elie Wiesel, "The Massacre in Lebanon," in *Against Silence*, 218.
29. Irving Greenberg, "The Third Great Cycle in Jewish History," *Perspectives* (New York: National Jewish Resource Center, 1981), 15–18.
30. Ibid., 21.
31. Ibid., 22, 23.
32. Ibid., 25.
33. Two books that articulate this theme carry almost the identical title. See Arnold Forster and Benjamin R. Epstein, *The New Anti-Semitism* (New York: McGraw-Hill, 1974), and Nathan Perlmutter and Ruth Ann Perlmutter, *The Real Anti-Semitism in America* (New York: Arbor House, 1982). For the latest addition to this type of literature see Harris O. Schoenberg, *A Mandate for Terror: The United Nations and the PLO* (New York: Shapolsky, 1989).
34. Irving Greenberg, "The Ethics of Jewish Power," *Perspectives* (New York: National Jewish Center for Learning and Leadership, 1988), 1.
35. Ibid., 4.
36. Ibid.
37. Ibid., 6.
38. Ibid., 9.
39. Ibid., 10.
40. Ibid.
41. Ibid., 15.
42. Ibid., 19.
43. Ibid., 24.
44. Ibid.
45. Ibid., 22.
46. Ibid., 23.
47. Ibid., 27.
48. For an interesting discussion of excommunication from the Jewish community regarding Israel, see Roberta Strauss Feuerlicht, *The Fate of the Jews: A People Torn Between Israeli Power and Jewish Ethics* (New York: Times Books, 1983), 281–82.

Chapter 2. Memory as Burden and Possibility: Alternative Views

1. Phillip Lopate, "Resistance to the Holocaust," *Tikkun* 4 (May/June 1989): 56.
2. Ibid. Lopate adds: "A good deal of suspicion and touchiness resides around the issue of maintaining the Holocaust's privileged status in the pantheon of genocides. It is not enough that the Holocaust was dreadful; it must be seen as *uniquely* dreadful" (p. 57).
3. Avishai Margalit, "The Kitsch of Israel," *New York Review of Books* 35 (24 Nov. 1988): 23.
4. Ibid.
5. Ibid., 24. All of this is also crucial for the marketing of Israel to the American Jewish

community. See ibid., 22. For Elie Wiesel's response to the trivialization of the Holocaust, see his "Art and the Holocaust: Trivializing Memory," *New York Times*, 11 June 1989. To the question of how one transmits the message without trivializing it, Wiesel responds, "Listen to the survivors and respect their wounded sensibility. Open yourselves to their scarred memory, and mingle your tears with theirs. And stop insulting the dead" (p. 38).

6. Boas Evron, "The Holocaust: Learning the Wrong Lessons," *Journal of Palestine Studies* 10 (Spring 1981): 16.

7. Ibid., 17, 18. For an illustration of the need for common struggle within the Holocaust, see Helen Fein, *Accounting for Genocide: National Responses and Jewish Victimization During the Holocaust* (Chicago: Univ. of Chicago Press, 1979).

8. Evron, "Holocaust," 17, 18.

9. Ibid., 19, 20. Evron claims that before the Eichmann trial Holocaust consciousness was waning and the ritualistic system of Holocaust commemoration was undeveloped. To immigrants from Arab lands and for Israeli-born youth, "the extermination was a matter of the Jews of Europe, not of Israelis" (p. 19).

10. Ibid., 21.

11. Ibid., 23.

12. Ibid., 26. For a fascinating response to Evron's article linking the so-called biblical right of the Jews to Israel and the expulsion of the Palestinians from the land, see Israel Shahak, "The 'Historical Right' and the Other Holocaust," *Journal of Palestine Studies* 10 (Spring 1981): 27–34.

13. Richard L. Rubenstein, *The Cunning of History: Mass Death and the American Future* (New York: Harper & Row, 1975), 69.

14. Ibid., 74, 76. For a detailed study of the Jewish Councils, see Isaiah Trunk, *Judenrat: The Jewish Councils in Eastern Europe Under Nazi Occupation* (New York: Stein & Day, 1977).

15. Richard L. Rubenstein, *The Age of Triage: Fear and Hope in an Overcrowded World* (Boston: Beacon Press, 1982), 135.

16. Ibid.

17. Rubenstein, *Cunning of History*, 11.

18. Ibid., 6, 94–95. Despite his differences with Wiesel, Fackenheim, and Greenberg, Rubenstein's radical analysis of the twentieth century leads him, as it does all Holocaust theologians, to a neoconservative political stance. However, his analysis of the Holocaust as a paradigmatic event also leads him to place less emphases on the state of Israel. Of all the Holocaust theologians he has written the least on Israel and not at any length since the 1960s. Even so, there is a similarity with Wiesel and Fackenheim: the central event is the Holocaust. For his conservative positions, see ibid., 96–97. For his fascinating piece on Israel, see *After Auschwitz: Radical Theology and Contemporary Judaism* (New York: Bobbs-Merrill, 1966), 131–44.

19. Shlomo Avineri, *The Making of Modern Zionism: The Intellectual Origin of the Jewish State* (New York: Basic Books, 1981), 3–13. On the origins of Zionism also see Arthur Hertzberg, *The Zionist Idea* (Philadelphia: Jewish Publication Society of America, 1959); Walter Laquer, *A History of Zionism* (New York: Schocken, 1976); and Ben Halpern, *The Idea of the Jewish State* (Cambridge: Harvard University Press, 1969).

20. Ibid., 112–13.

21. Ahad Ha'am, *Nationalism and the Jewish Ethic*, ed. Hans Kohn (New York: Herzl Press, 1962), 74–75.

22. Ibid., 67.

23. Ibid., 203.

24. See Avineri, *Modern Zionism*, 120.

25. Ibid., 122–23.

26. Quoted in Gary Smith, *Zionism: The Dream and the Reality* (New York: Harper & Row, 1974), 31.

27. Ibid., 36, 37. For an extended discussion of Ahad Ha'am's philosophy, see Bernard Avishai, *The Tragedy of Zionism: Revolution and Democracy in the Land of Israel* (New York: Farrar Straus Giroux, 1985), 45–66.

28. See Arthur A. Goren, ed., *Dissenter in Zion: From the Writings of Judah L. Magnes* (Cambridge: Harvard Univ. Press, 1982), 1–57. Also see Norman Bentwich, *For Zion's Sake: A Biography of Judah L. Magnes* (Philadelphia: Jewish Publication Society of America, 1954).

29. Ibid., 226.

30. Ibid., 227.

31. Ibid.

32. Ibid., 276.

33. Ibid., 279, 277.

34. Judah Magnes, *Like All the Nations?* (Jerusalem: Herod's Gate, 1930), 22. Magnes wrote: "Whether through temperament or other circumstances I do not at all believe, and I think the facts are all against believing, that without Palestine the Jewish people is dying out or doomed to destruction. On the contrary it is growing stronger, for, Palestine without communities in the Dispersion would be bereft of much of its significance as a spiritual center for the Judaism of the world" (p. 22).

35. Ibid., 27.

36. Ibid., "Toward Peace in Palestine," *Foreign Affairs* 21 (January 1943): 239.

37. Ibid., 240–41. Magnes felt America's "moral and political authority" to be crucial to solving a crisis that the parties to the crisis could not: "In view of the intransigence of many responsible leaders on both sides the adjustment may have to be imposed over their opposition" (p. 241).

38. Goren, *Dissenter*, 53–54. For Arendt's analysis of the rise of totalitarianism, see Hannah Arendt, *The Origins of Totalitarianism* (New York: Harcourt, Brace, 1951).

39. Hannah Arendt, "To Save the Jewish Homeland: There Is Still Time," in *The Jew as Pariah*, ed. Ron H. Feldman (New York: Grove Press, 1978), 181.

40. Ibid., 187.

41. Ibid., 182, 184, 186, 188, 189.

42. Ibid., 192.

43. Ibid., 221–22.

Chapter 3. A Tradition of Dissent

1. Roberta Strauss Feuerlicht, *The Fate of the Jews: A People Torn Between Israeli Power and Jewish Ethics* (New York: Times Books, 1983), 5, 287.

2. Howard Greenstein, *Turning Point: Zionism and Reform Judaism* (Chico, CA: Scholars Press, 1981), 1.

3. Ibid., 129.

4. Ibid., 128.

5. Ibid., 29.

6. Ibid., 56.

7. Elmer Berger, *The Jewish Dilemma* (New York: Devin-Adair, 1945), 39–40. For a more recent statement of Berger's views, see his "Zionist Ideology: Obstacle to Peace," in *Anti-Zionism: Analytical Reflections*, ed. Roselle Tekiner, Samir Abed-Rabbo, and Norton Mezvinsky (Brattleboro, VT: Amana Books, 1988), 1–32.

8. William Zukerman, *Voice of Dissent: Jewish Problems, 1948–1961* (New York: Bookman Associates, 1962), 141. I am grateful to Wes Avram, who introduced me to Zukerman and his dissent.

9. Ibid., 151, 154.

10. Ibid., 158.

11. Ibid., 35.

12. Ibid., 296–97.

13. See I. F. Stone, "The Harder Battle and the Nobler Victory" in I. F. Stone, *In a Time of Torment 1961–1967* (Boston: Little, Brown, 1989), 441–45; Michael Selzer, ed., *Zionism Reconsidered: The Rejection of Jewish Normalcy* (New York: Macmillan, 1970); Noam

ad, *Return to Judaism: Religious Renewal in Israel* (Chicago: Univ. of Chicago
For an example of such conversion literature and its limitations in the
s, see Arthur Waskow, *Godwrestling* (New York: Schockev, 1978).
or the Land and the Lord: Jewish Fundamentalism in Israel (New York: Council
elations, 1988), 2.
r a discussion of how religious and secular ultranationalists work together
rinzak, "The Emergence of the Radical Right" *Comparative Politics* 21
9): 171–92.
assessment of Jewish fundamentalism's long-term political damage, see
nd the Lord, 177–84.
sting discussion of progressive religious Zionism, see Michael Rosenak,
f Trouble: Reflections of a Religious Zionist," *Tikkun* 3 (May/June 1988):
27. Rosenak thinks that religious Zionism has an important role to play in
irth "namely to maintain its essential Jewishness and to negotiate the
required within the tradition by virtue of the return of part of the Jewish
land." The problem, for Rosenak, is the promulgation after the 1967 war of
orthodoxy combined with messianic fervor (p. 60). The latest response of
religious Zionists can be found in a booklet titled *You Must Not Remain*
ally at the Jerusalem Khan 7 February 1988 (Jerusalem: Oz VeShalom-Netivot
9). Also see the interview with Yeshayahu Leibowitz, "Israeli Philosopher-
American-Arab Affairs 26 (Fall 1988): 75–77.
ris, *The Birth of the Palestinian Refugee Problem, 1947–1949* (Cambridge: Cam-
. Press, 1987), 210.

23.

an, "Four Decades of Blood Vengeance," *Nation* 248 (6 Feb. 1989): 155.
56.

, "The Night of the Broken Clubs," *Ha'aretz,* 4 May 1989.
iro, "You Will Get Used to Being a Mengele," *Al Hamishar,* 19 Sept. 1988.
enberg, "The Third Great Cycle in Jewish History," in *Perspectives* (New
onal Jewish Resource Center, 1981), 25, 26. See also Emil Fackenheim, *What*
An Interpretation for the Present Age (New York: Summit Books, 1987); Arthur
and Paul Mendes-Flohr, eds., *Contemporary Jewish Religious Thought* (New
Press, 1987).
, *A Jew Today* (New York: Vintage, 1978), 121, 122.
127. Also see Wiesel's letter "To a Brother in Israel" in ibid., 129–37. The
lves almost completely around the question of why a Diaspora continues
e is a Jewish state. Unfortunately, Palestinian Arabs are mentioned only once
ssing.
l and Albert Friedlander, *The Six Days of Destruction: Meditations Toward Hope*
ergamon Press, 1988); Greenberg, *Jewish Way.* A major theme of Wiesel and
er's book is that Christians need to integrate the Jewish experience in liturgi-
nd therefore they provide a set of guidelines for such liturgy and a sample
t the same time, even the most recent public articulation of Holocaust liturgy
around the placing of a Catholic convent at Auschwitz and the removal of the
ll elicits no discussion of the Palestinian people. See "Elie Wiesel Speaks Out
witz" *National Catholic Reporter,* 15 Sept. 1989, and Elie Wiesel, "I Fear What
nd the Wall," *New York Times,* 17 Nov. 1989.
n Seders (New York: New Jewish Agenda, 1984), 61–62.
alidi, *Before Their Diaspora: A Photographic History of the Palestinians, 1876–1948*
ton, DC: Institute for Palestine Studies, 1984), 13. For a study of earlier forms

Chomsky, *Peace in the Middle East: Reflections on Justice and Nationhood* (New York: Vintage, 1974).

14. Chomsky, *Peace,* 57–58, 75, 34. For the heavy attacks on Chomsky and other dissenters, see Chomsky, *Peace,* 153–98.

15. Noam Chomsky, *The Fateful Triangle: The United States, Israel and the Palestinians* (Boston: South End Press, 1983), 43, 45.

16. Ibid., 48, 49.

17. Ibid., 202–4. As Chomsky points out, the invasion of Lebanon was linked to further repression in the occupied territories. See pp. 205–9.

18. Ibid., 334–35. For Israel's mistreatment of prisoners, patients, and refugees, see 228–40.

19. Ibid., 404. Also see Ze'ev Schiff and Ehud Ya'ari, *Israel's Lebanon War,* trans. Ina Friedman (New York: Simon & Schuster, 1984), 250–85. For the Kahan Commission Report see *The Beirut Massacre,* intro. Abba Eban (New York: Karz-Cohl, 1983).

20. Jacobo Timerman, *The Longest War: Israel in Lebanon,* trans. Miguel Acoca (New York: Vintage, 1982), 158, 9. Timerman writes: "Today in Beirut Arab children have their legs and arms amputated by candlelight in the basements of hospitals destroyed by bombs, without anesthetics, without sterilization. It is eleven days since proud veteran Israeli troops cut the electricity and water, and food and fuel supplies" (p. 162). For Earl Shorris's dissent, see his *Jews Without Mercy: A Lament* (Garden City, NY: Doubleday, 1982). Also see Amnon Rubinstein, *The Zionist Dream Revisited: From Herzl to Gush Emunim and Back* (New York: Schocken, 1984). The war precipitated a new level of dissent within Israel. See *The Other Israel* no. 2 (August 1983): 1–4 and ibid., no. 3 (September-October 1983): 1–6.

21. Jacob Neusner, "The Real Promised Land Is America," *International Herald Tribune,* 10 Mar. 1987.

22. Ibid.

23. Jacob Neusner, "It Isn't 'Light to the Gentiles' or Even Bright for Most Jews," *International Herald Tribune,* 11 Mar. 1987. For two longer treatments of the subject, see his *Stranger at Home: The Holocaust, Zionism, and American Judaism* (Chicago: Univ. of Chicago Press, 1981), and *The Jewish War Against the Jews: Reflections on Golah, Shoah and Torah* (New York: KTAV, 1984).

24. For a fascinating look at Judaism in the nineteenth century and the events that reshape it in the twentieth century, see Jacob Neusner, *Death and Birth of Judaism: The Impact of Christianity, Secularism and the Holocaust on Jewish Faith* (New York: Basic Books, 1987).

25. The tradition of dissent is almost endless and thus deserves a book-length treatment of its own. Still, a mention must be made of Israel's influence on American foreign policy and the pioneering work done by Alfred M. Lilienthal, begun in the 1950s and culminating in his massive volume *The Zionist Connection II: What Price Peace* (New Brunswick, NJ: North American, 1978). This work has been carried forward by Cheryl A. Rubenberg in her book *Israel and the American National Interest* (Chicago: Univ. of Illinois Press, 1986). For Israel's foreign policy, see Jane Hunter's journal *Israeli Foreign Affairs,* which began publication in 1987, and Benjamin Brit-Hallahmi, *The Israeli Connection: Who Israel Arms and Why* (New York: Pantheon, 1987). Also see Aaron S. Klieman, *Israel's Global Reach: Arms Sales as Diplomacy* (Washington: Pergamon-Brassey's, 1985).

26. Alexander Schindler, "To the President of Israel," in *AS Briefings: Commission on Social Action of Reform Judaism,* March 1988, Appendix A; Albert Vorspan, "Soul Searching," *New York Times Magazine,* 8 May 1988, 40. Two days after Schindler's telegram Irena Klepfisz, a feminist poet, spoke critically at the Israeli Consulate in New York. See Irena Klepfisz, "Hurling Words at the Consulate," *Genesis 2* 19 (Spring 1988): 18–20.

27. Yehuda Amichai, Amos Elon, Amos Oz, A. B. Yehoshua, "Silence of American Jews Supports Wrong Side," *New York Times,* 21 Feb. 1988; "Israel Must End the Occupation," *New York Times,* 21 Feb. 1988. For three other interesting positions publicized at the same time, see "Remember When It Was a Symbol of Hope?" *New York Times,* 27 Apr. 1988; "Why Must Jewish and Arab Blood Be Shed: It's Time to Call It Quits," *New*

York Times 15 Feb. 1988; "Time to Dissociate from Israeli Policies," *Nation*, 13 Feb. 1988, 193.

28. Arthur Hertzberg, "The Uprising," *New York Review of Books*, 35 (4 Feb. 1988): 32; idem., "The Turning Point," *New York Review of Books* 35 (13 Oct. 1988): 60. Also see his essay "The Illusion of Jewish Unity," *New York Review of Books* 35 (16 June 1988).

29. Elie Wiesel, "Let Us Remember, Let Us Remember," *New York Times*, 1 Apr. 1988; idem., "A Mideast Peace—Is It Possible?" *New York Times*, 23 June 1988.

30. Wiesel, "Mideast Peace."

31. Ibid.

32. Arthur Hertzberg, "An Open Letter to Elie Wiesel," *New York Review of Books* 35 (18 Aug. 1988), 13.

33. Ibid.

34. Ibid.

35. Ibid., 14.

36. Michael Lerner, "The Occupation: Immoral and Stupid," *Tikkun* 3 (Mar./Apr. 1988): 7.

37. Ibid.

38. Ibid., 7, 8.

39. Ibid. Lerner comments: "Once the perception fades that Israel stands for moral values, those of us who want to provide for Israel's defense may be unable to convince the United States to supply the latest and most sophisticated military hardware and Israel may be unable to keep up with Arab armies supplied not only by the Soviet Union but also by Japan and Europe. As a result, Israel may be vulnerable to serious military attack" (p. 8).

40. Ibid., 9.

41. Ibid.

42. Ibid.

43. Ibid., 10, 12.

44. "The Twenty-first Year: Convenant for the Struggle Against Occupation," *Tikkun* 3 (May/June 1988): 68.

45. Ibid., 69. The covenant concludes: "Refusal is the only morally and politically sound form of participation in Israeli society during the Age of Occupation. Refusal is a way out, a source of hope for our moral integrity as Israelis" (p. 69). For a chronicle of Israeli protests that emerged with the uprising see *The Other Israel* no. 30 (January-February 1988): 5–6 and *Israel and Palestine Report* no. 139 (January 1988): 17.

46. Israel Shahak, "Collection: Atrocities as a Method," n.d., 1. These monthly translations and commentaries from Israel are published by the American Educational Trust, P.O. Box 53062, Washington, D.C. 20009.

47. Israel Shahak, "The Givati Brigade: Its Misdeeds and the Politics Behind Them," *From the Hebrew Press* 1 (Jan. 1989): 2.

48. Ibid. As Shahak comments, "The Arabs understand 'nothing but force' is a very common racist stereotype in Israel, as is the belief that public humiliation is the 'right' way of 'dealing with the Arabs'" (p. 2).

49. Tikvah Parnass-Honig, director of the Alternative Information Center in Jerusalem, details this solidarity of Palestinians and Israelis in her unpublished paper delivered at the United Nations in June 1988, "Another Aspect of the Intifada: Stepping up the Occupation Policy—Repression of Any Public Activity of Palestinians and of the Inevitable Cooperation Between Them and Israelis."

50. Simha Flapan, *The Birth of Israel: Myths and Realities* (New York: Random House, 1987), 5.

51. Ibid.

52. Ibid., 7, 8.

53. Ibid., 8, 9.

54. Ibid.

55. Ibid., 235–36.

56. See Avi Shalim, *Collusion Across the Jordan* (New York: Columbia Univ. Press, 1988); Ilan Pappe, *Britain and the Arab-Israeli Conflict, 1948–1951* (New York: Macmillan/St. Antho-

ny's Press, 1988); Tom Segev, *1949:* [...]
Morris, *The Birth of the Palestinian* [...]
Univ. Press, 1988). See also Benny [...]
Its Past," *Tikkun* 3 (Nov./Dec. 1988 [...]

57. Morris, *Palestinian Refugee*, 288–89. [...]

58. Ibid., 292, 293–94.

59. Segev, *1949*, 26–27.

60. Ibid.

61. "Territory for Peace—Bad Deal: Int [...]
14 Mar. 1988. With Shamir's visit [...]
message was published. See "An Op [...]
York Times, 15 November 1989.

62. Jack Mondlak, "To the Jews of Amer [...]
Times, 12 May 1988. Cynthia Ozick, t [...]
movement. See "To Mr. Arafat: Ston [...]
For Ozick's attempt to address the [...]
"Peace Group to Refute Mideast 'My [...]
there are those within the Jewish co [...]
circle the old city of Jerusalem with a h [...]
Palestinians," *New York Times*, 31 Dec [...]

Chapter 4. Toward an Inclusive [...]

1. David G. Roskies, *Against the Apoca* [...]
Culture (Cambridge: Harvard Univ. Pr [...]

2. Ibid., 212.

3. Ibid., 202.

4. Irving Greenberg, *The Jewish Way: Livin* [...]
368–70. Greenberg writes: "One can say [...]
able without tzedakah. In the light of t [...]
not a matter of money, fund raising [...]
answer that one gives to the question: D [...]
of the total assault on life in the Shoah [...]
God/life, or for Satan/death." For Gree [...]
1938 as a response to the Holocaust and [...]
ment of Israel, has become "the central v [...]
is worth" (p. 371).

5. See Ilya Levkov, ed., *Bitburg and Beyon* [...]
History (New York: Shapolsky, 1987), 22 [...]

6. Irving Greenberg, "Some Lessons from [...]

7. Ibid., 4.

8. Ibid., 4. Not content with protest, Green[...]
Reagan should have given at Bitburg recc [...]
Greenberg addressed five audiences: th [...]
1945, the veterans and families of the A [...]
world. See his "The Speech Ronald Reag [...]
tives, Spring 1985, 5. For the internation [...]
Bitburg.

9. Elie Wiesel, "'Your Place Is With The [...]
Bitburg, 43.

10. Ibid., 44. Not everyone agreed with the [...]
vigorous criticism, see Jacob Neusner, "R [...]
Bitburg, 386–87. Neusner starts his essay [...]
my advice about what to say to President [...]
him this: Remember, not everyone in the [...]

11. See Janet Av[...]
Press, 1983) [...]
United State[...]

12. Ian Lustick, [...]
on Foreign [...]

13. Ibid., 126. F[...]
see Ehud S[...]
(January 19[...]

14. For Lustick'[...]
For the Land [...]

15. For an inter[...]
"In a Time [...]
56–60, 124—[...]
national rel[...]
innovations[...]
people to its[...]
an uncritica[...]
progressive [...]
Indifferent: [...]
Shalom, 198[...]
Prophet," [...]

16. Benny Mor[...]
bridge Uni[...]

17. Ibid.

18. Ibid., 211.

19. Ibid., 222—[...]

20. Ibid., 229.

21. Ibid., 231.

22. Ibid., 233.

23. Amos Ken[...]

24. Ibid., 155—[...]

25. Ibid., 156.

26. Yossi Saric[...]

27. Gideon Sp[...]

28. Irving Gre[...]
York: Nati[...]
Is Judaism: [...]
A. Cohen[...]
York: Free[...]

29. Elie Wiese[...]

30. Ibid., 126[...]
letter rev[...]
when the [...]
and in pa[...]

31. Elie Wies[...]
(Oxford: [...]
Friedland[...]
cal acts, [...]
liturgy. A[...]
revolving[...]
Berlin W[...]
on Ausc[...]
Lies Bey[...]

32. *The Shal*[...]

33. Walid Kh[...]
(Washin[...]

of Palestinian national identity see Muhammad Y. Muslih, *The Origins of Palestinian Nationalism* (New York: Columbia University Press, 1988).

34. Ibid., 14.

35. Elia Zureik's chart displayed in Edward Said, *After the Last Sky: Palestinian Lives* (New York: Pantheon, 1986), 111. Also see Elia Zureik, *The Palestinians in Israel: A Study in Internal Colonialism* (London: Routledge and Kegan Paul, 1978).

36. Edward Said, *The Question of Palestine* (New York: Vintage, 1980), 51. Also see Edward Said and Christopher Hitchens, eds. *Blaming the Victims: Spurious Scholarship and the Palestinian Question* (London: Verso, 1988).

37. Ibid., 57, 59, 34.

38. Hanan Mikhail-Ashrawi, "The Coming of Age: An Anatomy of the Palestinian Intifada" (Paper delivered at the United Nations Nongovernmental Conference on the Question of Palestine, June 1988), 1. For an extended discussion of these themes see Mikhail-Ashrawi, *From Intifada to Independence* (The Hague: Palestine Information Office, 1989).

39. Ibid., 11–12.

40. Muhammad Hallaj, "The Palestinian Dream: The Democratic Secular State," in *Beyond Occupation: American Jews, Christians and Palestinians Search for Peace*, ed. Rosemary Radford Ruether and Marc H. Ellis (Boston: Beacon Press, forthcoming.)

41. *Punishing a Nation: Human Rights Violations During the Palestinian Uprising December 1987–1988* (Jerusalem: Al Haq/Law in the Service of Man, 1988), 343–44. As the second year of the intifada came to a close in December 1989 the number of deaths had reached 824, injuries 80,000. This information can be obtained from the Data Base Project on Palestinian Human Rights, 4753 N. Broadway, Suite 930, Chicago, Ill. Also see the human rights report compiled by the U.S. Department of State, "Country Reports on Human Rights Practices for 1988, 'The Occupied Territories,' " (Washington, D.C.: U.S. Government Printing Office, February 1989), 1376–87.

42. "Affidavits on Sexual Harassment and Violence Against Palestinian Women" (Jerusalem Database Project on Palestinian Human Rights, 1989), 121–22.

43. Jean Corbon, George Khodr, Samir Kafity, and Albert Lahham, "What Is Required of the Christian Faith Concerning the Palestine Problem," *Biblical and Theological Concerns* (Limasol, Cyrus: Middle East Council of Churches, n.d.), 11. Also see Jean Corbon, "Western Public Opinion and the Palestine Conflict" in *Christians, Zionism and Palestine* (Beirut: Institute for Palestine Studies, n.d.). Corbon's lecture was presented in February 1969.

44. Ibid., 11, 12.

45. Ibid. This understanding of Zionism as a form of racism was adopted by the United Nations on 10 November 1975. For an interesting discussion of this theme see *Zionism and Racism: Proceedings of an International Symposium* (Tripoli, Libya: International Organization for the Elimination of All Forms of Racial Discrimination, 1977).

46. Ibid., 13.

47. Ibid.

48. Ibid. The theologians thus address Christian Zionism: "It is, therefore, a total misunderstanding of the story of salvation and a perversion of God's plan for a Christian to want to reestablish a Jewish nation as an exclusive political entity."

49. Gabriel Habib, "A Statement," in *Auschwitz: Beginning of a New Era?* ed. Eva Fleischner (New York: KTAV, 1977), 417, 418, 419. George Khodr echoed these sentiments this time in reference to the Lebanese War. See his "Christians of the Orient: Witness and Future; The Case of Lebanon," *WSCF Journal* (May 1986): 35–42.

50. Naim Stifan Ateek, *Justice and Only Justice: A Palestinian Theology of Liberation* (Maryknoll, NY: Orbis, 1989), 9–10.

51. Ibid., 33–34, 48.

52. Ibid., 63–64, 66, 69.

53. Ibid., 77.

54. Ibid., 74–114.

55. Ibid., 134–38.

56. Ibid., 168.
57. Ibid., 170. For other sources of local Palestinian theology contact the Al-Liqa Center-Jerusalem, Jerusalem-Bethlehem Road, P. O. Box 11157.
58. Mubarak Awad, "Statement," *Database Project on Palestinian Human Rights,* Jerusalem, 5 June 1988. For a discussion of his understanding of nonviolence see Mubarak E. Awad, "Nonviolent Resistance: A Strategy for the Occupied Territories," *Journal of Palestine Studies* 13 (Summer 1984): 22–36.

Chapter 5. Holocaust, Israel, and Christian Renewal

1. Edmund Wilson, *Black, Red, Blond and Olive* (New York: Oxford Univ. Press, 1956), 462–63.
2. Reinhold Niebuhr, "A New View of Palestine," *The Spectator,* 6 Aug. 1946, 162.
3. Reinhold Niebuhr, Letter to the editor, *New York Times,* 21 Nov. 1947.
4. Richard Wrightman Fox, *Reinhold Niebuhr: A Biography* (New York: Harper & Row, 1987), 209–10.
5. Reinhold Niebuhr, "Jews After the War," *Nation,* 21 Feb. 1942, 215–16, 28 Feb. 1942, 254.
6. Ibid., 254, 255.
7. Gregory Baum, Introduction in Rosemary Radford Ruether, *Faith and Fratricide: The Theological Roots of Anti-Semitism* (New York: Seabury, 1974), 7, 11. Actually, it was at this time that the seeds of a more critical Christian response were being planted by the Christian social activist Daniel Berrigan. See *The Great Berrigan Debate* (New York: Committee on New Alternatives in the Middle East, 1974).
8. Alice and Roy Eckardt, *Encounter with Israel: A Challenge to Conscience* (New York: Association Press, 1970), 15.
9. Ibid., 200, 201.
10. Ibid., 244, 249. The Eckardts' comment: "The religious man repeats, 'He brought us forth from Egypt.' The secularist proclaims, 'Masada shall not fall again.'. . . The nonreligious individual celebrates the biblical Exodus from Egypt, and the religious person celebrates the transreligious, post-biblical epic of Masada. Existentially speaking, the two are sharing one experience" (p. 248).
11. Ibid., 256–57. For an extended discussion of these themes, see Franklin H. Littell, *The Crucifixion of the Jews: The Failure of Christians to Understand the Jewish Experience* (New York: Harper & Row, 1975).
12. Ibid., 259.
13. Ibid., 262, 263. See also A. Roy Eckardt, *Elder and Younger Brothers: The Encounter of Jews and Christians* (New York: Charles Scribner's Sons, 1967); idem., *Long Night's Journey into Day: Life and Faith After the Holocaust* (Detroit: Wayne State Univ. Press, 1982). For their later, more critical work see Alice L. Eckardt, "Forgiveness and Repentance: Some Contemporary Considerations and Questions," in *Remembering for the Future: Jews and Christians During and After the Holocaust* (Oxford: Pergamon Press, 1988), 571–83 and A. Roy Eckardt, *Black, Woman, Jew: Three Wars for Human Liberation* (Bloomington: Indiana University Press, 1989).
14. Paul M. van Buren, *Discerning the Way: A Theology of the Jewish Christian Reality* (New York: Seabury, 1980), 41.
15. Ibid., 42–43.
16. Ibid., 170, 190, 187, 182, 176, 177.
17. Paul M. van Buren, *A Christian Theology of the People Israel, Part II* (New York: Seabury, 1983), 202–3.
18. Robert McAfee Brown, *Elie Wiesel: Messenger to All Humanity* (Notre Dame: Univ. of Notre Dame Press, 1983), 2–3. Brown dedicated his book to Wiesel; it reads in part: "You have said that to be a Jew means to testify; such must also be the obligation of a Christian. And you have taught us all—Jews, Christians and all Humanity—that

before testifying ourselves, we must listen to your testimony. And now I feel obligated . . . to testify."

19. Robert McAfee Brown, "Christians in the West Must Confront the Middle East," in Rosemary Radford Ruether and Marc H. Ellis, *Beyond Occupation* (Boston: Beacon, forthcoming). Also see Brown's earlier article "Speaking About Israel; Some Ground Rules" *Christian Century* 105 (6 Apr. 1988): 338–40.

20. Ibid.

21. Ibid.

22. Ruether, *Faith and Fratricide*, 258, 225. Ruether ends her book with a proposal to reform current theological curricula about the Jews. She includes teaching the Jewish scriptures from a Jewish perspective, correcting the stereotypes of the Pharisees and thus the myth of blood guilt, and studying the way theological anti-Jewishness has been translated into social and political oppression (pp. 259–61).

23. Rosemary Radford Ruether, "Anti-Semitism and the State of Israel," *Christianity and Crisis* 33 (26 Nov. 1973): 240–41.

24. Ibid., 242, 243. Ruether concludes: "The development of new conditions for the Palestinians' existence and a commitment to Israel's secure survival are indissolubly linked together. Each cause really depends on the other. Anyone committed to one must also become committed to the other" (p. 244).

25. Rosemary Radford Ruether and Herman Ruether, *The Wrath of Jonah: The Crisis of Religious Nationalism in the Middle East* (New York: Harper & Row, 1989), xix, 244.

26. Ibid., 20.

27. Rosemary Radford Ruether, "Beyond Anti-Semitism and Philo-Semitism," in Ruether and Ellis, *Beyond Occupation*, (forthcoming).

28. Ibid.

29. Ruether & Ruether, *Wrath of Jonah*, 237.

30. Ibid., 238.

31. Annette Daum, "Christians Respond to West Bank/Gaza" *Interreligious Currents* 7 (Winter/Spring 1988): 1, 2, 8.

32. David Biale, "The Philo-Semitic Face of Christian Anti-Semitism," *Tikkun* 4 (May/June 1989): 101. A similar desire for normality is found in an interview with the Israeli novelist A. B. Yehoshua. See "In Praise of Normality," *Jerusalem Post International,* 30 Sept. 1989.

33. Ibid.

Chapter 6. Beyond Innocence and Redemption

1. Thomas L. Friedman, "How Long Can Israel Deny Its Civil War?" *New York Times,* 27 Dec. 1987, 3; quoted in Alan Cowell, "Three Palestinians Killed in Protests in the Gaza Strip," *New York Times,* 17 June 1989, 6. For Friedman's recent discussion of these issues, see his *From Beirut to Jerusalem* (New York: Farrar Straus Giroux, 1989).

2. Joel Brinkley, "Israel Defense Chief Sees Failure in Quelling Uprising," *New York Times,* 5 Dec. 1989. Also see Kenneth Kaplan, "Intifada 'Under Control,'" *Jerusalem Post International,* 16 Dec. 1989.

3. For Arthur Waskow's analysis of the situation, see his "Peace and the Palestinians," *Genesis 2* 19 (Spring 1988): 8–12. Waskow essentially supports Michael Lerner's positions articulated in chapter 3, though his mix of biblical imagery and contemporary politics distorts the reality of the situation.

4. See Eugene B. Borowitz, *Liberal Judaism* (New York: Union of American Hebrew Congregations, 1984); Michael Wyschogrod, *The Body of Faith: Judaism as Corporeal Election* (New York: Seabury, 1983); David Hartman, *A Living Covenant: The Innovative Spirit in Traditional Judaism* (New York: Macmillan, 1985). The challenge to see the Palestinians at the center of Jewish history and theology has been ignored. See Marc H. Ellis, *Toward a Jewish Theology of Liberation: The Uprising and the Future* (Maryknoll, NY: Orbis, 1989);

idem., "Solidarity with the Palestinian People: A Jewish Theological Perspective," *New Outlook* 32 (Feb. 1989): 40–41. For Hartman's latest views, see "The Uprising: Israelis Address American Jews," *Tikkun* 3 (Mar./Apr. 1988): 19–20, and his comments in Shelley Kleiman, "On Moderate Ground: An Alternate Image of Judaism," *Jerusalem Post International*, December 1989. Analysis of these and other Jewish theologians will figure prominently in my next book on the future of Jewish theology.

5. Roberta Strauss Feuerlicht, *The Fate of the Jews: A People Torn Between Israeli Power and Jewish Ethics* (New York: Times Books, 1983), 284.

6. Of course, the other side of Jewish privilege is discrimination against Palestinian Arabs. Though most of Jewish writing on the problems of Israel does not mention Palestinians, when they are mentioned it is in relation to the West Bank and Gaza. However, the challenge from the beginning has been Palestinians within Israel, now approximately 18 percent of the population. Essentially three politicies have been applied to Palestinians within the Jewish state: expulsion, ghettoization, and second-class citizenship. For discussion of the forgotten ones, see Fouzi El-Asmar, *To Be an Arab in Israel* (Beirut, Lebanon: Institute for Palestine Studies, 1975), and Ian S. Lustick, *Arabs in the Jewish State: Israel's Control of a National Minority* (Austin, TX: Univ. of Texas Press, 1980).

7. For two perspectives on Jewish influence on United States foreign policy, see Paul Findley, *They Dare to Speak Out: People and Institutions Confront Israel's Lobby* (Westport, CT: Lawrence, Hill, 1985), and Edward Tivnan, *The Lobby: Jewish Political Power and American Foreign Policy* (New York: Simon & Schuster, 1987).

8. It is interesting that despite the past and contemporary suffering in Jewish history, Jews have continually chosen to live among others in pluralist situations. This choice was reaffirmed after the Holocaust and is reaffirmed again today even with a Jewish state. Thus American Jews remain in America, and Russian Jews consistently prefer America to Israel, that is, the great majority of Jews seek the challenge of freedom and the creativity of pluralism. For an interesting discussion of these themes, see Jacob Neusner, *Stranger at Home: The Holocaust, Zionism, and American Judaism* (Chicago: Univ. of Chicago Press, 1981).

9. Simha Flapan's discovery of the continuity of policies of David Ben-Gurion and Menachem Begin in relation to Palestinians underlines the essential logic of a Jewish state. It needs to be spoken of in unequivocal terms: a Jewish state within the pre-1967 borders or encompassing the occupied territories demands the refusal of equal political, cultural, and economic rights to Palestinians. This discussion, present in the early dissenters in Zion, is largely absent among contemporary dissenters.

10. Feuerlicht, *Fate of the Jews*, 287.

11. In this regard, see an interview with Emil Fackenheim "Western Jews' Attitude Disappoints Fackenheim," *Canadian Jewish News*, 3 Nov. 1988, 9. For Israel's ability to carry others with them, see Shai Feldman, *Israeli Nuclear Deterrence: A Strategy for the 1980s* (New York: Columbia Univ. Press, 1982), and Aaron S. Klieman, *Israel's Global Reach: Arms Sales as Diplomacy*, (Washington: Pergamon Brassey's, 1985). For the necessity of Israel's nuclear capability see Robert Harkavy, "Survival Imperatives," *Transaction: Social Science and Modern Society* 23 (January/February, 1986): 63–72.

12. Thus I would part company with those who argue the primacy of the American experience, or any national experience, for the Jewish people, including that of Israel. At this point in history Jews, like others, live within nation-state systems, but no state has an ultimate claim on our identity or loyalty. As Jews we live in America, France, or Israel, but our history existed long before and will (we hope) long after these particular forms of social organization disappear. A major task of the renewal of Jewish life is to relativize these forms of social organization, which also means that our links with state power must be questioned in Israel and the United States. Because I believe that Jewish empowerment is important and thus a return to Jewish orthodoxy (the synagogue) or an "advance" to Jewish liberalism or neoconservatism (state power) is impossible and/or a mistake, the content and means of empowerment is in need of a lengthy discussion. Suffice it to say here that this position takes issues with the positions represented by Elmer Berger, Arthur Waskow, Jacob Neusner, and Irving Greenberg.

Though the content of the policy of the Jewish Committee on the Middle East is appealing, its foundational principle is not. See "Time to Dissociate from Israeli Policies," *Nation* 249 (3 Oct. 1988): 292.

13. Elie Wiesel, *A Jew Today* (New York: Vintage, 1979), 16; Irving Greenberg, "Cloud of Smoke, Pillar of Fire: Judaism, Christianity and Modernity After the Holocaust," in *Auschwitz: Beginning of a New Era?* ed. Eva Fleischner (New York: KTAV, 1977), 23, 29.

14. For a discussion of these themes of solidarity, see Marc H. Ellis, *Toward a Jewish Theology of Liberation: The Uprising and the Future* (Maryknoll, NY: Orbis, 1989), 79–84.

15. Hannah Arendt, "The Jews as Pariah: A Hidden Tradition," *Jewish Social Studies* 6 (Apr. 1944): 99–122; Ron Feldman, "The Jew as Pariah: The Case of Hannah Arendt" in *Hannah Arendt, The Jew as Pariah: Jewish Identity and Politics in the Modern Age*, ed. Ron H. Feldman (New York: Grove Press, 1978), 18–19.

16. Elizabeth Young-Bruehl, *Hannah Arendt: For the Love of the World* (New Haven: Yale Univ. Press, 1982), 229, 224.

17. Ibid., 338.

18. Hannah Arendt, *Eichmann in Jerusalem: A Report on the Banality of Evil* (New York: Viking Press, 1964), 279.

19. For the exchange of letters between Scholem and Arendt, see "Eichmann in Jerusalem," *Encounter* 22 (January 1964): 51–56. In her response Arendt also recalled a conversation with Golda Meir, later to become prime minister of Israel, though she agreed to leave her name out of the published letters and even to change her gender. "Let me tell you of a conversation I had in Israel with a prominent political personality who was defending the—in my opinion disastrous—nonseparation of religion and state in Israel. What he said—I am not sure of his exact words any more—ran something like this: 'You will understand that, as a socialist, I, of course, do not believe in God; I believe in the Jewish people.' I found this a shocking statement, and being too shocked I did not reply at the time. But I could have answered: the greatness of this people was once that it believed in God, and believed in Him in such a way that its trust and love toward Him was greater than its fear. And now this people believes only in itself? What good can come of that?—Well, in this sense I do not 'love' the Jews, nor do I 'believe' in them; I merely belong to them as a matter of course, beyond dispute and argument" (p. 54).

20. Hannah Arendt, "To Save the Jewish Homeland: There Is Still Time," in Feldman, *Pariah*, 181–82.

21. Martin Buber, *Eclipse of God: Studies in the Relation Between Religion and Philosophy* (New York: Harper & Row, 1952), 129.

22. For Gershom Scholem's critique of Buber's understanding of Hasidism, see his "Martin Buber's Interpretation of Hasidism," in Gershom Scholem, *The Messianic Idea in Judaism* (New York: Schocken, 1971), 228–50. For Buber's response to Scholem's accusation of Buber's propensity for "religious anarchy" as well as his understanding of Jewish law, see Maurice Friedman, *Martin Buber's Life and Work: The Later Years, 1945–1965* (New York: E. P. Dutton, 1983), 191–94.

23. Martin Buber, "Genuine Conversation and the Possibilities of Peace," *Cross Currents* 5 (Fall 1955): 292–93.

24. Ibid. Buber continues: "I believe, despite all, that peoples in this hour can enter into conversation, into a genuine conversation with one another. A genuine conversation is one in which each of the partners, even when he stands in opposition to the other, heeds, affirms and confirms him as this existing other; only thus can the opposition, certainly not be removed from the world, but be humanly arbitrated and led toward overcoming" (p. 296).

25. Cited in Friedman, *Later Years*, pp. 358–59. For the various responses to Buber, 358–60. For the dialogue of Arendt and Buber, see 361–63.

26. Walter Benjamin, *Illuminations*, ed. Hannah Arendt, trans. Harry Zohn (New York: Schocken, 1969), 257–58.

27. Ibid., 264.

28. For a fascinating detailed exploration of these themes in the form of a memoir, see

Gershom Scholem, *Walter Benjamin: The Story of a Friendship*, trans. Harry Zohn (Philadelphia: Jewish Publication Society of America, 1981). Like Benjamin, Franz Kafka is interesting for the dialogue of religious and secular. See Marthe Robert, *As Lonely as Franz Kafka*, trans. Ralph Manheim (New York: Schocken, 1986). Both Scholem and Robert explore Benjamin's and Kafka's relation to the Jewish tradition and their ambivalent feelings about Zionism.

29. Greenberg, "Cloud of Smoke," 54. For a contemporary dialogue that may speak to the revival of the hidden tradition along the lines of Arendt and Buber, see Robin Morgan, *The Anatomy of Freedom: Feminism, Physics and Global Politics* (Garden City, NY: Doubleday, 1982), and Judith Plaskow, *Standing Again at Sinai: Rethinking Judaism for a Feminist Perspective* (New York: Harper & Row, 1989).

30. Johann Baptist Metz, *The Emergent Church: The Future of Christianity in a Postbourgeois World*, trans. Peter Mann (New York: Crossroad, 1981), 18, 19.

31. Ibid., 19.

32. Ibid., 20.

33. Elie Wiesel, "Greeting," in Marc H. Ellis and Otto Maduro, eds., *The Future of Liberation Theology: Essays in Honor of Gustavo Gutierrez* (Maryknoll, NY: Orbis, 1989), 40.

34. Gustavo Gutierrez, *On Job: God-Talk and the Suffering of the Innocent*, trans. Matthew J. O'Connell (Maryknoll, NY: Orbis, 1987), xiv.

35. Ibid., 15.

36. Ibid., 10.

37. Ibid., 92.

38. Ibid., 93.

39. Ibid. For a dialogue on Jewish theology and Latin American liberation theology see Otto Maduro, ed. *Jews, Christians and Liberation Theology* (Maryknoll, NY: Orbis, forthcoming).

40. Isabel Carter Heyward, *The Redemption of God: A Theology of Mutual Relation* (New York: Univ. Press of America, 1982), 199, 54–59.

41. Carter Heyward, Anne Gilson, et al., *Revolutionary Forgiveness: Feminist Reflections on Nicaragua* (Maryknoll, NY: Orbis, 1987), 108.

42. Ibid., 104.

43. Ibid., 103–10. Heyward concludes: "In Nicaragua, we began to see that forgiveness cannot happen unless people give up images of themselves as alone, set apart, or different and join in the struggle to build a social order in which every person and living creature is respected" (p. 110).

44. Rosemary Radford Ruether and Herman J. Ruether, *The Wrath of Jonah: The Crisis of Religious Nationalism in the Israeli-Palestinian Conflict* (San Francisco: Harper & Row, 1989), 238, 239.

45. For earlier reflections on solidarity between Jews and Christians in the struggle for liberation, see Ellis, *Jewish Theology*, 73–75. For difficulty with religious language in the face of oppression, see Joan Casanas, "The Task of Making God Exist," in *The Idols of Death and the God of Life: A Theology*, ed. Pablo Richard et al., trans. Barbara E. Campbell and Bonnie Shepard (Maryknoll, NY: Orbis, 1983), 113–49. To those who fear Christian interaction with Jewish theology in the present, a historical view is important. See Jacob Neusner, *Judaism in the Matrix of Christianity* (Philadelphia: Fortress, 1986).

46. "Palestinians Under Occupation Present Steps Toward Peace," *New York Times*, 15 Mar. 1988, 20.

47. Naim Ateek, *Justice and Only Justice: Toward a Palestinian Theology of Liberation* (Maryknoll, NY: Orbis, 1989), 168–73.

48. An example of this was the use of the American Jew John J. Pollard as a spy for Israel, which raised the question of dual loyalty for American Jews but, more substantially, the willingness of the Israeli government, like all governments, to deceive. See Fred Axelgard and Peretz Kidron, "Pollard: The Flak Flies in the U.S. and in Israel," *Middle East International*, 20 Mar. 1987, 2–6. Israel's involvement in the Iran-contra affair is another example of deception. See Jane Hunter, "The Iran-Contra Affair: Ollie's Off-the-Shelf Enterprise: Was Israel to Walk Away with It?" *Israeli Foreign Affairs* 3 (Aug.

1987): 1, 5. For a much earlier example of deception, this in relation to the Holocaust and high-level Israeli government officials in the 1950s, see Ben Hecht, *Perfidy* (New York: Julian Messner, 1961). His book is a meditation on the theme of how the conditions of state and the human condition in general are also found in the Jewish state and Jewish individuals.

49. Yehoshafat Harkabi makes a similar point when he cautions against Israel's feeling its army can overcome any adversary: "The problem is that, if Israel is so strong, it can allow itself to follow any policy perceived as being to its benefit, while ignoring possible reactions in the world and among the Arabs. The emphasis on Israeli might is thus liable to be an impediment to rational thinking. The paradox here is that, in order to survive, Israelis must free themselves of the myth that their survival is guaranteed in all circumstances and conditions. . . . From this perspective, it may be that the Lebanon war has been an invaluable lesson." See Harkabi, *Israel's Fateful Hour*, trans. Lenn Schramm (New York: Harper & Row, 1988), 44.

Afterword. The Task Before Us

1. Bernard Avishai, *The Tragedy of Zionism: Revolution and Democracy in the Land of Israel* (New York: Farrar Straus Giroux, 1985), 4–5.
2. Ibid., 359, 298.
3. For an interesting analysis of the Israeli-Palestinian conflict, see Yehoshafat Harkabi, *Israel's Fateful Hour* trans. Lenn Schramm (New York: Harper & Row, 1988). Much of Harkabi's book revolves around the need to combat right-wing religious messianism in Israel. He writes: "The explicit assertion that a certain period is the beginning of the Redemption arouses a hope that can only be destructive. Paradoxically, no idea poses a greater menace to the survival of the State of Israel than that which links Zionism with Redemption and Messianism" (p. 167).

Index

211